LETTING GO

——An Anthology of Attempts ——

LETTING GO

—An Anthology of Attempts —

M.E. Hughes, *editor*

BACON PRESS BOOKS
WASHINGTON, DC
2016

"Isolation" by Martha Hughes originally appeared in *Out of Her Mind: Women Writing about Madness*, edited by Rebecca Shannonhouse (Random House, 2000).

Published in the United States by Bacon Press Books, Washington, DC
www.baconpressbooks.com

Cover Design: Alan Pranke
www.amp13.com

Book Layout and Design: Lorie DeWorken
www.mindthemargins.com

ISBN: 978-0-9971489-0-9

Library of Congress Control Number: 2015960976

PRINTED IN THE UNITED STATES OF AMERICA

For writers I have known . . .

Introduction

In my grandparents' kitchen there was a drawer with a sliding, tin top once used to store bread. Post-World War II, it housed brown paper bags. For some reason, I was in love with the shiny, sliding, tin top, and the quiet protest it made when pulled open. I also was in love with my grandmother. When she took out a brown bag, held it in one hand and whacked off a piece with the other—to wrap a package for mailing or to make a round piece for the bottom of a cake pan—I thought her magical and powerful for making something out of nothing.

In that house in the 1940s and many others throughout the nation, everything was saved; nothing went to waste. Rationing was slow to lift. Not ten years had passed since The Great Depression, so people did not let go lightly of people, places or things; they might not get them back.

Today, we have become a "throw away" society. Nobody expects anything—from vacuum cleaners to T-shirts—to last. Such items are easy to find and often cheap to buy. People are harder to replace. Life has speeded up so much that social media or text messages seem adequately to take the place of sitting down to talk together, but in my opinion, over time, this will loosen the bonds of relationships and make them easier to "throw away," too.

When I called for manuscripts on the topic of letting go, I asked people to write about the process of letting go; I didn't care if they were successful; I was more interested in how they went about trying, rather than the result. (For real struggles to let go, take a look at Joe Levine's "Finis" or Terry Purinton's "Dragon Lady.") I emphasized that this book was not a "how to." Instead, it was designed as a collection of essays in which readers could explore the very real—sometimes funny, sometimes painful—efforts we all make throughout our lives to let go.

I expected to receive many essays on letting go of things or bad habits. I was wrong. (Although Joan Scott's humorous piece, "The Paper Room," details the difficulty of getting rid of her paper obsession.) Is it possible we have all read so much about letting go of possessions—shoes and clothes, antique furniture, fine linens, nice china—and habits—smoking, boozing, drugging, overeating—that such things no longer plague us?

There's another reason for the subjects these writers chose to write about, as well as the style in which most wrote: The thirty essays are from writers of fiction—novels and short stories. I have worked with them all, except for Ugandan writer Marione Malimba Namukuta ("The Battle Within") who, except for a visa, would have been my student. At one time or another we have worked on their fiction together in: The Peripatetic Writing Workshop, Inc., a writing intensive, which meets at home and abroad; in my private workshops; in classes I teach at New York University; or as private editing clients.

Fiction is their "first love." The overwhelming passion of their lives is to tell stories, often with themes echoing problems of the material world, as well as strong, timeless metaphysical or psychological questions. (Witness the novel way Roz Kuehn faces a painful divorce in "Commencing Being Fearless.")

The style of the "life stories" in the collection makes them seem made-up. They are not. (George Farrell's stunning

"Hoarding Memories" on a father's betrayal cleverly mixes the fictional techniques of dialogue and scenes with a straight-forward essay style. In Julie Strong's "Acadie," because of the fictive style she uses, we feel we are standing in a corral, as a woman tries to let go of her long-held fear of the on-coming horses. The story seems "too beautiful" to be true; but it is.)

So you might ask, why would a teacher of fiction ask fiction writers to write nonfiction essays? Selfishness is the answer. I do not know how to let go of anything. Not of people, places and things. I come by it naturally, still having a gunny sack full of my great-grandfather's desk contents—old letters, pieces of string, rubber bands, broken pens, newspaper clippings, address books, pencils, a political button from a forgotten, local race—emptied out in 1939 on the day he died. No one, including myself, ever had the heart to throw them away. The question in the air is: Does the inability to let go of ideas, people, places and things sometimes drag one down? After all, we are no longer in the Post-Depression Era; most of us don't really need to save brown bags any more.

I believe readers will find answers to that question in Lisa Wohl's "Outside In" and the many other thoughtful essays in this collection, which show us that freeing oneself by letting go of everything from worn out ideas about yourself to material possessions is not only possible but often necessary for enjoying the fullness of life. Via their stories, these fine writers, with whom I've shared so much of my life, give us valuable food for thought on letting go or, for those still not convinced, permission to stop forcing oneself to try.

M.E. Hughes
January 2016

. . . OF SHOULDS

The Perfect Mother

Emily Tsokos Purtill

The key problem with having been a lawyer for eight years before I was a mother (and just being myself, in all the years before then) is that there was only one way of doing things—perfectly. All or nothing. Following the rules. I had quantifiable goals and knew whether I had reached them. My high school teachers, university professors, supervisors at work and clients always summed me up: "Excellent attention to detail." But it took me a long time to realize it doesn't always work with being a mother.

Of course, I had fully intended to return to work after my maternity leave. But then, the day arrived when I held my baby. He was perfect. And I couldn't let go.

Before I realized it, I had rules. No bottles or pacifiers. Nobody, other than my husband or I, putting him to sleep (no rocking). No photos of him on Facebook. Whole food. Nothing from a packet. Nothing with too much sugar or salt. No TV or iPads. Outside play. Imaginative play. Play dough. Play dates. Painting. Crafts.

Two and a half years and a baby girl later, we crossed the world from Perth to live in New York for a year for my husband's work. I had abandoned my international legal career, which had taken me to Paris and was the centre of my life for so many years. When I became a mother, that whole previous life seemed irrelevant. Oh, I had let the side down by staying home, but I felt so overwhelmed with emotion for these little ones that I couldn't give them to anyone else while I went to work.

I am not particularly conservative or think women *should* stay at home. It makes perfect sense to return to work. But I literally couldn't. I knew we could live comfortably on one professional salary. The thought of leaving the children to spend twelve hours at the office brought me to tears. I just didn't have it in me to return.

Perhaps I should go back to the first month of my little boy's life. He had "breast refusal." Even though midwives and lactation consultants told me I was doing everything right, and he would eventually get it, his mouth remained firmly closed. So I spent six weeks expressing every two hours, trying to get him to latch on, persisting. I couldn't give up so easily on everything going perfectly; I just needed to keep trying. Eventually, after six weeks, he decided to nurse. I had succeeded and in doing so became an urban legend. *Don't give up. You too can be the perfect mother.* And when he spoke at ten months, of course it was my amazing parenting! I had stayed at home with him. He was rewarding me for unfaltering dedication to his life.

When it was time for our son to start eating solid food, my husband and I grew vegetables in our own garden. Carrots, spinach, beans. I would pick them every afternoon, steam and puree them for the baby's dinner. He never had anything from a jar or packet. *Perfect, perfect, perfect.*

Like everyone else, I had always wanted to live in New York. I dreamed of browsing shops in Soho, having brunch in the East

Village at a child-friendly hipster café, making friends with Carrie Bradshaw, as I waited in line for my morning coffee, taking the children to art and music classes in the cultural epicenter of the world. I couldn't wait to go.

We arrived in the thick of summer, gazing up at the green canopies of oak trees in Central Park, and soon found an apartment on the Upper East Side in a building buzzing with children. On the first day my husband left us for work, I strapped the children into our new, red double stroller and headed to Central Park. The sidewalk on the park side of Fifth Avenue didn't want to be friends with the stroller and bumped the kids up and down until their tiny teeth chattered like cartoon characters. At the park amongst the Ralph Lauren collection of toddlers playing in the sprinklers and chubby babies napping in the strollers, I was the only mother of the children I was with. Most had been mothers but not of these children. I tried to make conversation, but they were cold.

I then signed up on "New York Mommy" e-mail lists but unsubscribed from most within a week. They were all about finding the "perfect caregiver" for your child. The women in our building posted ads on the notice board hoping someone would share information about good nannies. Few women wanted to talk about their children or spend time with them. My idea of mothering life in New York was melting fast.

The sticky weeks of summer continued with long days at the park, but it wasn't the best long-term arrangement. My six-month-old daughter was cranky if she didn't nap enough in the stroller. My toddler was tiring of the same playground. On very hot days, I bundled us all into a taxi to enjoy the air-conditioned museums with the baby in the sling and toddler in a stroller, but it was always short-lived and exhausting, rendering me useless for the rest of the day. We tried story time at the main library in midtown. My little boy appreciated the lions and plethora of books, but the baby wailed non-stop. We didn't have grandparents or cousins or friends to visit. My husband worked late. It dawned on me how different my social life in Perth was, and how many people I knew there. And now it was just going to be my children and me for a long year ahead.

On the odd occasion when there was another mother at the playground or library, we became instant friends, swapped phone numbers and arranged play dates around nap times. It's easy to bond and roll your eyes at the nannies. Make snide remarks about the absent mothers who had babies, then handed them over to nannies in the delivery room, so they could check e-mails and get back to their *real lives*. Because, of course, we hadn't.

I found out about toddler music classes. As I was about to pay for the term, half-jokingly I said to the girl at the desk, "Oh, and it's fine to bring the baby, too, right? She's only six months old."

"Well, nobody's ever asked that. It's meant to be one-on-one with your toddler. I'll have to call the director of parenting."

"No, you can't bring the baby," she reported ten minutes later. "You have to leave it with the nanny, so you can give your toddler your full attention."

"I don't have a nanny. I just moved here from Australia."

She leaned towards me. "I think you'll find most moms on the Upper East Side have nannies. It's too hard without any help," she whispered.

Hard is what I do best! Give me hard any day!

"Well, I'm sure that some people find it hard," I said and left.

I watched the nannies in Central Park with the toddlers and babies. Some were loving and warm with the children. Some stared vacantly in another direction. Most were on cell phones.

I couldn't imagine giving my children to someone roaming Central Park while talking on a phone. Of course, nobody in New York was perfect enough to look after my children. And what kind of mother would I be if I entrusted their well-being to a total stranger? But. Everyone else did. Perhaps New York had a different standard of perfection. It was about keeping your career going, only being available to your children after business hours and on weekends. It was not nursing-on-demand or home-made baby food or unlimited affection. How had I got it so terribly wrong? I had nothing in common with the other mothers and everything in common with the nannies. I was not a Manhattan mother with a real life to get back to. I was a nanny.

A few weeks after this discovery, my mother flew the twenty hours from Perth to New York to visit us in the week I decided to replace regular with whole grain pasta and bought a vegetable steamer. "I don't like this pasta," my little boy said, chewing a piece of whole grain penne and spitting it back into his plate next to his semi-chewed steamed carrots. Perhaps the pasta was a little fibrous and the carrots slightly rubbery.

"Why are you feeding him this weird brown pasta? Why don't you just buy normal pasta?" my mum asked.

"Because this is healthier."

"Just give him normal pasta and put some butter on it," she said.

"Then he won't eat anything else."

"So, what? It's pasta."

"He needs to eat whole grains and more vegetables."

Mum shook her head and said, "I'll make dinner tomorrow night."

So she bought rice (the unhealthy white kind), butter (salted) and a chicken (Kosher, because we were in New York). When

I saw the ingredients I knew she was cooking pilafi—a dish of a Greek village long since immigrated to English-speaking places. Comfort food. "I'll show you how to make it," she said.

"I know how to make it. I've watched you make it a million times. I just choose not to make it, because it's so unhealthy."

"It's rice cooked in chicken broth. It's very healthy."

"It's white rice cooked in chicken fat then coated in fried butter. It's pure high-glycemic carbohydrate in saturated fat. Why don't I just order McDonalds?"

She added butter to the hot frying pan. It sizzled, scorched and blackened. The smell is always overpowering, addictive, beautiful and wrong all at the same time.

I sank to the floor to play with the children while she finished dinner. For five minutes they were smiling, kissing, laughing, sharing and then biting, crying, snatching, screaming.

"Dinner's ready!" Mum called out and put it on the table.

My son sensed the butter and shoveled it into his mouth as fast as he could, the soft, black-flecked rice snowed on the chair and the floor, a nightmare to clean up. I will need to pick it up grain by grain, I thought.

"You see, he likes it better than the whole grain stuff you cook," my mother said.

"Of course he's going to like it better. It's pure butter. It's a calorie-laden food with no vegetables. I may as well have ordered American fried chicken like the other mothers."

"It's good for him." She scowled at me when I refused to eat it.

"I would like some more pilafi please, Mummy," he asked in his best polite voice, having finished his plate.

"Good boy, I'll get you some more," Mum said, and whisked his plate off the table to refill it.

"Nice dinner, Mummy," my little boy said.

The days dragged on. I was tired of Central Park. We had visited all the museums several times. The polar bear at Central Park Zoo died the day after we visited, which I took personal responsibility for. I yelled at my mother for buying my son a frosted chocolate cupcake instead of a whole grain zucchini muffin. I yelled at the children when they didn't sleep. I was not acting particularly perfectly. I was exhausted. Dragging two children around Manhattan was killing me.

"You're doing a good job, but maybe you should get some help," my mum said, loading our freezer with pilafi before flying back across the world.

"I've been suggesting the same thing since we moved here," my husband said. "You're so hard on yourself."

Yes, but it was as though I needed permission from *her*. She had done it perfectly, albeit with a little more refined sugar than I was willing to sprinkle into their lives.

When the leaves in Central Park began to redden and crisp and spiced pumpkin lattes appeared on the menu in Starbucks, I knew my time was running out. Since forbidden by New York mother/nanny laws from attending classes all together, something had to change. I finally relented and posted an ad on a nanny website. My inbox was flooded from applicants declaring how much they loved children and never talked on their cells while babysitting. I still didn't intend to leave them alone with someone else. I just needed the nanny to help with dinnertime, which was a constant scramble of placating overtired children, keeping them away from boiling water on the stove, assembling a healthy meal of lean protein, whole grains and multi-colored vegetables, or pilafi from the freezer, as the aroma of burnt butter filled the apartment and reminded me of my mother's absence. I eventually found a soft-spoken college graduate to help me. I would tidy and clean the apartment before she arrived (*see how perfect I am!*). When she was around, the baby would be glued to me, unwilling to acknowledge this stranger. I would fold the laundry, make afternoon tea for everyone, cook dinner with the baby on my hip (*perfect, perfect, perfect!*), while she relaxed on the couch and read a book and did puzzles with the older one. This wasn't what help was, was it?

"I've done everything by myself," I loved to hear myself say. What was wrong with me? I still had to be the perfect mother, even to a twenty-two-year-old babysitter? I couldn't just go and have a nap or go to the gym or order dinner from Seamless, like everyone else in our building? The children would cry for me. The food would be too salty and damage their kidneys. It wouldn't be perfect.

Even I, in the height of my delusions, knew this wasn't the solution. At least one of us had to learn to separate.

I heard about a little international pre-school a few blocks away that still had vacancies, even though fall was edging closer, so my husband, my son and I paid a visit. There were colorful, summer mosaic collages on the walls, photos of smiling children having a picnic, eating pizza, finger-painting. I was willing to concede on the pizza, since they seemed to be doing all kinds of craft activities I no longer had the patience for.

"Do you want to come to this school?" I asked him.

"Yes, Mummy, I want to play here."

And now I was one of those parents who let her two-and-a-half year old decide his future.

DAY ONE

I cried as I cut up a rainbow of fruit for his morning snack and put it in a little Tupperware container. I made pasta. And sandwiches. I used all the Tupperware. We walked to the school and met his teacher.

"Does he really eat all that food?" she asked, as I unpacked his bag and loaded it into the fridge.

"Sometimes," I lied, coloring.

"Maybe tomorrow you don't need to make food for the whole class," she said. "Give yourself a break."

But I don't need a break! I tried to smile and looked over at my baby boy, who was now dressed for pre-school and doing a jigsaw.

"The teacher seems very capable," my husband said. Yes, but she's *not me*.

"Well, Mummy's going now, but I'll get you later," I said.

"OK, Mum," he said to his jigsaw puzzle, not looking up. I hugged and kissed him. "Mummy will get you later," I said again.

Apparently he cried when he realized I wasn't there. It broke my heart to think of him crying and my not being there to comfort him. How could I do this? It was fixable. I could just take him out of the school, and we could find some other way to make things work. I was fine. Really, I could handle them all day every day. Of course I could. I'm their mother.

"Give it a chance, Em," said my husband, as I sobbed to him that night and watched the last of the lights go out on the skyscrapers of my old dream.

DAY TWO

"I can look after your son, but I can't look after your wife," the teacher told my husband quietly, as I cried saying good-bye at the school and all the way down Park Avenue past the line-up of white-gloved doormen.

I wasn't perfect any more. Or maybe I never was to start with. I put the baby down for a morning nap in her crib. I enrolled in a writing course at NYU, made myself a coffee and didn't empty the dishwasher as soon as it was finished.

DAY THREE

My son cried, but I didn't.

DAY FOUR

He asked to go to school. Neither of us cried. I finally relaxed.

For three hours in the mornings my little boy was happy playing with his friends, learning letters and singing songs. The baby had a longer morning nap in her crib and was more pleasant for the rest of the day. I had time to finish a still-warm coffee, write a little, breathe. Was it about him or was it about me? Why had admitting I needed time to myself been so difficult? I couldn't control everything. I wasn't the perfect mother. Is there a perfect mother? On the spectrum of perfect, where was I? Does it matter?

Everything about New York was so much more fun once I was able to pretend in the mornings that I was a writer, not the only stay-at-home mom with a frozen legal career in my nannied-up building. I was easier on the children, and I was easier on myself. Still, I was always the first mom at lunchtime pick-up. Even in the polar vortex, I found myself standing in the arctic blizzard of Park Avenue a few minutes early with my cheeks feeling as though slapped by evil fairies. But seeing my little boy's smile told me that it was all okay.

By the time spring poked its reluctant head out of ten feet of snow, there were only weeks left until we returned home. But it didn't feel like we were going home. In the middle of this vibrant city, we had all found our places. This was our home now—big, loud, crazy New York. I had let go a little bit and gotten so much more back. The Manhattan mothers had taught me a lot. I stopped setting myself unrealistic standards of motherhood perfection. They were all doing it their way. And whatever way it was, it was the best way for them.

These days, when my mother offers to look after the children and make them pilafi for dinner, I smile and nod and thank her. I fight the urge to lecture about whole grains and vegetables. And, at birthday parties when my children are inevitably first in line at the food table, shoveling as many treats into their little mouths as they can, sometimes I just take a deep breath and let them.

Emily Tsokos Purtill has won several Australian awards for young writers, including the prestigious Tim Winton Award for Outstanding Achievement for Young Writers. Her winning story was published in the anthology HATCHED (edited by Tim Winton, Fremantle Arts Press, 2013). She holds a bachelor of laws and a master of laws from the University of Western Australia and has recently returned to writing after working as a lawyer for eight years in Australia and Paris. In 2014, Emily was living in New York where she participated in an advanced fiction course at New York University. She currently lives in Perth, Western Australia, with her husband and children. She can be contacted at em_tsokos@hotmail.com.

What You Are Expected to Expect When You Are Expecting

David Turnoff

One day many years ago in graduate school in Cleveland, your friend was describing his girlfriend's family. She had two sisters, whom he had met along with her parents, before going out on a date. You don't know why you recalled the conversation so often through the years. It meant nothing to you overtly, but there was something there to prioritize its storage in a place of readily accessible memory.

While they were talking, your friend said, her father just sat there, shoulders hunched over, saying nothing. "He's beaten down. Four women and him. He can't get a word in edgewise," he said. And then you, a young man just starting graduate school, an adult on paper, but really just an aging boy with no sense of your place in the world, much less any deep understanding of family dynamics, replied, "The poor sonofabitch."

You and your friend had a good laugh over that. Why it seemed funny at the time, that comment, you couldn't exactly say. It just felt funny. Your knowledge of living in a house with four adult women as an adult yourself was, to say the least, limited. In hindsight, it was probably just an attempt to sound agreeable to your friend. But you said it, and it should have been a throwaway line, like the dozen or more everyone makes each day. And yet for some reason this one stayed with you.

Through the years, you recalled it on occasion, usually for no apparent reason, the way random, often distant memories percolate up during relaxed moments—a long car ride, a walk on the beach, a particularly pensive sitting on the toilet. "The poor sonofabitch." Just a harmless thought passing through a quiet mind.

Life proceeded. You moved to New York and met someone. You dated her, but it didn't work out. A few more years went by, and you met her again. Same girl, different life. You dated again and, oh boy, this time it felt right, and you made it official. Then boom, boom, boom. One potato, two potato, there were one, two, three children. And lo and behold, they were all girls, beautiful, happy, living girls.

Now when the recurring, fleeting memory returned, it came with implications. During those early years of parenthood, that old conversation with your friend (now married himself and a father of three boys) showed itself for what it was—a slow-moving, temporal, rhetorical boomerang, patiently working its way through the years, innocently enough, until it rose up and clocked you on the head with the substance of your own words. And then you knew. It hadn't been about some old friend's girlfriend's parent, a man you never met who meant nothing to you. He was only a place-saver, a totem of misdirection. The words, somehow, prophetically, were meant for you. You were the poor sonofabitch all along.

Was it true? Were you now the victim (or father) of unhappy circumstances? At the very least, it needed considering.

First of all, was it something that even mattered to you? Did you really care whether you had a boy or a girl, or a combination of the two, or a slew of one but not the other? Had you even thought about having children in that degree of detail?

Didn't you want a son? You had thought about it, certainly, but that's not necessarily the same thing as wanting one. You grew up in a family of predominantly women. Your father worked long hours, and you were home mostly with your mother and two sisters. That was the norm. But through the years, whenever you thought about having children, when you imagined yourself interacting with your own children, you saw yourself interacting with a single child, and it was always a male child. But was that a dream based on a desire, or was it just a passive idea, a reverse extrapolation of how you had experienced your own childhood as someone's son?

So maybe it didn't matter to you. That felt right. But any relief you experienced in reaching that conclusion (the most reassuring conclusion given the circumstances) did not last long. What you quickly discovered is that it didn't matter what felt right to you. It was about what was expected of you, the role you were expected to play. And from the point of view of others, it was expected that you should care, you should care very much. Any statement from you to the contrary was met with an amused expression of doubt.

The comments started soon after the second child was born. It started with your wife's aunt, who informed you that the reason you had not had a son was because you had not eaten enough chestnuts in the lead up to pregnancy. This was a common theme from your wife's family: Somehow the outcome of your children's gender implied a kind of "fault" on your end, one that more often than not was implicated by your dietary choices. Your wife was happy with having girls, but even she suggested you ate too much soy.

Meanwhile, your friend with the three boys offered to "lend" you some of his semen. And both friends and family seemed compelled to tell you about the articles they had read on any number of factors that tip the balance one way or the other. It was true, you conceded, that your X and Y chromosomes had determined the gender for each child, breaking the tie of your wife's double X's. But then you tried to explain how in all cases the winning chromosome, the one that makes it through the gauntlet of procreation, succeeds as a random event. If one tosses a quarter three times and it comes up heads all three times or tails all three times (two outcomes which have a combined probability of one out of four) would they assume the coin was rigged? The answer, when it came, always surprised you: Yes, yes they would. More commonly, you wouldn't even get a reply. They would just smile at you, sympathetically, skeptically. You could almost see the images of soy and chestnuts reflected in their eyes.

And if having to parry with friends and family over issues of procreation was not enough, both casual acquaintances and complete strangers seemed happy to make up the difference and join in the fray. "Are you going to try for the boy?" was a common question received while waiting in check-out lines or while spotting one of your little daredevils underneath the monkey bars at the playground. "It looks like you have your hands full," was another common refrain (read between the lines as "you poor man"), conveyed with a mix of humor and pity spoken readily, always in passing, along the streets of New York City.

But if you're going to have a family of girls, at least your timing can't be faulted. From a practical perspective, the strength of the historical reasons for wanting a boy over a girl in this country are perhaps at an all-time low. The opportunities and responsibilities available for women have never been as varied and plentiful as they are today. The fruits of an old promise are ripening, and you can be excited for your girls in ways your grandparents or even your parents could never feel about your mother or your sisters when they were young.

That all sounds reassuring, but what about the name factor? Don't you need a boy to carry on the family name? A boy will keep it going for one more generation, at least. And then what? Another generation, another crapshoot. When we think through worry and uncertainty, and where blame lies, there's usually a twenty- to forty-year window that feels tangible, a period of time that can relate to you and any perceived responsibility you carry. Grandchildren, great-grandchildren and whatever happens after are elusive hypotheticals. It can't be too much of a concern.

So how important is it to you now? Still not sure? Maybe try to expand your perspective. Get input from the descendants of some former big shots like Marcus Aurileus or Marco Polo to hear their thoughts on things. Or take the pulse of some Browns or Smiths, or Patels or Kims, if you can track any of them down. And by the way, did the dinosaurs have surnames? OK. Fair enough. The name is not a game changer for you.

A friend recently asked you if you had any regrets in your life. You used to be full of them. Regrets over worrying too much, for not investing time in developing skills that would have served you better in life, for not mapping out plans more concretely. But now when you are asked that question, you don't hesitate. There are no regrets. More specifically, there can be no regrets. Everything that happened in your life was necessary to lead you to meet her and date her and marry her. And everything after that led you to have your one, two, three girls. Any changes in any of it could have changed everything. One sperm out of millions finds one egg and makes one child. You go back in time and sneeze or scratch your behind, and your timing is off by a few seconds and another one in a million sperm wins. Change any of it, and you would not have known these girls.

But you wouldn't have known the difference, your friend replied. You would most likely have had other children you would have loved just as much. "That's true," you said. "But I don't know those other children. And I don't want to."

You remember the time a few years ago when your oldest, who is now nine and wants to be an astronaut, asked you where the first person came from. You told her she came from a monkey. And that the monkeys we were went away when we became the people we are.

She thought about it for a minute. Then she said, "I wish I could be the last person in the world."

"Why?"

"Because then I would see who the next people will be. The new people who will be here after us. I would be the one who gets to see them before we all go away. No one else would know about them except for me."

And one, two, three, that's when you truly knew. There can be no regrets.

_____

David Turnoff was born in Philadelphia and raised in Miami, Florida. After living in various parts of the Northeast and Midwest, he settled in New York City, where he met his wife, Theresa, and their three children were born. While living in New York, David began writing short fiction and attended several writing workshops, most consistently with Martha Hughes. After many happy years in New York, an impending space issue following the birth of their third child and a subsequent late October hurricane prompted a move. He currently resides with his family in Berkeley, California. In his spare time, he continues to write short fiction.

Outside In

Elizabeth Wohl

When I was a child, we moved. My father's checkered career as a middle manager for assorted corporations meant he was always being transferred or downsized or fired. We'd pack everything we owned into boxes and follow the moving van to Delaware, Illinois, Indiana, New Jersey, home office to field office and back again and out again, first the motel, then the rental, then the mortgaged new house. By the time I was in seventh grade, I'd been to eight schools, public, private and parochial. One year, I'd be in a one-room grammar school with a dirt playground. The next I'd be at a Catholic girls' school curtseying to nuns whose idea of gym was a decorous walk around the block in two straight lines à la the children's book heroine, Madeline. I was always the new kid at school, and the thing I wanted to learn, more than history, math or anything, was how to fit in.

I learned to talk about bird dogs, runaway chickens and sick hogs the year my father, fed up with business life, bought a farm in Indiana, but wild onions got into the rye and ruined it for sale to the whiskey distillers. The farm lost more money than we had. We were in trouble and a well-connected great-aunt used her pull to find my father a new, even-less-good-than-before corporate job in my mother's hometown. My father was radically unhappy, but I was thrilled. At last we would settle down.

I'd underestimated my mother. After years of packing and

unpacking, of politely offering tea when the Welcome Wagon lady showed up with local businesses' coupons at our latest new house, my mother was not ready to admit defeat. Maybe my father's career was going nowhere, but her family could still move up in the world. She embarked on her own career as a volunteer, which made new friends in the right places. Soon I was out of the town's more or less progressive public school and into an elite private school on a scholarship.

This was a much-appreciated correction to my sketchy early education. I went from A's to D's in math, but kindly old Dr. Conwell tutored me on the side. The headmaster handed me a biography of George Sand, suggesting Sand and I might have writing in common. But when Winkie's (or was it Muffie's or Babbie's?) father drove up to school in a brand new MG convertible and handed his Sweet Sixteen the keys to the car as a birthday gift, I realized once again, I was a stranger in a strange world.

My classmates, it seemed, got new cars the minute they passed their drivers' tests. On the other hand, no one seemed to expect me to show up driving a forest green Austin Healy when I turned sixteen. I was, however, expected to be "attractive," the secret, I slowly figured out, to success among my new friends and importantly, their parents.

"Attractive" was code for upper class, white, Anglo-Saxon Protestant manners and style. One was either attractive or one was not. Only the attractive fully understood the code's many nuances and conventions. I was Irish and a Catholic, lapsed but a Catholic nonetheless, and from a family anything but upper class. I was also a quick study. Soon I was saying "sofa" instead of "couch," and "curtains," not "drapes." A house, no matter how huge and pillared, was never a "mansion" but simply "a house." You said, "How do you do?" and shook hands upon first meeting. "How nice to see you," was the usual good-bye. Above all, an attractive woman did not "make a spectacle of herself," nor was she "bold." Attractive wives joined the Junior League and sat on civic boards. Their husbands ran the chemical companies that dominated the town's economy, or they were doctors and lawyers or had inherited money and owned land. A few were artists, adding a quasi-bohemian flair to a staid society. Attractive young children were invited to dancing class and later to parties and large debutante dances, where they met other young people who were attractive enough to marry. The not-attractive were tolerated with a patient, if insufficiently veiled, disinterest and included now and then only if they had some special skill or knowledge that advanced the interests of their betters. They did not get into the country club, nor were their children invited to dances and parties, and their rise to any sort of social and professional eminence was pretty much doomed.

I found myself leading two lives. My father, with time on his hands, had become a relentless do-it-yourselfer at the modest subdivision house we called home. He'd draft me for projects like painting the porch or retiling the basement. After we'd finished, I'd spend hours using this or that noxious chemical to get the paint out of my hair or the tan-colored grout from under my nails before I headed off to visit friends who kept horses and had pools and tennis courts of their very own, who griped about having to spend summer weeks at the family compound on Martha's Vineyard or Maine, who skied out West after Christmas and always spent spring break at some tropical beach.

My outsider mentality quickly alerted me to the insularity of this world. The large, affluent Jewish neighborhood on the other side of town had homes almost as stately as those of my friends, but no one ever spoke of anyone who lived there. Under the code,

Italians were marginally attractive, Irish a bit more so, especially if they acted like the Kennedys, who'd sent their sons to Choate and Harvard and their daughters to curtsey before King George. African-Americans, especially children, might be the beneficiaries of some charity, but in the world of "attractive," they did not exist. All of which was not very attractive. I knew that, but this was high school, and I wanted to fit in. I began to take pride in knowing the ways of this arcane world—what constituted a "decent" (as in strong) drink, how to write a proper regret for a tea dance, whom to talk to when at a formal dinner. Above all, I learned to assume an air of amiable distance when my friends talked about sports I didn't play (golf, paddle tennis), places I'd never seen (Bermuda, Paris) and people I didn't know (mostly even richer kids who'd gone to boarding school in tenth grade). Overheard adult conversations were the most interesting, as serial tumblers of scotch on the rocks lubricated an endless accounting of who knew whom, who'd married whom, and *sotto voce*, how the money had been made.

My comeuppance came one hot, humid July evening when an "attractive young man," (Andover, Yale) invited me to dinner at the country club. I bought a new dress, shoes to match and the afternoon of the date, I even paid my younger brother to iron my wild, black Irish hair. After an hour with my head on the ironing board, my face next to hot steel, and my brother improvising a monologue about the stupidity of girls, my hair was finally smooth enough to qualify as attractive. I counted on the club air conditioning to keep it that way.

Alas, my date had arranged for dinner on the club terrace. We ordered gin and tonics and watched white haze steam up from the golf course in the ninety-plus degree heat. Soon my pale blue shift dress was damp under the arms. My hair made its move, frizzing into a mop growing ever larger until I saw, reflected in the horror on my date's face, my hair as one of those dandelion puffballs that would never be allowed to intrude on the club's impeccable green turf. All around me tawny brown or bright blond hair maintained pageboy good manners. My hair was making a spectacle of itself. I rushed to the club's ladies room. There, in a sea of pink and green chintz, I whacked at my mane with comb and brush. When that failed to tame it, I tried watering it down, only to get water stains all over my dress. When I came out of the ladies room, my date took one look at bedraggled me, drained his drink and stood up. An urgent phone call he'd forgotten to make, he said, hustling me out of the club. I never saw or heard from him again.

Today I see that scene as something out of a sitcom, but at the time, it hurt. I had failed to be attractive. I couldn't fake it until I could make it. I went off to college chastened, determined to be myself. *Authentic*, as they say. I spent endless hours in coffee shops with self-styled campus radicals—one always wore what he called his "Stalin shirt"—mulling over the great issues of life and death. What would I have done in the Holocaust? Could capitalism survive? Would passive resistance work in a militarized world? I was eighteen and didn't have a clue. My provisional views were often shaped and reshaped by the smooth-talking young men I met. But my little band of outsiders made me feel something of an insider, albeit one who hedged her bets. "Stay as sweet as you are," the dean of women told us all at freshman orientation, and although there were a few wild ones among us, most of us tried to do, or tried to appear to do, just that.

But then came India—the land of liberation to all those Westerners who trek to ashrams in search of inner peace. A post-college grant sent me to the Balwant Vidyapeeth Rural Higher Institute outside Agra, where for a year I taught English to young men from nearby villages. They were preparing to bring some Western ideas— improved sanitation and farming methods, for example—to rural India. But they were also firmly rooted in their own ways. "This is India, Madam, not America," they would tell me, making it clear the code I'd so assiduously studied and tried to imitate back home meant nothing here.

At first, I felt oddly disoriented. The whole idea of dressing to be "attractive"—-the right hemline, the right fabrics, the right styles—was meaningless when almost every woman I saw wore a sari. My wild hair? Who cared? All around me women wore coconut oil-tended long black braids. Some of my students felt sorry for me because I wasn't married yet, though I was only twenty-two. Some warned me against "love marriage," asserting that an arranged marriage would be more likely to last. But when I said Americans preferred love marriage, their attitude was one of amused acceptance. They didn't expect me to change my mind. And sometimes, I couldn't change theirs.

One assignment I gave was to write a letter to their fathers and begin with the salutation, "Dear Father." My students balked. "Oh no, Madam. We would never 'dear' our fathers," one of my students protested. He insisted on "Sir," and so did everyone else in the class. "Sir" was appropriate for business correspondence, according to the manual I taught from, but "Dear Father," in my classroom became, "Sir."

A rattletrap bus rode between the Institute and Agra, where my fellow grantees and I often went for cold coffee with cream. Women sat in the front of the bus, men in the back. One young California couple insisted on sitting together in front, an attempt to teach the locals the proper relationship between the genders. They braced for a challenge, but none ever came. My Indian fellow teachers and students had none of that American cultural evangelism in which we validate ourselves by insisting others be like us.

Now, I'm not defending gender segregated buses or the caste system in India, or the class system in England or America for that matter, but after a childhood and youth of trying to fit in where I didn't and couldn't belong, my students' open and calm acceptance of difference came as a gift.

They welcomed me into their homes where we sat on wood and string beds, the only furniture they had, with the laundry and maybe some Technicolor calendar pictures of Shiva or Ganesh, hanging from the dried mud walls. Even the poorest house would offer me food. I'd demur. They'd insist. I quickly figured out it would be insulting to refuse, and soon I'd be downing a bit of curry, a chapatti and ghee, the clarified butter that was a luxury in these homes. Sometimes the whole village would watch me eat, pointing at my blue eyes and laughing, but in a friendly way, as I entertained them with my ineptitude at eating curry with my (always right) hand. Their relaxed tolerance of an outsider's ways, probably acquired after many millennia of foreign invasions and the rise and fall of a vast variety of internal cultures, was freeing. I was more comfortable as an outsider in India than I'd ever been in the conformist West. My outsider status was the way in which I belonged.

My students' amused tolerance threw my own customs into high relief. I came to see them for what they were—arbitrary, provisional and sometimes out of date. In any culture, what may have made sense in one context becomes calcified in another. Like many Indians, I might hold cows sacred if my ancestors had endured famine, and if I relied on dairy products for protein, cow dung for fertilizer and fuel, and the animal's strong back to plough next year's crops. Maybe we should think of those bloated McMansions and tank-like SUV's that clog our highways as American sacred cows. In a culture where workplace competition is an extreme sport, it becomes very important for round-the-clock strivers to find ways to advertise their "success," global warming be damned. And the code of "attractive?" Well, learning it certainly didn't make me better than anyone else. It was simply a way of signifying and preserving membership in a local power elite. It was a tool, and I came to see that if I wanted to build a life that had meaning for me, I'd better choose the right tools.

"This is *India, Madam, not America.*" It's almost a mantra. Outwardly this realization didn't change me much. Some summers I straighten my hair. (Professionally, thank heaven!) I tend to say "black tie," instead of "tuxedo," and I never pick up my fork until everyone at the table is served. Of course, in Europe, each person eats right away so food doesn't get cold, but I can't get comfortable doing it. Maybe that and other Pavlovian inhibitions explain why social anxiety still finds me sometimes reaching for that second glass of wine. But whenever I need to let go of that old, odd woman-out feeling, I remind myself that life is much more interesting when the struggle for acceptance yields to an effort to understand.

What once was a source of struggle now seems a series of opportunities, a chance to explore different ways of being in this world. As one of my favorite poets, Frank O'Hara, put it, "Grace/to be born and live as variously as possible."

Elizabeth Wohl was a journalist for many years, as an Associated Press reporter, a Ms. Magazine *contributing editor and during the Vietnam War, a freelance reporter for the North American Newspaper Alliance. Her fiction has been published in* The Quarter, Fiction *and other literary magazines. She lives in Brooklyn and is hoping the wisdom in this anthology will help her stop revising and let go of her novel.*

. . . OF ANGER AND FEAR

Acadie

Julie Strong

I am standing in a muddy field, weeping into the mane of an Icelandic pony. It is mid-April 2005 at a riding centre near where I live in Nova Scotia's Annapolis valley. Nova Scotia is the hour-glass-shaped land sticking out from Eastern Canada.

I am here for a women's weekend with Icelandic ponies. It is for women who would like to ride were they not afraid of regular-sized horses. I am fifty-six, divorced and an MD with three grown children. I am afraid of horses; however, I need to connect with one.

When I was four, my mother died shortly after giving birth to my baby sister, Gillian. The following summer I was playing on a beach when a cantering horse kicked me in the head. It wasn't a bad injury, but I have no memory of my mother, and I reckoned if a horse took it away, then a horse might give it back.

Most likely my lack of memory is because our father threw away all our mother's belongings and never spoke her name again. How I yearned to remember something about her. And bar being kicked in the head again, I felt I had nothing to lose. In fact I did lose something, or rather was able to let go of something: part of the heavy weight of mother-loss I have carried for many years.

As a physician in general practise, I relate well to adults; however, when I have to give a child an immunization, my insides freeze up. I hate injecting a needle into her arm. Worse, I sometimes feel envious when her mother kisses and soothes her afterwards. When I was little they could have chopped off my arm, if only my mother had been there to comfort me. But then, with only one arm, I wouldn't be going to a riding weekend.

As I drive into the centre I see two women in a field stroking a couple of ponies. I park, lace up my hiking boots and fill my pockets with carrots. Olga, the centre's owner, leads me to the field and introduces me to Jarpi, an Icelandic pony with a chestnut brown coat and long, shaggy, black mane with bangs that wisp over his eyes. He radiates perfect serenity, as he nibbles on the new blades of grass sprouting from the ground, his tail giving the occasional swish. Perfectly content in the moment, Jarpi is the opposite of me with my past roiling around inside like a can of barbed worms.

Jarpi looks up as Olga speaks his name. I am five-foot-three, and Jarpi is thirteen hands tall, so we are pretty much eye-to-eye. I offer him a carrot. He nuzzles it with soft, velvet lips, and I feel his warm breath on the palm of my hand. His lips retract to reveal huge yellow teeth the size of piano keys. I shudder yet hold my hand still as he takes the carrot and chomps appreciatively. I stroke his neck and run my hand down over his flank. He is plump in the middle; he looks pregnant. The last time I saw my mother, she would have been very pregnant, but I am a doctor, and doctors know boy horses don't get pregnant.

I bury my fingers in the downy fur at the base of Jarpi's mane and inhale his good, earthy, horse smell. I hug him tight. Something about this huge creature being gentle with me, tolerating my presence, when with one flick of his hoof he could send me flying, moves something inside of me. I begin to cry. Olga murmurs about ponies being okay with grief and leaves. I look up to make sure the other women aren't looking my way. They are not, and Jarpi's chomping drowns out the noise of my weeping. After a minute, I loosen my grip on his neck; my past should not give Jarpi indigestion.

Jarpi's thick winter coat is coming away in clumps, and his back and rump are caked with dirt. Rolling in the now-molten mud is the ponies' favourite spring activity. Even though his coat is mired and shaggy, his big brown eyes and long black eyelashes make him look beautiful.

The last time I felt beautiful, or even really pretty, I was three. Photos at that age show me in frilly dresses, frilly socks and lacy sweaters. With my mother gone, Daddy put me in dungarees or anything else he could find; I knew I looked dirty and ugly, but so was my mother, from living underground. Served her right for going there.

Daddy smelled nice, of shaving soap and cigarette smoke. I stood beside him with the matches for when he wanted to light another cigarette. There was no more throwing me in the air or bedtime songs. He sat hunched over the kitchen table in front of his cold cups of tea, smoking. It was always dark in there with the curtains closed. He murmured over and over, "I should never have let her carry that bag of potatoes. That's what did it." Well, I could carry a bag of potatoes just fine and knew it could never hurt a grown up. Maybe if I dropped a bag on the baby, it would go away, then Mummy could come back, but I would go to jail.

When Daddy looked up and saw me, he looked away, like I had hurt him. I hated that. Sometimes I even wanted to hit him, but I put on the smiley face he liked. If he ever found out how angry I was, he might decide to go away, too. Auntie said Mummy had gone to sleep, so why did Daddy let them put her in the ground? Daddy was our Prince. The dwarfs in Snow White knew only the prince could wake her. Since I loved her the most, I shouldn't have let them do it. It's my fault she's been buried alive. I would have a horse one day, and cry out like the Lone Ranger, "Hi Ho, Silver!" I would get her out, bring her back and together we would gallop off.

Olga returns with a bucket of brushes. There are five: one for getting the big clods of mud off the ponies, one for polishing their coats, one for getting the tangles out of their manes and two for I haven't a clue what. We lead the three ponies to the fence and tie their halters to a railing so they don't roam away. We enjoy grooming them; the rhythmical circular movement is hypnotic, and we derive pleasure from divesting them of their grimy old winter coats and bringing their new undercoats to a brilliant shine. The ponies seem to like being brushed, and we women relax along with them, imbibing their sense of being totally at one with their surroundings. We even manage to brush out their tails and not be kicked while we are at it.

The finishing touch is to remove the pebbles from their hooves. There is a special pick for this. A horse's hooves are the same as our fingernails. You can trim the hoof, no problem, but the nail quick is super sensitive. In a horse, this is called the frog, and it's there where pebbles get caught. But if you touch the frog while trying to extract the pebble, the horse's immediate reflex is to kick out. We participants, in unison, decline to perform this task, so Olga does it. I watch, thinking how much better the pony must feel once the pebble is out. I think about the stone in my heart, and how I have to have something that connects me to my mother, even if it's only to fill the void. I don't care if I will feel better if I let it go. It's all I've got of her.

We saddle the ponies and clamber up. Mounted on Jarpi, I am nearly seven feet high, a veritable giantess. It is satisfying to be able to see over bushes and rocks and survey the world from this new perspective. We riders are instructed how to maintain "power position" in the saddle. This means having our hands rest on the reins and imagining our feet connected to the earth through the stirrups. We breathe into our center, which for women approximates to the womb space. We learn the difference between using "hard" and "soft" eyes. Hard eyes are when the vision is focused on a specific object that you want to reach; soft eyes are for peripheral vision, for being on low alert for things such as fallen branches and deep puddles. This idea of a soft gaze is familiar to me from ten years of practising mindful meditation. I am thankful for anything familiar, such as knee-deep mud, manure and horseflies, in this world of strange objects, including five types of grooming combs and brushes, three types of bridles and electric fences.

Riders need to develop clear intent. Our intent is to go riding. The ponies' intent is to stop and eat as much grass as possible along the way. Also, we must be on the alert for a type of pond weed that the ponies will gorge on, given the chance, but it causes bad stomach cramps; we are to steer them away from this. Another potential hazard is the recently-sighted mother bear with her cubs. A pony will bolt if he sees a bear; this makes sense. Olga says he can also startle at any sudden movement, like a garbage bag caught on a bush or tossing in the wind. If the pony shies beneath us and takes off at a gallop, we are to lean forward and grab hold of his mane until he slows down. We women swallow our trepidations and head off onto the trail in the woods.

It is a pleasure to feel at one with Jarpi as he steps confidently over winter's fallen twigs and piles of old brown leaves. I inhale the scent of damp earth coming back to life. A pair of crows caws from a pine tree. I feel as if Jarpi and I, together, make up that mythological beast, a centaur, but I've never heard of any female centaurs, just males, and how randy they were—gate-crashing weddings and making off with the women guests. My satisfaction at being a centaur is short-lived. Farther into the woods, the potholes become broader and deeper, with big fallen branches strewn over them. Every dozen steps, Jarpi loses his footing. After a few minutes of being churned around in the saddle, I totally forget about breathing and hang onto the reins for dear life. A twig pokes Jarpi in the belly and when he startles, I nearly fall off into a water-filled ditch. Twice he veers off into a clump of trees and a branch pokes me in the eye. I wonder if this pony is trying to kill me. The next time Jarpi startles, it is as if I know what to do and simply do it. I bend forward from the hip onto his neck and grasp his mane. He slows down, and I can breathe again, knowing I can respond to the unexpected. I have learned not to take it personally. Jarpi isn't trying to get me off his back; he just has his own issues. Besides, he seems quite happy to be stroked and calmed down over whatever it was that spooked him. It strikes me as odd that a big animal like a pony would be scared of an imaginary creature.

I remember being terrified of the witch under my bed, just after I started grade primary. I would dream about Mummy. But then she would take off her face, and it would be the witch underneath. Then the witch would take off her mask, and it would be Mummy. I would be so relieved and happy. Then she would take off the Mummy mask, and the witch would appear again. Then I stopped dreaming of either of them.

When I was six, our father moved us all to Colwyn Bay, a little town in north Wales. Daddy gave me a book of Greek mythology.

I read how Hades, the god of the underworld, came in his chariot drawn by six coal-black stallions and abducted Persephone. Her grief-stricken mother, Demeter, the goddess of the harvest, threatened the world with famine unless Persephone was restored to her. Eventually a bargain was struck. For five cold months, Persephone would live in the underworld, but in spring she would return to earth and the embrace of her mother. So each spring when the ground thaws and hyacinths and anemones burst into bloom, it is a sign that Persephone has emerged from the darkness and stepped on the still-frozen ground. For me, Mummy was Persephone, living in the underworld until she could come back. She was a goddess and could catch a train to Colwyn Bay whenever she wanted. I wished she would hurry up and decide to come back soon. I missed her so badly. I wouldn't mind how dirty she was or eaten up by worms and insects. I would pretend I didn't notice.

A kind teacher wanted to adopt Gillian. Gillian was pretty with blond hair. I had mouse hair and was ugly from the pain and confusion and anger inside me. No one would ever want to adopt me. I pretended I didn't care about not having a mother. But if a woman had baked a cake or done anything especially for me, I would have taken her hand and never let it go. And if she ever dared try to leave me, I would eat her alive.

We are deep in the woods; little clumps of snow persist only in the darkest crevices. It is wonderful to see coltsfoot, that harbinger of spring, sprouting from the ground. Its yellow flowers look like squashed dandelions, as if emerging from the still-frozen ground sapped all their energy, leaving them impotent and unable to fully open their petals. The blossom sits atop an anemic-looking grey, skinny stalk. Coltsfoot is a sorry, leafless excuse for a flower, but it is Nova Scotia's equivalent to Persephone's hyacinths and their appearance in spring.

The pony in front of us stops to pass water. A torrent flows downhill towards us. Jarpi decides to empty his bladder, too. Olga instructs us to lift our bottoms up out of the saddle to take the weight off their kidneys while they micturate. The ponies then all look up and sniff the air. They break into a tolt, because they know we are approaching home and fresh hay and freedom. Tolting is a gait specific to Icelandic ponies. It is half-way between a trot and a canter. It feels like riding a washing machine set on spin cycle when the towels have bunched all to one side. It takes a few minutes to get used to, then becomes quite pleasurable.

We return to the stables and unsaddle the ponies. I rub Jarpi down and give him another carrot. We bring over fresh hay; the ponies have a nibble then run off into the field where they drop and roll in the mud, rise up, look at us and give a snort and whinny. We laugh about all our grooming going to waste, then stagger into the farmhouse to rest.

The next day it rains all morning, but clears by noon and becomes warm enough to eat lunch outside. We are sitting on a bench beside the two fields where Olga keeps a handful of retired horses. Three white and two black mares live in one field. One of the black horses has a diamond on her forehead, while the other is entirely black. The one with the white diamond is Lisa and the black one is Acadie. Olga says that Acadie is eight years old and has never yet been ridden. When she came to the centre two years ago, she would not allow any horse or person near her, probably because she was mistreated in the past. Acadie now permits Lisa close but will bite the other horses and nip at people, too.

In the other field, an elderly chestnut gelding paces up and down. Olga glances over at him.

"That's Turk. Acadie must be in heat," she says.

We look over to admire Turk's fine erection then return to our coffee.

Afterwards, Olga invites us to enter the mares' field and each of us chooses a horse to approach. We are to pay attention to our feelings and to our own and the horse's breathing. We are to start a conversation with our horse and see what transpires. I want to talk to Acadie, on account of her past. I want to talk to her especially about anger.

When I was ten and Gillian, six, our father took us to Australia. How would Mummy ever find us now? No one had ever said she was dead. People murmured things like, "Poor kids, they lost their mother." Or, "Your mother has gone to live with God and look after the baby angels." Even though she was my goddess, how was she going to catch a plane? And I knew she didn't swim that well. That's when I despaired. She might just as well be dead. My heart congealed to stone, and I swore I would never trust anyone again so long as I lived.

I feel very small in the big horse's field. As I squelch through the mud and get closer to Acadie, I become more and more nervous about how tall she is and whether she will let me near her. What if she suddenly decides to trample me to death? I realise I am holding my breath and make myself breathe in and out. She allows me to hug her around the neck, and I murmur into her mane that I am sorry for what happened to her. For what happened to both of us. She waits until I am done, then accepts a carrot and walks away.

I return to the fences. "How was it talking to Lisa?" Olga asks.

I feel very foolish. I thought I was talking with Acadie but had approached the wrong horse. Still, I am glad to have been able to express anything about how I feel to anyone at all.

To wrap up the weekend, Olga suggests we try riding one of the big horses bareback. I love the idea, and since I have already met Lisa, I volunteer to take her halter and bring her from the field. Again I am seized with anxiety; the horses are so huge. Then Acadie notices me and begins walking in my direction. This time, I know it is Acadie, because she is entirely black. Her coat glistens with anthracite sheen and with each step, her long mane wafts back and forth. She halts beside me, and I notice that her hips are swaying a little. I try to explain to her that I have come for Lisa, but I know I cannot walk away from a horse that has never yet permitted anyone to hug her, let alone ride her. My hands fumble with the halter, but my reach is not long enough, so Acadie bends her head to allow me to slip it over her neck. I am overcome by her trusting me in this way and begin to cry as I lead her over to the fence where Olga is waiting.

"That is Acadie, not Lisa," she calls out.

"Well, she wanted to come," I say, adding, "I would like to ride Acadie bare back."

"She has never been ridden before," Olga protests.

I blurt out, "Well that makes two of us," not knowing what I mean but sensing it is about trust. I am sure that Acadie hasn't invited me to bring her here just to slough me off. She stands quite still, and I am ready to mount her. However, Olga has been with horses for over fifty years, compared with my few hours, so I do pay attention to her advice.

"OK," says Olga, amazed that Acadie has come this far with a stranger. "Put your arms around her."

I stroke Acadie's neck, feeling the muscles rippling beneath her skin, then reach over and hug her.

Olga hesitates a moment. "All right, you can lie across her back while I hold your legs."

Tears are falling down my face onto Acadie, and my nose is running, but she doesn't move. I hang over her like a sack of wheat, feeling the warmth of her broad back and girth against my belly and thighs. Something shifts inside me. I cry some more. A pebble drops from my heart. My mother wasn't the only source of mothering in the world.

It lasts just a couple of minutes. But it is enough.

Afterwards, Olga says this was a tremendous first step for Acadie in learning to trust people. I wondered whether a part of Acadie's coming to me was because she was in heat. Acadie interpreted my open grief as passion, and that was enough. She invited me to cover her, as if I were her mate. I, in turn, felt supported by her greater size and strength as if I were a little girl again and she, my mother. In that brief space of time, the closeness of sex and the closeness of mothering became the same thing.

Making the connection with Acadie seemed a little like a re-enactment of the myth of Demeter and Persephone. Only this spring time the Earth Mother goddess came as a black mare looking for a mate and found instead a motherless daughter. Two sentient creatures took a chance in trusting each other and afterwards walked away lighter.

Since that weekend I have found it easier to enjoy my own children and my medical work. I started telling Greek myths to inner city kids. Mostly they enjoy the gorier tales, such as Hercules's slaying of the Nemean Lion, but I usually manage to get the story of Demeter and Persephone in, too.

Julie Strong is a physician and shamanic healer in Halifax, Nova Scotia, and holds a medical degree from Trinity College, Dublin; a BA in classics, Dalhousie University, Halifax; and is trained in psychosynthesis, a transpersonal psychology fostering wholeness and creativity.

Her "Athena in Love" won the 2012 Canadian Atlantic Fringe Festival's new playwright award; she received the 2010 Atlantic Writers' Federation Award for short story; The Medical Post of Canada *has published her articles. She has presented on madness and creativity in America and Europe and teaches shamanic healing workshops, helping others find their power animals and spirit teachers. Strong was born in England.*

The Boy Who Saved Me

Kerry Guerin

Insomnia is God's gift to worry. For a year there was no getting away from it, not with drugs or therapy or meditation.
During the day worry massaged my brain with: 'What about
this?' 'What about that?' At night, I would sit bolt upright in
bed from something far worse than worry. Staring at the crim-
son 2:00 a.m., stabbing me from the clock atop my husband's
dresser, fear flung me out of bed and propelled me down the
hall to my son's room, where I threw open the door, terrified he
would be hanging or lying in blood-soaked sheets with slit wrists
or in a drug-induced coma, never to wake.

I'm lucky. That's not what met me when I'd fling open his
door. There are parents who have flung open bedroom doors only
to find those images weren't fantasies. Their sons and daughters
took their lives not because of being gay, but because communities,
schools, friends and even their families couldn't deal with homo-
sexuality. Those young lives were lost to hopelessness that grows
from bullying, rejection and being informed by everyone—from
relatives to the law—that if you're gay, you aren't worth protecting.

Putting distance between the homophobia my son experienced has been for me an experiment in letting go. Complete
success I wouldn't call it; occasionally, I still feel that familiar
anger, but where I choose to put my focus is the only aspect
of daily life I get to control. In part, choice has allowed me to

recover, let's call it, from that nightmare.

Liam came out when he was twelve on a summer's evening before the start of seventh grade. He had spent the day with friends, and I rushed out the door to pick him up with dinner already on the grill. As I pulled up to the house and rolled down the window, he and his friends were standing on the front lawn, glancing covertly at each other while one boy counted, "One, two, three."

"Liam's gay!" they shouted, smiled nervously and searched my face for the reaction. In that moment I wasn't happy or angry or shocked. I had known for quite some time Liam was gay. I was a little sad, because I wanted his coming out to me to be done in private. I knew we needed to talk; he needed to talk, so a quick reply and quicker getaway seemed in order.

"That's great. Get in. Dinner's on." I gave a vague smile to the crowd on the front lawn but focused on Liam's face. His mix of excitement and fear was palpable. By the time we reached the corner, he was wiping away tears. I tried to comfort him on the way home. After all, it wasn't like comforting a child who had lost something, gotten left out, had his feelings hurt—those moments belong to all children and adults who parent them. This moment was ours, unattached to any experience of his friends or any of the parents I knew.

The three-minute ride home led to forty-five minutes of sitting in the car and talking. I'll never forget it and have shared little of what was said with few people. I will keep that moment between us, mother and son, thankful for a child with enough courage to be authentic and grateful that something right had been done for him, despite the craziness of divorce and remarriage. I saw that some positive expression of living had taken hold in him, which nurtured and gave him strength to stand up and be recognized.

I won't tell you that fear of his being physically assaulted didn't grip me. It was the only bell that went off when he told me he was gay. Something visceral shot through me while we sat in the car that night. I had visions of him walking into the school bathroom and being jumped, his head smashed against a sink or toilet, blood everywhere. I let go of those images, because I was missing what he was saying about what it meant to him to be gay. I shook off those visions and listened to a scared yet thoughtful boy who was becoming a man who owned himself.

When Liam came out to his stepfather Joe and to his sister Jillian, little did I know they would be the most prescient family members. Jillian, ever the realist, said, "Yeah, that's great, but I'm telling you not to tell anyone at school, because there are hillbillies, and I don't mean rednecks, I mean real hillbillies, who will want to hurt you. Assholes. You know what I mean?"

"I appreciate what you're saying, but I can't do that. I can't hide," was Liam's mantra for the days following his revelation. He came out to Joe in private. They both told me Joe ended the conversation with, ". . . and if someone hurts you, we'll hurt them back, and I don't mean physical violence. There are ways to deal with people who hurt you because you're gay." Liam was happy and relieved he had a family who admired him for knowing himself. Liam's father Arthur had the wisest and sweetest response. "Ah, Liam, it's about time. I love you."

Shortly after it became public that Liam was gay, my fears came true. He was assaulted by a fellow seventh-grader. The boy who attacked him was suspended for three days and sent Liam a message on Myspace that went something like: "Fuck you, you stupid faggot Jew, I am going to kill you." His page said Hitler was his hero, and he had an entire page of 666. There was a family court hearing, orders of protection and a permanent suspension for the student, more so because of anti-Semitism than homophobia. You see, gays weren't a protected class under New York law, another reason to feel outraged.

Rage provides a terrible cover-up for fear. I hate feeling fearful, but I was full of it. So, I mastered the art of pushing fear aside with rage, which occasionally softened on the good days into spitting anger and contempt. I talked about this assault on my son all too often, feeding the rage a little more each time. But that wasn't the worst thing: It was seeing reality sink in that some people wouldn't like or accept him because of who he was. I tried to comfort Liam and myself with words I had said to him and his sister over the years: "Go where you're wanted. Don't go where you're not wanted." In other words: Find your friends, find your community. They're out there. But those words were little comfort. Those words provided little comfort to me as well, knowing the risk he took every day he went to school. Yet, he kept going, at least for a while.

Many of Liam's peers liked him. He is smart, finds history and politics particularly interesting. He had friends at school. But after a while friends and interests weren't enough to keep depression at bay. I don't know if it was the effect of hearing a barrage of homophobic slurs every day that finally depressed him to the point of immobilization, or not having a young, gay community of his own while his straight friends were dating and going to parties, or both, that made getting out of bed an act of futility. He began sleeping sometimes sixteen hours a day. Anxiety had him up in the middle of the night, pacing and formulating tactics to get through the next school day. Those school days eventually stopped coming.

I am grateful Liam often confided in me about his feelings. I didn't have to guess much about why he was sleeping a lot and camping out in his room. What to do about it was the breeding ground for my own frustration. When depression first took over my son, I was guilty of saying things like, "You will meet many assholes in life. You have to learn to let them go." Ha! I was telling him to let go of feeling bullied and unsafe, yet I couldn't let go of one iota of what was happening to him at school. The difference between Liam and me is that I enjoyed hating people. He didn't. He did what we had asked of him as a child: Don't hit anyone. Use your words. Tell an adult. That advice wasn't giving him relief, so depression moved in. The more depressed he became, the more hateful I became.

Unfortunately, there were many to hate. The high school principal was high on the list. During our first meeting to discuss solutions for Liam, the principal said, "IF this is happening," referring to Liam's account of the homophobia he was experiencing. It was everything I could do not to use that "if" to springboard across the table at him. I was sitting between my husband, a retired New York Police Department Special Victims detective, and my ex-husband, who practiced law for thirty years. They were calm, pointed and confident. I was confident only that the fight was on. I was juiced. That's what the fear for my son did for me. It was invigorating, like morning coffee, dangerous, too; I couldn't see that blind rage would harm my efforts to protect Liam. If I didn't get down from the ledge, I would never realize anything positive for my son.

During the tenth and beginning of eleventh grade, Liam would come many nights to our bedroom door. "Mom, Mom, Mom, can you come out here?" I'd close the door so our voices wouldn't wake Joe, and Liam and I would end up on the living room couch. I held him when he wept and breathed a little better when he would sit in one corner of the couch and map out how he would manage school. Those were the times he was toughest, not paralyzed by the homophobia waiting for him daily. I never left the couch unless he fell asleep or went to bed. I would stay there, calculating murder. Well, not murder, but I began to understand the meaning of crimes of passion. The most pain came when I realized my pain was nothing in comparison to my son's.

My life became a series of head-jerking experiences woven into unremarkable daily life with its trappings of middle-class living: a couple of used cars, jobs, school nights, births, deaths, joys and heartbreaks. Bolstered by a silent belief running through it all that even though things were tough, I felt tomorrow everything would be okay. Yet, tomorrow, as the remedy for a day gone wrong, seemed less and less certain. Punched in the back of the head, threatened with death, intimidated nose-to-nose at his locker, called a faggot, queer, cocksucker so often that being asked to quantify it in the law suit he took against the school, was a joke. This became Liam's average day. Most days he hung on with false bravado—really liking to learn—and a push from home (regretted in retrospect) to move forward no matter what. My regret comes from finally understanding that telling someone to "shake it off" is akin to saying, "it's no big deal." It was a big deal.

The weight of being the mother of the boy who stood up for himself, being the mother of a boy who might not survive, being alone on the couch at two in the morning, formulating conversation after conversation with various students, parents, and administrators, which began, "Let me tell you something, you ignorant bastard . . ." all of that weight after four years has lessened. How? How did I get to a place where only on occasion does that visceral anger and negativity still take over?

Although wary of sharing with everyone, I talked to my friends and family. I feared receiving a bad reaction or worse yet, silence from the more conservative members of the clan. I didn't shy away when someone in the community asked me what was going on with Liam and school. I tried my best to remain calm and not rant, at least not in public, and I pushed my son to look at his life a different way. Who says you have to graduate with your class, immediately head to college, etc., etc.? Then I talked to attorneys, investigated civil rights, the legal aspects of what was happening, spoke to the New York American Civil Liberties Union, all in the hope of arming myself with information instead of a razor-sharp tongue.

The most crucial aspect of attaining a less hateful place wasn't something I did. My son did it. Liam thrived. Some would say he thrived because he has a supportive family. True enough. Still, there are many supportive families who lose gay sons and daughters to suicide. Liam is a survivor. Maybe he gets that from his gene pool. Wherever it came from, his courage to keep going was the essential ingredient in my own recovery, which I learned from watching my son negotiating one foot in this world and one foot out.

Fortitude was something we talked about often in this family, not a fake version of it, like a Sesame Street jingle—"Today's word is Fortitude!" It came up whenever someone was struggling. Forge ahead; don't let the bastards get you down—that kind of thinking. Fortitude isn't the same as letting go. Fortitude means using the shit that's been handed to you and planting a garden, preferably in view of the one who handed you the load in the first place.

Letting go, something you'd think I'd know about since I had been sober for more than twenty years, has always been elusive. To me, letting go means no more anger, no more hate. Letting go exists in some spiritual place I strive to reach when the shit pile is too high to manage, and I am imagining myself knocking someone out with my imaginary shovel. I don't get on my knees and pray for the willingness to let go, so I can transcend to a higher plane. I simply talk myself out of saying or doing the unforgivable, not in the interest of serenity but mostly, because I don't want to embarrass anyone. I have felt serenity at various times in my life, but usually because of being in nature, never as a result of calling someone an ignorant bastard. During this period of our lives when Liam was under attack, I tried many times to counter despair by counting the joys in our lives. I allowed myself to feel honestly grateful for what my family and I have. I laughed; I loved. I dug deep into the basics I learned when I got sober. Most important, I didn't give up. I attribute that to my DNA, something I was reminded of by watching my son in his moments of willingness to forge ahead.

Liam has always been interested in every aspect of who he is. A few years previous to his coming out, on one of those usual Saturday's full of laundry and cleaning, I stood at the washer and opened the back door, happy to see spring arriving just off the patio. Liam was nine then. Walking back and forth from the washer to the fridge to his room, he had something to say or ask on every trip. "So, if you're Irish and Dad's Jewish, what does that make me?" he asked. I didn't hesitate. "A tenacious little bastard; like a dog with a bone, you'll never give up." Some would say it's inappropriate to talk to a young boy that way. But irreverence has a place in our house, and bad language is the least of my worries. Serious conversation followed when I told him about the toughness of the Irish and Jews, what they endured throughout history and their achievements in America.

My own parents ventured here from Ireland and England just after World War II. My ex-husband Arthur's grandparents were Northern European Jews who arrived before the war. We always made it a point to tell our children about their ancestry and reminded them that our people came here because their rooted beginnings provided less than desirable prospects. They looked to America not to make a fortune but simply to have a life where they could be Jewish or Irish without fear. They could make a living, worship how they wished, maybe have a family and certainly have a life. They could be authentic. There was nothing Disney about their lives. They worked hard, weren't always rewarded for it, were the occasional targets of hatred, and I am sure doled out some of their own vitriol on some unsuspecting, poor bastard. They were tenacity in spades. I doubt they were serene. There was no room for serenity in a life informed by survival.

Because my son couldn't live a life without fear, some eighty years after our ancestors, I made it my mission to wear armour and wield the sword. That's my gene pool, and fortunately, it's Liam's, too. That basic, snarling survival and suspicion is how I approached anyone who had anything to say about my son. On Liam's good days he believed, as his ancestors did, that life could and would be better.

Time moving through daily life and, when nothing was left, unadulterated hope turned my all too frequent musings about revenge into vague, momentary blips. I discovered the more time I devoted to hate, the more I was missing life: Not only a son, but a daughter who was engaged and planning a wedding, four step-children, grandchildren, a husband, family, a job, friends, my friends' worries and joys. With so much to focus on in the moment, time eased out those terrible fantasies, made me put the shovel behind the door. Now, especially since the lawsuit against the district for deliberate indifference to homophobia was settled, I don't or won't spend time hating people who aren't in my life or in Liam's. There are people I have no desire to speak to. I don't go out of my way to make a point of silence. I simply don't have them in my life, including some relatives.

Maybe it's a sign I haven't fully let go? There's an argument in my head, which goes something like this: You don't like that my son is gay, and that's okay. We don't have to talk about it. That's your cross to bear. I'm walking away." Then the revenging angel steps in and says, "Who are you to judge? Fuck you. Stay away from me." I don't know if the arguing voices will ever quiet. Most days, the best I can do is not to give voice to my darker angels.

After a series of incidents, including being hit with an ice ball in the head and being called a faggot, an incident, mind you, the assistant principal saw and admitted that Liam was targeted, we presented Liam with the option of quitting school. Six months later he took the option. It took that long to decide, not because he was a masochist looking for more pain, but because he was a child raised to believe education is vitally important and quitting wasn't an option. I helped him get there by doing my own research and discovering a high percentage of gay teens drop out of school, but I didn't want him to be a drop out. I wanted him to get an education and thrive. If it was going to happen, then I had to change my own ideas about school and success and begin by being open to helping my son find another path up the mountain. In doing so I began to sleep longer and lash out less. Watching my son, not only land on his feet but achieve the extraordinary for a young man his age, went a long way to helping me put away my imaginary shovel.

In the final days of Liam's high school before he quit in the eleventh grade, Liam's English teacher put a quote from Walt Whitman on his school website page. I don't recall it verbatim, but it tied together learning and responsibility. I appreciate Whitman, like poetry, write some, and was an English major in college. What I do recall about the quote was its implication that if the learner failed to learn, it was the learner's fault.

I had a son who was writing at twelfth-grade level in eighth grade and made it into Harvard Model Congress three times. He received the Triple C Award granted by the New York State Congress for Community, Commitment, and Citizenship. He testified before the New York State Senate on DASA: Dignity for All Students Act. Even better, he was everything he was supposed to be as a child and teenager, sometimes wonderful, funny, smart, well mannered, and sometimes not. Yet, the daily homophobia, never addressed in any meaningful way by the school administration, put an end to his high school career. He wouldn't have a senior year, go to prom, get a high school ring, or proceed to college in the same way throngs of students do every fall. Those missed milestones weren't the learner's fault. Dropping out of school wasn't his failure; it was theirs.

Since quitting high school, Liam received his GED, began community college before his peers graduated high school, interned for a United States congressman and was appointed the Deputy Supervisor of Woodstock, NY, at eighteen. Currently enrolled at The George Washington University's Elliot School of International Affairs in Washington, DC, he is bright, beautiful and living an authentic life.

I don't believe I can fully let go because that requires forgiveness. Yet, there is something about being a mother that stops me from getting there. How can I forgive those who hurt my son? I should probably tell you my spirituality is stuck in neutral, and I regret it, but that would be a lie. I know how to forgive. I have to want to, first. What I have done to combat my own hatred is to recognize those individual teachers and counsellors who championed him, such as the high school social worker, now retired, a guy who was doing what the universe meant him to do and did it well. What I don't do is engage everyone I meet and tell them the story and name names of the hated. During the process, of course I did, with my closest friends, but I didn't and don't have a soapbox. Soapboxes can get dangerously comfortable.

I admire those who fight for a cause, who don't get swallowed up in the process. I admire the true survivors, the ones who turn someone else's ignorance into a reason to live well, as Liam did. As for me these days, I have met with success at letting go in the moment when not engaging the hatred. What that means is I stop myself from taking pleasure in revenge fantasies, like being an Irish Joan of Arc wielding a sword. I have been truly humbled by watching my son become who he should be and not who they wanted him to be. I know some things my young son doesn't, but I don't know everything. Protecting the world from evil, real or perceived, is a collective effort. Simply put, if I want justice, or compassion, or to be heard, then I have to be willing to give it, even to those I think are undeserving. I am a mother who loves her children. I am only one among many. My best road now is to do no harm.

Today, the boy who saved me is forging ahead with grace. My steps may not be graceful, but I will take them anyway.

Kerry Guerin has had an interesting, if not terrifying, ride so far but hasn't published her first novel yet. It's time now. Besides, she reports, her husband says, "You're a nicer person when you're writing." Another reason to forge ahead. So, that's her goal—finish and get published. She also began writing poetry last year, under the guiding wisdom of poet Susan Sindall.

Guerin lives in Upstate New York, where she attended Marist College, before completing her undergraduate degree at St. Patrick's College in Maynooth, County Kildare, Ireland. If she had to choose, she'd do all four years in Ireland. Of course, that was a time in her life before she got sober . . . and eventually met her husband, Joe Muldoon. Between them they have six children. Don't call after 9:00 p.m. They're really tired.

Lionheart

Maria R. Ostrowski

Her name is fear.
I know what she is and why she haunts me, but it took three decades, my best friend's death, war, miscarriage, the Berlin Wall and mental illness to understand: Fear comes like the Reaper whenever I am faced with the unknown.

Fear is hardly a stranger. We first met in 1986 at a bus terminal in Austria. I was four years old. My brother Leo and I were standing side-by-side with our young US Air Force officer father, mother and grandparents. Although Leo was eighteen months younger, we were often mistaken for twins. We looked like Hummel's with round, healthy faces, big brown eyes, blunt cut bangs and oftentimes matching sweaters. When my mother turned her head for a moment, a slender woman with dark, curly hair and black sunglasses approached. Crouching eye-level with Leo and me, she smiled, popped a piece of candy in our mouths and slunk away.

Having been raised on, "Don't talk to strangers," I promptly spit out the candy and whispered to Leo to do the same. I forget if I alerted our mother.

We got on the bus. I was sitting on the aisle and spotted a mass of dark, curly hair a couple of rows ahead. The woman with the black sunglasses turned and smiled.

Then, as I walked up the hill in Innsbruck hand-in-hand with my grandfather, the woman appeared again and grabbed my other hand. I looked up, and she smiled wide, showing her teeth, scowling at Grandfather. I knew instinctively I should fear her. This unknown woman wanted to steal me.

This bizarre, tense encounter lasted only moments before my mother intervened, but the strange woman remained, lurking in the shadows of memory, never far, never forgotten, and as time passed, my fear of the unknown grew with me, stretching in spurts like my skin and bones. Throughout my life in times of turbulence or loss, I would remember this stranger who threatened to take the life I knew and loved.

Alice's was a life I knew and loved; she was my best friend.

Awake in bed on Sunday, November 7, 1999 sunlight eclipsed between the venetian blind and the window frame, I heard the phone ring downstairs and Mom scream, "Oh my God, Terry!"

Terry was Alice's mother. I went cold. I knew Alice had gone out with her boyfriend the night before. The stairs creaked beneath my mother's feet. *Stay away. Don't come to my door.* She depressed the old-fashioned metal latch; it fell, heavy; her tears, her words; my heart. I howled the primal, shredded cry of life ruptured.

"My world has been smashed . . ." reads my journal a week after Alice died in a car accident. I was seventeen and in a state of shock. She had been my closest friend since we were seven years old. I couldn't process the idea of her death. I wrote to her, left the letter open on the desk, so she could see it. The funeral, returning to school and waiting for her at our locker, seeing her bedroom turned into an office—these events were nightmares. Why wasn't she there? Why was I going through this alone? This confusion over where she was and the gripping fear that it was true—she was gone, she had been taken—continued for a long time.

I did not want to believe in a world without her. This unknown, new world smashed all security, all certainty. Everything familiar, including people I saw and places I went, was twisted and darker, even happy events, like graduating high school, going to senior prom, crossing the street for ice cream, waking up, were no longer guaranteed. I did not talk about it; I did not seek help but pleaded in each letter: "Please come back, Alice. Let me know you can read this. Please don't forget me. Let me know you are with me," I wrote, believing she would read them, just as we read notes we passed to each other in study hall. She would read them, because that was what we had always done.

Ten of Alice's notes remain after all these years, having survived many moves and cleaning purges. She lives in these notes folded into palm-sized squares and decorated with doodles of rainbows with puffy clouds, stars and smiley faces. They are full of inside jokes, references to boys and concerts, snarky comments on school assemblies and schemes for weekend sleepovers. When I look at them, I recall the light in her eyes on the last day of school and her nose-crinkling giggle. I will never let go of these gentle, loving memories of my best friend.

With the passing years as I grew into an adult, I built a wall inside myself to keep at bay all destructive emotions and experiences, which I felt would destroy me. I graduated from college, married a wonderful guy, but life, as everyone knows, is never smooth sailing, and so fear and trauma kept growing behind my inner wall.

One such traumatic event for me and my family began on a warm and sunny day in 2005, when my husband, Todd, and I were visiting his parents in Connecticut. I glanced at my cell, one of those silver flip phones everyone owned ten years ago; the caller ID read, Leo. Wondering if he was okay, I picked up my cell and answered.

For the last several years my brother had been having trouble with ordinary things, like running out of gas and money. He felt alienated from the world around him and a complete lack of motivation, but had no words to explain it, except the despairing phrase, "It's all my fault."

Teachers noticed his increasing incoherence. He started failing classes and broke up with his girlfriend, but determined to graduate, he took summer courses and saw a counselor, who introduced him to cognitive behavioral therapy and the antidepressant, Zoloft. In 2001, he graduated high school and got a job fixing bar-code scanners, until his condition negatively impacted his performance, and he was let go. Leo was devastated, but came home with a plan: He would join the military to get his "butt whipped into shape." But after reviewing his mental health file, the Navy deemed him unfit. Leo became distraught and feared his future.

Still, he persevered, looking for ways to help himself. He tried yoga, vitamin therapy, acupuncture and hiking. He enrolled at Manchester Community College and spent time with a new girlfriend who introduced him to the writings of C.S. Lewis. Her religious beliefs influenced Leo. He joined her church, studied religion and philosophy and continued to find work, trying to function with a condition he didn't understand.

He then tried construction, but his worsening dissociation made it difficult to grasp real-life things, and he accidentally shot himself with a nail gun. His condition escalated. Leo now believed most foods were toxic and also began taking all electronic devices out of our house.

"I can't take it anymore. I can't," Leo said, sounding out of breath and anxious. "Just hang on," I said, catching Todd's eye. "We're leaving right now. We'll get there as soon as we can, okay?"

"Let's go." Todd grabbed his keys. Minutes later, I sat beside him in his Chevy, neither of us speaking. He was a firefighter at that time, and when I looked over at him behind the wheel, I saw the firm set of his jaw and brows, the stern line of his mouth and the fixed look in his eyes concentrating on the road ahead. He drove down roads I knew every stretch of, yet nothing looked familiar, as I sat there thinking, Hang on, Leo, hang on.

When we pulled into the drive, I sprinted to the back door. A note lay on the cream-colored countertop. I froze. Todd snatched it, wouldn't let me see it. "He's at the hospital. He couldn't wait," Todd said.

That wasn't Leo's first hospitalization or his last. I remember those early institutions only in flashes: Johnson Memorial, Natchaug, Manchester Memorial, St. Frances and Bidwell, before the final diagnosis in 2006 of schizophrenia.

Shortly after he was diagnosed, I visited him at a psychiatric ward. I stood in front of secured double doors thinking, This is unreal. Was my brother—a good-looking, gentle soul who respected women, loved his family and had many friends—really behind secured doors? Finally, I was admitted to a room full of people in off-white scrubs pacing or sitting at tables. I stared straight ahead and gripped my black leather handbag. I was not prepared to see my brother like this. I wanted to bolt. Instead, I gritted my teeth. I was afraid if I didn't see Leo, I would lose him.

I will visit my brother, dammit, I said to myself. Through denial, I was determined to keep this thing out of our lives.

I sat across from him at a table with my stomach in a cold knot. We didn't say much; we played cards. Slouched in his chair, he glanced at me and offered a side smile that looked like it cost a lot of effort, as if all his muscles were heavy.

When I left, I felt angry. And I continued to feel it. At first the medical profession kept getting the diagnosis wrong. Once properly diagnosed, they couldn't find the right medicines and kept trying out this medication and that. I wanted to shout, "My brother isn't a test rat!" I couldn't see him as a person with a complex disease undergoing intense treatment.

Seeing one's beloved kinsman suffering, as if invaded by a foreign force, left me scared not only for him, but also for our family, I wondered who else would develop this frightening condition. Would I, too, fall prey? Even so, all during those early years after Leo's diagnosis and worsening condition, I fooled myself into thinking I was safe behind my "wall."

One day thumbing through photos Dad had snapped in May 1988 when we visited Berlin, I stumbled across photos of the Berlin Wall, scarred with graffiti. The wall, erected during the Cold War to divide the city in two, had evolved into a collage of angry-looking symbols and messages: Here a raised fist; there a crazed, cartoonish face; crude, ghostly-white stick-figures with bound wrists and ankles; monsters with gaping mouths. All their anger, anxiety and fear Berliners gave to the wall day after day, asserting the painful existence of their lives.

I zoomed in on one message spray-painted black with the final word in red: *Wo wir sind, geht alles schief, und wir sind überall!* (Where we are, all goes wrong, and we are everywhere!)

I stared at the photo with this unsettling message and

recognized the wall inside of me. And yet, I could not abandon it. Where fear is, all goes wrong, and fear is everywhere. Everywhere, like God Himself, I thought.

For a short time when I turned thirty-one, I had never felt so beautiful or alive. Then one Saturday evening in March, my husband Todd and I went to Mass to pray that I would not lose the baby. Suddenly, I went cold, and I knew. We left Mass early.

The next day I lay on the couch, shocked and exhausted, my howl from the night before still rattling in my empty womb, a beautiful life gone. What was left of me was shaken and lost. In the following weeks, I tried to steel myself by diving into writing, fighting feelings of worthlessness. On good days, I called myself strong. "I survived. I do things. I have a social life and my work. I won't talk about it or think about it. Now, get back to work," I told myself. But this was just spray paint on my wall, like the Berlin Wall graffiti, messages to cover the bleakness and give the world a show of life and strength.

In truth, the miscarriage shattered my confidence. I'd had no control over my body. That I was athletic, strong and healthy, yet could not stop it from happening, frightened me. Without any knowledge about miscarriage, I was completely unprepared for how deeply I would grieve the little life, my ghost baby, as well as the mother-to-be inside me, who I did not know existed until then. I believed I had failed them both. I blamed myself completely. There had to be something wrong with me. These were the damaging messages written on my inner wall.

When flashbacks began a couple of months after the miscarriage, I didn't want to acknowledge them and felt I could manage on my own. So, I denied help when Dr. Carpenter, my

Ob-Gyn, called to check on me. "Thanks, but I'm fine . . . I exercise . . . I'll be all right," I said.

My husband clued me in on how contradictory I sounded: "Which is it?" he'd say and grin. "Are you fine now, or will you be fine later, after exercising, because you are not fine now?"

All I wanted to do was detach myself, push these feelings behind the wall, and keep going. But when the flashbacks and panic attacks became a bombardment, I knew I was far from fine. My wall was crumbling. I would be in my writing room, then suddenly, I was a teenager again. A ghost phone would ring, my mom scream, "Oh my God, Terry!" I felt the funeral parlour's stagnant heat, the gray disbelief of a November graveside and anger that told me I was still alive.

And a strange woman with shaded eyes turned in her bus seat and grinned.

I was terrified, but I knew I couldn't hide anymore. All of the experiences and emotions I had pushed behind the wall were pushing back, breaking through and coming after me. The broken pieces of myself would cripple me, if I did not acknowledge and learn to let them go.

This understanding came with the realization that someone close to me had gone through this process and didn't let his fear and anxiety stop him from trying to get well. Reflecting on that day in 2005 when Leo called, I remembered that Leo had taken himself to the hospital, talked about his problems with medical professionals and kept trying, despite his real fears, to get help. I saw that his example could serve as my guide.

I had no knowledge of schizophrenia and in my ignorance associated the word with multiple personalities and scary movies.

After all, I was only a year out of college, where terms like "psycho," "schizo" and "insane" were callously misused to describe everything from ex-boyfriends to exams and parties. Luckily, my boss Marty, whose own son was schizophrenic, generously began to school me about this fearfully misunderstood illness.

Caused by a combination of genetics, stress, and a neural circuitry disorder, schizophrenia reveals itself through a variety of symptoms, including hallucinations (hearing voices), delusions, and thought disorders. Also, negative symptoms often resemble depression; cognitive symptoms as impaired decision-making skills, lack of concentration, the ability to retain and apply information.

Schizophrenia "does not cause a split personality, but can cause a split with reality," Marty explained. Untreated delusions and hallucinations cause suffering from paranoia, panic and depression. Many schizophrenics hear white noise and garbled sounds, like radio interference and voices, which obstruct the ability to read or converse.

Tragically, the disease often strikes during the promising years of young adulthood. As she spoke to me, I finally understood why Leo, who had built a computer as a gift for me in his teens, now had difficulty in his early twenties managing workaday life.

Marty told me that one in every one hundred people have schizophrenia, which is roughly one percent of Americans, according to websites of the National Alliance on Mental Illness, the National Institue of Mental Health, and Schizophrenia and Related Disorders Alliance of America.

Over time, Marty shared her experiences coping with her son's journey. She gave me articles to prepare me for the confusing, lengthy and discouraging process of diagnosing the illness, which is full of trial and error and misdiagnoses. She also taught me to hope. With proper treatment, support, and medication, some people recover from schizophrenia's symptoms and build healthy lives, especially those suffering early-onset schizophrenia. Learning about schizophrenia did not make it any less tragic, but it dispelled misconceptions. I learned that education was a crucial part of letting go.

Leo had grasped this from the beginning. When diagnosed, he educated himself on the illness, did homework to prepare for therapy sessions and over time became knowledgeable in managing setbacks and panic. He participated in support groups and explored various therapeutic activities like community gardening, which he thought of as "unconventional education."

Today, whenever I think of Marty, I am reminded of something Leo said. "You find fellow travelers along the way . . . people who let themselves get in touch with the fear."

He was referring to friends he made in his rehabilitation programs and his Schizophrenics Anonymous group, but he was voicing for me the steps in the process: Find strength, share, and learn from others.

It is hard to convey the frantic search for logic and attendant, helpless awe one experiences on becoming conscious of the mind's delicacy, especially when it happens to someone you love. As Leo once told me " . . . there's no logic behind the beast."

I hardly ever spoke about this, even with Todd. I was too frightened. I wondered why Leo? Could I get it? If I had children, could they have it? I was frightened of schizophrenia, which could make me lose connection with my world, the people I loved, and the ability to discern between fantasy and reality. This illness, this unseen force, was taking Leo's mind, his youth, his future life and relationships and holding them hostage. I feared this unknown illness like the God I blamed and yet prayed to, begged and bargained with in the irrational, desperate search for a reason.

At Christmas that year we celebrated at the rehabilitation center, where my brother lived. The whole family came and sat at a long cafeteria table, joking and laughing. Leo did not say much, but we all reached out from our different worlds to be together. We were a family—with problems and sorrow, repressed anger, frustration and disappointment and love, patience and hope for each other. Fear wasn't at that table, and in this warm moment, I glimpsed all that I had.

By September Leo had moved into a group home, which offered independence and a sense of community. That fall when Todd and I married, Leo was an usher and danced at our reception. And for the past six years, he has held a steady job.

Leo's Facebook cover photo is a lion's head. The scrolled lettering beneath it reads, "Lion Heart." Nothing describes Leo's spirit better. He continues to this day to study "the nature of the beast (schizophrenia) and treat it."

Being with Leo is humbling. He lives simply and gives freely of his time to help others. He visits my grandparents and parents often—"The Elders," he calls them with a twinkle in his eye. He is a compassionate soul. He doesn't realize it, but for those open and ready to see, he teaches that letting go of fear means the difference between living and functioning; letting go of fear opens one to find and grow compassion for fellow travelers and those who have yet to start their journey. I should know; because of my brother, I am now well on my way.

Maria R. Ostrowski, a full-time fiction writer, is currently working on Cliffwood, *an atmospheric mystery set in 1930s New England following the historic Fairfax and Pinthis shipwreck. She has taught poetry workshops through the Bushnell's Partners in Arts and Education Program and traveled and performed nationwide at the Brave New Voices poetry festival. After receiving a degree in English at the University of Connecticut, she assisted in coaching young adults in performance poetry through the Connecticut Youth Poetry Slam Team. During this time, Ostrowski also worked as a marketing strategist and consumed excessive amounts of coffee. She lives and writes in Springfield, MA, with a husband who patiently accepts the chaos of a household run by a writer. For further information see MariaOstrowski.com.*

. . . OF DREAMS
AND OBSESSIONS

The Paper Room

Joan Scott

Relinquishing paper used to fill me with dread. I'm not talking about discarding steak house coupons (I'm vegan), or gourmet dog food coupons (I don't have a dog), or exotic river cruise coupons (I can't swim), nor am I talking about recycling. I mean, I am never able to let go of paper in all its shapes, formats and colors.

Paperless office was never in my dictionary. My home office was crammed with pristine pages, in white plus every rainbow color, waiting by the printer. Post-it notes, monogrammed paper and scribbles on the backs of envelopes that never made it to the recycle bin, were always strewn across the desk. And what about the mounds of it on the floor: three grocery bags full of months of pink *Financial Times* and stacks of outdated *New Yorker's* with their award-winning covers and cartoons, which I couldn't part with. Six years of the quarterly magazine, *This England*, with its reminiscing and war poems amidst country settings I held close to my heart to remind me of grandparents and home. *Bon Appetite* editions for all those recipes I meant to try. *Travel & Leisure* for vacations I could never afford but loved to explore on paper. *Vogue, Vanity Fair* and *Oprah*, artistically photographed and full of literary information, gossip and well-being tips too hard to discard, as well as boxes of printed e-mails, because pressing the delete key immobilized me with fear in case I needed the information stored on past e-mails, which elevated my inbox to ten thousand messages (by then the data geek squad threatened to close my account).

Did I mention the paper in books on writing that took up four bookcases, including John Steinbeck's journal, *Working Days,* which he wrote while working on *The Grapes of Wrath,* which reminded me of the punishing journey toward artistic fulfillment; *The Marshall Plan Workbook* by Evan Marshall, which showed the steps in starting and finishing my novel; *The Art of Dramatic Writing* by Lajos Egri, which gave it life; and *Writer's Digest* sourcebooks, complete guides for the writing process; *Webster's* and *Oxford Dictionaries* and *Roget's Thesaurus* for spell checking, editing and refining my work; and the *1996 Writer's Market 75th Anniversary Edition* to help me sell it? (After storing it for almost twenty years, perhaps it was time to let go and navigate the digital world.)

I had a vintage collection of "How To" books on endless computer versions, because pressing the Help key on the computer only added to my frustrations, so it was better to keep the books, even though they were out of date, but so was the computer sitting in the closet. Someone just might need both if they were into vintage computing, I reasoned.

People accused me of being a paper hoarder when they saw boxes of new greeting cards—get well, retirement and sympathy versions—ready to send because I didn't do e-cards. I didn't care; I wanted my family, friends and colleagues to fondle the envelope, notice the color and decoration that matched the card inside and have them admire the Forever stamp selected for its investment and meaning: an animal for the pet lover, a flower for the gardener, the flag for the patriot and a movie star for the cinema buff. Tucked in the boxes were packets of seasonal stamps: ice skaters for New England recipients, exotic foliage for West Coast sun worshippers and islanders, the world for overseas mail and Mickey and Minnie Mouse characters for the little people in my life. I thought of the recipients, slicing open the envelope, with an ornate letter knife, or, excitedly, ripping it open to reveal a card chosen just for them, personalized with a handwritten message from a fine pen. I always sensed the pleasure it gave.

But not all the boxes held new cards; some stored old cards and letters. Every airmail letter my mother wrote me since I left England, tears still marking the pages. Letters asking when I would be returning, and those, ten years later, when both parents finally realized I'd made my home in America and was never moving back to my birthplace. Satin-covered cards with pressed flowers my father sent to my mother when they were courting during World War II. Soldier poems he wrote about me before and after I was born, his excitement and hope for a second child who never arrived. All treasured when they'd both passed on and too painful to let go.

On another shelf were files of my school reports handwritten in ink and signed by my headmistress, Miss Brown, an old-school Downton Abbey character; a copy of the alien card that allowed me to work in the US; citizenship papers next to the stars and stripes paper flag I waved, after I'd pledged my allegiance; and the corporate identity badge that marked my life and soul with a number.

After I'd vacated my cubicle at work, I swore someone probably closed the entrance with yellow tape: DANGER, DO NOT ENTER, because no one wanted to be responsible for throwing away the evidence of a life well-earned in the corporate world. My colleague in the adjacent cubicle, who was into Feng Shui at the time, used to light a scented candle to help her "Om" her way through the politics, and I am convinced my boss had been tempted to "accidentally" drop it over the partition into my "fire hazard" so he could get rid of my paper mess and blame my colleague. But I was not ready to let go, so the papers piled up until we went digital and my secretary took over the new paperless office procedures. When I finally walked out of my corporate home of eight years, I was reluctant to leave that part of my life behind, so I took a lot of it with me: Brochures I'd written, minutes of meetings that changed the face of the international world I lived in, adaptations of promotions, customer testimonials, in case I needed samples for my new consulting role. I didn't. I used to look at them, longingly, from time to time, for the evidence of my success. This is how my home office became The Paper Room.

Oh, I tried to let go. I hired a friend who staged houses for re-sale to de-clutter my "paper storage closet." Yes, the one containing reams of printing paper, green hanging files and beige folders, envelopes, all sizes in two colors, and labels. My staging friend looked wistfully at the closed door at the end of the hall but kept quiet. I muttered it needed clearing, and she offered my services to the Paper Room, just one hour a day, she mumbled. That's all it would take. Do I have that many years left to spare an hour a day?

When friends visited for the first time and did the tour, they remarked, "Your house is so uncluttered," and when they came to the end of the hall and asked, "What's in there?" I replied, "No one enters that room." They said nothing because, obviously, it led to a room off-limits, possibly a shrine to a member of the family who had passed on.

A realtor friend once suggested that should we consider selling our house, we could advertise it as a four bedroom, two and one-half bathroom, Tuscany kitchen, entertainment room, with a caveat:

Comes with Writer's Historical Paper Room with artifacts from the Forties through the Sixties. (Research notes on the Swinging Sixties for my novel, receipts of mundane items like baked beans and reams of Word Perfect drafts). My excuse for not de-cluttering was a dream of fame. My fans would clamor to view the Writer's Room, just as they flock to Pacific Grove, California, to see John Steinbeck's studio or the Florida Keys, where Hemingway toiled away his writing hours or to Virginia Woolf's shed in East Sussex. With their neat desks, comfy armchairs, orderly book shelves and views, their spaces never resembled The Paper Room, so I guessed my fans would be disappointed, but I reckoned without The Paper Room I'd have lost my sole reason for living. I never let go of all the paper because I envisaged that when the time came, my husband would hold his hand on his heart, wipe a tear from his eye and be able to confess "an author lives on in that room." I owed him that much for my procrastination.

I recently came across old Post-it notes suggesting how I might let go of my paper hoarding:

YELLOW–*Let go of outdated books, magazines and newspapers.*

(Result: I regretted throwing out information I knew I'd never miss, such as recipes, lists of good websites for writers or investors, but I stopped waffling over my old, paper friends by asking: If you had only one hour left of life, would you spend it reading this magazine? If I answered no, then I let it go.)

BLUE–*Learn the NEW, no matter how scary.*

(Result: I signed up for a master class on navigating the paper-less digital world and graduated with a paper certificate, which I am not ready to discard, just yet.)

WHITE–*Understand that—if I de-clutter the Paper Room— then one day, someone will enjoy going through (and be able to find) what's left and the best work of my writing life.*

PINK–*Relinquish procrastination so my husband will value me as a dedicated writer.*
(Result: I did, and he does.)

Joan Scott *was born in England. At fifteen she wrote a prize-winning essay about a trip to Paris. The newspaper prize paid for a baguette and a croissant. Years later when the writing life paled and the rent was due, she honed her creative writing skills with London advertising agencies, taught tango to VIPs, marketed wines and left rainy England for a Californian drought, where she became 'Nanny Joan' resulting in a nonfiction proposal,* We Don't Just Go Places, We Experience Them, *for caregivers and grandparents to bolster children's creativity.*

Moving to Boston, she promoted textiles, wrote poems and articles on beekeepers, burying beetles, and ballerinas, then joined corporate America to build a career in international marketing communications. While being paid to travel, she continued writing on sampans, helicopters and high-speed Japanese trains. She has let go of paper with her slice-of-life blogs: "When Life Gets in the Way of Writing the Great British Novel," and is becoming a fearless flyer, navigating social media with her psychological suspense, debut novel, Who Is Maxine Ash? *She can be contacted on joanscott.uk1@gmail.com*

Finis:
Farewell to a Novel
Too Long in Progress

Joe Levine

A writing teacher of mine said that a novel is like a pyramid: The possibilities for how to begin can cover wide ground, but the end point must be inevitable.

In novel writing, then, like life, choice is fateful. You can erase, cross out, go back to a previous point and begin again—and with computers, mix and match older versions—until you go mad. But in choosing a direction, there remains an element of commitment. You don't go there in a day. You must convince yourself that opening up this facet of character, that detail of the past, this scene in the present, is worth the effort. You have to believe, or at least suspend disbelief, just as, some day, you will ask the reader to do. In the end, you can't really go back, because the choice becomes real. You can't say—to yourself, at any rate—*no, he didn't live in a house with an old lady. She didn't have a lover named Emmet. Strangers didn't make her cross and suspicious of snooping.* You can choose not to include those things, but they still happened off-stage and still shaped the people you are writing about, because you know them. If they didn't, you'd be writing about different people—and that, as the saying goes, would be another story.

❧❧❧

I have been writing a novel—the same novel—on and off for twenty-three years. The joke I make—that what began as contemporary fiction is now a historical novel—is not really a joke. I began it in the fall of 1984, when that year still sounded futuristic, at the end of my first summer in an MFA writing program, now long since defunct. One of the two Writers who led it is now dead; the daughter of the other, whom I knew when she was five years old, has since published two novels, to favorable review in the *New York Times*.

Also:

The Berlin Wall has crumbled.

The Soviet Union has fallen.

AIDS has swept the globe.

The World Trade Center, then twelve years old, has toppled.

We have entered the computer age.

I have married, fathered children and acquired an apartment, two cats and a career that, while it involves writing and editing nearly every minute of the day, is not Writing and never will be.

Through it all, however, there has been this book—the wildcard. What, after all this time, do I have to show for it? Not a published line, not a dime. Yet it has had major consequences for my life and that of others. I have declined jobs that would have left me too little time to write; I have asked my wife to put off having children.

Why? And why has it taken so long? This isn't a masterwork; I'm not breaking new ground. Research would likely reveal among first novels, my subject—first love and losing it, the effort after to move on to some other present—is the most common of all.

The answer, in part, is that convincing myself that I am a writer has been a lifelong process. I have wanted to be one since I read Steinbeck's *The Wayward Bus* and *Sweet Thursday* at age twelve and was impressed and charmed by what I thought was his gritty, manly take on real life—hobos, diners, whores, the road, the sun, the sea. But because that wasn't my own life, I have never believed in my heart of hearts that I am one. I am the son of comfortable people, one in public relations, the other in advertising, who themselves dreamed of being Writers. I have a stack of my father's youthful short stories in my filing cabinet; my mother took classes at the New School, where she collaborated as the librettist on an attempt to musicalize the novel *Babbitt*. As that same teacher once told me, we tend to gravitate toward the worlds we know. Mine were those of public relations and advertising. I knew I would never be the kind of adventurous, self-effacing observer who lands himself in wars, foreign cities or lonely garrets. I would have no great stories to tell of other people and places, rich in universal truths.

Nor, I was convinced, did I have it in me to Make Things Up—to spin a tale from a chance view of an old man silhouetted on a street corner, or from an odd newspaper story of a bizarre crime or of an abandoned old house. In writing classes and workshops, the woodenness, the lack of voice, spark and authenticity in unsuccessful attempts of this kind made my heart sink and angered me. I wasn't going to suffer this fate. I would know my material and my limits, so that no one's time would be wasted. (Young as I was, it never occurred to me that those unsuccessful attempts might be first drafts. That this was what real Writers do.)

Of course, for material that left me only a narrow range of people, places, events, which I had actually experienced. From time-to-time in a fiction writing class, I dipped into that well for short stories that seemed to please others, but I seriously doubted I'd ever have the patience or courage to sit still and simply listen, alone, to what was inside me. I was too social, too needy. I did delight in solitude, but the solitude I enjoyed derived from escaping my network of commitments. Also, writing of this kind seemed too difficult to do on a sustained basis—the literary equivalent of trying to look at the top of your own head by standing on a chair. At best, you get occasional glimpses of the remoter slopes but never the whole thing and mostly come away with a crick in your neck. You wrestle with the constant dilemma of how to come at your perennial subject. Head on, dropping all pretense of distance? Where, then, is the line separating what you are doing from confessional journal writing? (Anais Nin and Frank Conroy are great writers of that kind, but I suspected even then that their journal writing and memoirs were better than their fiction.) Or by changing things, working from the outside in, pretending there's a difference between character and self— at first just for the sake of changing them, as a wise older friend suggested to me, to convince oneself to believe, which after all is job number one? Because you can't very well expect to catch the reader up in your spell if you haven't first caught up yourself.

The answer, for me, came clear, with the first real short story I wrote in college. It was about a man named Reddick—the name just popped into my head one night—a struggling writer and would-be musician living in Greenwich Village. He was thirty-one, an age that had seemed to me appropriately ancient and past prime. He had grayish hair that flopped on either side of his head "like beagle's ears." He was in love with a woman who didn't love him back, and there was a manuscript by the side of his mattress on the floor, which was the source of unrelenting misery but also "represented spiritual salvation."

From that experience, I learned that however close something might seem to my own life, there must come a moment where I believe in the thing as a separate entity, or else, like all the failed attempts that preceded Kitty Hawk, the whole big clumsy edifice would never leave the ground. For that to happen, my imagination must be sparked by something only half understood that points toward greater truths and mysteries, even as it points back toward myself.

But: Would anything Big Enough, Important Enough, of that kind ever happen to me that would merit a novel to tell it?

The spring and summer I was twenty, I worked as a newspaper reporter on a weekly paper in a small town on the Connecticut shoreline. I had taken a year off from college, partly because I wasn't learning anything. I spent most of my time in dormitory lounges, playing the piano and, later, practicing with a band, partly because I was in a state of exquisite misery over a girl who was willing enough to sleep with me but not to the exclusion of two other men. She was wild, independent, the daughter of a lawyer who'd represented rock musicians; her family was turbulent, and it seemed at times as if she had no parents, and at others as if she were raising them. My pursuit of her took place in a student co-op house, amid a lot of music and drugs and even, one weirdly warm day in late February when we all took our clothes off, up on the roof. Eventually it struck me the ship was sinking, and I'd better get off, at least until repairs could be made.

At that paper I met another reporter a few years older than myself, who, in certain, exaggerated ways, seemed to mirror my own personality and problems. Though not at first glance. He was an ascetic who lived in a log cabin on the backwoods property of a University of Connecticut professor. He made his own soups and breads and talked about James Agee and Henry Adams. More impressively, he had actually read them. He rode his bike wherever he could and ran in long-distance races; he gardened and talked about disappearing ways of American life. When I asked whether he didn't want to move up to a bigger paper in a larger town or city, he admonished me that small towns were *real*; you could get your arms around them, see and know the people behind the institutions. Even better, you could slow things down from the pace of modern life and live just for living instead of trying to measure up on some public stage.

This prickly, somewhat self-important person seemed to me to be everything I was not: disciplined, principled, serious, tough, and above all, emotionally self-sufficient. He did have a girlfriend—the curator of the local historical society—but she seemed of a piece with him: lean, a runner, a hard worker. They came into the newsroom together on my first afternoon on the job, and I thought they were two kindred souls: Ma and Pa Kettle. She rented the ground floor of a little colonial house that belonged to an elderly couple. Proprieties were observed, appearances maintained—and with them, distances. He did not stay over often, though that seemed to be his choice more than hers, and sometimes I wondered if they had sex at all.

But if he was the lone traveler that I was not, I had a talent he lacked. Because I was lonely and needed friends, and these two were the only candidates, my chameleon-like nature allowed me to adapt to them, especially as they were a couple. (My only child to their mother and dad?) I was able to work on him, chip away at his flinty heart, until finally, after weeks of saying *we really should take you for that beer*, or *have you over for dinner*, or *meet up Sunday for a bike ride*, he actually made good on one of those offers, and soon I was a regular in their lives. She was glad to have me around, too, it seemed, because he could be a bit stern. I added a little comic relief. I brought him out of himself.

Then one weekend not long before I left to go back to school, I learned from her that a woman from his college days was in town; the two of them were off spending the weekend together; and this person was the great love and obsession of his life. And it seemed a revelation. He had vulnerabilities. The sternness, the Puritanical nature, the extolling of Spartan, small-town life were armor against feelings that threatened the stability of his world.

During that period, I was rooming in an old house up in the hills that had once been run as an inn frequented by artists and musicians. The old woman who had run it still took in the occasional boarder, mainly to have someone able-bodied living in the house with her and her elderly friend. The house was filthy and filled with objects, compost smells, cat shit, dust and stories un-guessed at. Why, when she seemed to have money, did she refuse to have the place cleaned? Was she Miss Havisham, clinging to her past by wallowing in it? Why was she so kind to me, loaning me her car, making me a special Thanksgiving dinner, but so sharp with a friend of mine and his girlfriend who had briefly moved into the area and stayed there before me? Did she want me to stay? Had there been a husband? (I was too naïve for it to occur to me that she and her companion were lesbians.) How could she be annoyed at me for my mess (a stopped toilet I was too embarrassed to report and too inept to fix) when her own was so exaggerated? And the barn kitten that I accidentally hit on the road one night—which survived and which, when I brought it into the house for her to look at, suddenly snapped upright, and darted off into the dim recesses of another room, never to be caught again—surely that was symbolic of something or other. The errant product of a union the two of us never achieved—not in a Harold-and-Maude sort of way, but in the sense of letting down our guards and becoming truly dependent upon one another?

I knew, in some way, I was gathering notes for Something Big, but just how I would write it and what it would all mean, I didn't yet know.

Five years later, I enrolled in a master of fine arts program at a New England college. On arrival, I discovered the eleven other students were women between the ages of thirty and sixty-five. While I was puttering with short stories, they all were in various stages of writing novels. Some were better than others, but what struck me—besides being like a young person watching children in a playground and badly wanting one of his own—was the *believedness* about what they had written. A critical mass, above all of character and place. And I was persuaded—because I wanted to be; because I decided it had to be true—that was how you wrote a publishable book. Cleverness, all right; plot, OK; language, yes; but people and place most of all, and if you simply kept at it and generated enough about them, fleshed them out, got to their essence, the rest was of less consequence. It would not matter if, as the famous meta-fictionist I'd studied with in college insisted, you had not considered all that had been written before you "at this late hour of the world," and you did not break new stylistic ground.

It was at that point an idea for my novel was born—or, rather, that I reached for it and found it waiting. He—my fellow reporter, the ascetic—would be her (the old lady's) roomer. Like she and I—and like he and I—they would do a dance of near intimacy, guessing at each other's pasts and internal truths. The book would be from her point of view, as she tried to lure him into staying on—even, perhaps into inheriting the house—yet perpetually running aground on his severity, judgmental manner, political correctness. His defensive overlay. She would have the same first view of him I did—with a girlfriend who seemed a kindred Puritan spirit. And then, one day, the other girl, the love of his life, would come to visit, and, despite her hazy eyesight, she would suddenly realize this was *not the same girl*; that he had weaknesses, obsessions, regrets, like her own—and his severity was a shield against his own feelings and vulnerabilities. And that, I thought, was the story.

Except that it wasn't. In other hands—Henry James's (*The Aspern Papers*); Philip Roth's (*The Ghost Writer*); Doris Grumbach's (*Chamber Music*); John Casey's (*Spartina*); Anita Shreve's (*Eden Close*), or any of the others who, at various moments, seemed to have written the Ur-text for what I was striving after—it might have been. However, between my inability to envision and render the inner minds of a possibly lesbian, eighty-four-year-old and a formidably tight-lipped young man with the demeanor of a Yankee parson, what I produced was a piece of writing that hinted at much but delivered little; that was so humorless and airless that a friend, upon reading it, said: "On the emotional meter, if red is overload, you haven't even reached black."

One of the two Writers, when I asked him at the MFA program's end if he thought I, too (with my pitiable one hundred twenty-five pages), had a publishable book, was more diplomatic and thus more cutting: *Mmm. I'd turn my attention to starting something new, I think. Eventually you'll break in.*

But the other writer—less polished, less well known, but funnier, crazier, more *haimish*, said, *I just want to tell you that on some level, you had me. I believed.* And that was it. I decided

I would stick with it, because, really, what else did I have to tell? This had been the most interesting, detail-rich period of my life—the part that seemed most like grist for something you'd read in a book—and again, I was not, as I saw it, someone who really makes things up.

Besides, thinking about my two main characters—what they would do or say, what their real issues were, the details of their histories—had become reflexive, something I lapsed into when running or on long walks, or in the shower, or on a plane or train ride with a pen and paper in hand. I had, in fact, finally slowed down and found that stillness I had always hungered for.

Still, it would be another eight years of farting around—this scene here, that one there—before I really committed. I was thirty-two when the moment finally came. Perhaps it was because I had just started dating the woman I would eventually marry, and with that loneliness filled, I was able to really concentrate for the first time. Maybe, too, I sensed the clock ticking in earnest on career, job, children—or maybe plunging more deeply into writing was a defense against yielding too wholly to domestic intimacy.

Whatever the reason, I started writing about how my ascetic had first met the girl who was the love of his life, and instead of that having happened in college, I discovered they had spent their childhoods together on an island off New England—and things began to flow. It was the first time the prose hadn't felt constipated; the first time I had fun with the story. I was making things up, but also drawing on places and experiences that were very rich for me—very present and at hand. It was like a baseball pitcher getting in a groove. I wasn't aiming the ball. I was just letting go. And what eventually happened was that over a period of years and with much prodding from wife, agent, friends, the book turned inside out. What had been the frame—his past and the relationship from which he'd fled—became the center, and what had been the center—the interlude of quiet reflection in the old lady's house that resonated with his memories of that relationship—became . . . not even the frame, but a moment in passing.

The true subject of the book had emerged, as well. It was that hole in him—and in me—into which the self disappears when another person becomes an addiction—and the attempt to move on from the moment in life when the bottom most beckons.

In some way, I'd always known this. In fact, in line with my teacher's dictum, I had begun my novel in some sense knowing its inevitable ending, if not how I would get there.

Life is sloppier than art, so it may seem odd to relate that, while I was living in the small town, escaping from the girl in college who had made me miserable, I also was letting go of another fantasy: a high school girlfriend whom, for various reasons, none of them particularly grounded in reality, I had once decided I was destined to marry. One weekend, during the summer I was living in the small town at the old lady's house, she invited me to her parents' summer place, a house on a lake, where as teenagers, we had spent some angst-filled hours. It was a painful visit, particularly as it wound down, and she began to withdraw as my desperation became apparent. The experience would have left me completely crushed save for one small, beautiful moment. Just before it was time to go, we went for a swim in the lake to escape the oppressive August heat. In the water, a certain natural clownishness between us reasserted itself. We spat streams and chased each other. And then, at the very end, we swam for what seemed like a very long time around the perimeter of the lake, in the warm shallows. There, I remember the sensation of her body near mine, the calm repetition of gliding along underwater; the peace that momentarily settled on me; the feeling that in some more timeless way we were together, even as we were saying good-bye.

I was still devastated two summers later when she wrote to tell me she was getting married and again not long after to say that she was pregnant. But the moment stayed with me. It seemed to embody a resolution of some kind, even if it was one I hadn't yet fully reached or understood. I knew when it was happening that I would use it someday in a piece of fiction, and as my novel took shape, I realized it was my ending.

And there you have it. The story of the writing of a story. A tale of valiant, writerly labor and rewarding discovery.

So why, after twenty-three years, does this book still not feel done? In one way, I've made the break. I'm in the process of sending the manuscript around to agents and publishers. But part of me still holds on. Is it because there's more to be discovered and written? A writer friend whose intuitive judgment I greatly trust has said to me many times, *It takes as long as it takes. You'll know when you're finished.*

Is it because I'm a perfectionist? There's no question that I've wanted the book to be absolutely as good as it can be because, after all, it might be my only shot. That's at least one reason why I ignored the advice of the lesser of the two Writers—the one who believed in me—who had said never to rewrite unless it was on someone else's dime. And it's why, while others I know have spit out new ideas whenever they've had them, I have chosen to use my free time to flesh out and refine this one idea, to the point where it seems the book that now exists is the result of simply tracing out every possible thread, expanding every moment, considering every alternative—*What if she died? What if he were black?*—to the point that the proverbial twelve monkeys could have achieved the same result.

Is it because I'll miss the company? Over the years, these characters have been there for me at so many moments that those times have themselves become memories. In Paris, the day I realized I could not marry the woman I had become engaged to, and I sat in a cemetery where someone famous was buried— Verlaine?—and thought, *The old lady would think about all the artists and writers she knew. Would have been involved with one of them, perhaps the other old woman who is her companion now.* Or the time in a half-converted barn on my parents' property when I typed what became the novel's opening scene—of him riding his bicycle up a hill. The stillness in the barn, the peace, transmuted into his morning. Or all those runs in Prospect Park; all those notebooks, filled with musings and scenes that turned into scenes halfway along.

But here's what I really think: As long as I'm working on this book, I am a Writer. I'm immersed in something I believe in, and I don't know if I have another such piece of writing in me. My pool of material is thin, and I have used some of the best of it.

Also, when I re-enter that world—the world of the young ascetic—I am him again. I am that younger self—the live-alone, traveler, observer self; the ride-my-bike-to-get-to-places guy; the runner; the cooker and eater of solitary meals, listening to ballgames on the radio; the guy in the diner, the coffee shop, the book store, lonely, self-sufficient, young, free. The twenty-four-year-old running in Prospect Park, the thirty-year-old biking in France, even the thirty-five-year-old living with my wife in Mexico, where once, twelve years ago, I hopefully typed the place and date after "The End" at the bottom of an early draft.

When I let this book go—when I stop writing it—I will have to acknowledge—not on paper in self-conscious prose but to myself—that I am no longer that person and will never be again. Even if I publish the book, I will still be a guy whose main gig is writing but not Writing; who is forty-nine and exercise-averse; whose first responsibilities are to wife, children and elderly parents. Passion and sex are no longer the animating forces of my life. That parents will die, children will grow up and live apart; I, too, will grow old.

I wonder, of late, what might have been had I done things a bit differently. What if I'd committed more to being a writer? Because I never gave myself to it wholly. I've always not only worked, as one must, but worked real jobs. Thrown myself into them, played office politics, cared, climbed the ladder. Never trusted myself to hang my hat entirely on fiction writing. Maybe if I'd lived the life more, I'd have pushed to an extreme—let my characters feel more hate, act with more lust, anger, perversion, malice.

Or what if I had *not* committed so fully to this particular story? What if I had not hoarded all energy for writing, rewriting, reordering this one book? Would something lighter, stranger, less obvious have popped out of my unconscious?

Or worst: What if I had it right the first time? That any novel would, at some point, have required the kind of deadly earnestness of just going at it that can cause anyone, however skilled, to lose his lightness of touch and sense of humor? Is it possible I've done that? Produced something that's solid and workmanlike, but also as an agent recently intimated just not something anyone can love?

I dunno. But on the positive side of the ledger, I also look back and see I have, after all, listened to what was inside me. I have, indeed, made some things up. I do need solitude, and I do need to write. Those are not inconsiderable lessons to have learned.

It may well be I can never again escape to a world as compelling for me, as that town, that time of life, that subject. It may be true, if I try to write a second novel, I will have to do it with a novelist's detachment—with more thought and less feeling. I will have to do a lot more making up this time around. How many times, after all, can you summon that wealth of memory—write about a sunset or an embrace with the intensity that comes of having been there? Doesn't writing ultimately become more of a chess game, a less heated intellectual exercise—and do I care enough to do that? Do I have the will and discipline to write about the grayer areas of life?

But that, too, is another story.

Joe Levine lives with his wife and daughters in New York City, where he toils in the spin trade. He wrote "Finis" about his unpublished novel, A Hole in the Bottom of the Sea, *in 2007. After subsequently sending the book to scores of agents without success, he has indeed let it go, although the characters live on in his mind. Recent events in his life have made him realize writing autobiographical fiction requires research, too—and the quest can be as perilous as any other.*

Slaying the Dragon Lady

Terry Purinton

I'm a caretaker on a wealthy suburban estate. I both work on the property and live there part-time. A long time ago, as in thirty years, I decided to let go of my caretaking job before even taking it. During the job interview, while sitting before my prospective boss as she described my duties, a thought bubble rose above my head saying, "Hmm, I'll stay six months max, then move on."

I was twenty-seven. I still had many jobs lying in wait, all leading to a career. There was the teaching career in creative writing, once I published a novel. There was the social work career, once I went back to school. There was a freelance journalism career, once I broke into the field. There was even a career as a physician's assistant, but the sum total of two college science courses, geology and horticulture, did not show a lot of promise in medicine.

So here I am, three decades later, still trying to let go of my job.

Whenever someone asks me what I do for a living, I hesitate and squirm before saying I'm a caretaker. I garden, cut lawns, remove snow, chauffeur, run errands, take care of pets, and am generally on call for just about anything that comes down the pike. All my tasks are menial. None produce particularly satisfying results, except the gardening, which is not particularly noticed by my jet-set employer. I can be beckoned on week nights and weekends to drive and am called upon to take care of most any task too trivial or time consuming for my employer, such as screwing in light bulbs. I've come to refer to her as the Dragon Lady. The older I get, the more I squirm, especially in front of a mirror.

But here's the thing. I'm a writer. I took this job so I could write. Caretaking has put me under a kind of house arrest, which forces me to do something meaningful between the meaningless duties. And it works. I have written and written and written.

I'm a writer first, a caretaker second.

But here's the other thing. When someone asks about my writing, I hesitate and squirm, because the question, often politely implied, is: What have you published? The answer is: Nothing. That's not completely true. I've published articles, contributed to books; I am proud of my nonfiction work. But my publishing history for what counts in my soul—a novel—is a big fat zero. After writing twice my weight in novels with nothing to show, my friends and family know not to ask.

I want to say it's just a matter of time before I publish a novel. It's just a matter of time before I let go of this job. But when? What is the right time? And how much time do I have?

I haven't let go of my caretaking job because I need the money, and at my age, I'm afraid of unemployment, or of ending up with work that pays less money and gives me less time to write. Plus, after 30 years, I've developed a sort of Stockholm syndrome with the Dragon Lady, where I mistake free time from my duties as an act of kindness.

Maybe it's not too late to go back to school and begin a fulfilling career. Maybe I can find something more worthwhile than writing novels. Books take too much time to write. If I let go of writing, I'll have time to pursue a meaningful way of making money.

Somehow that rings false.

I once met a backhoe operator who claimed caretaking was his idea of a dream life: "Free from nine-to-five, living off the grid, a caretaker is unconventional, independent and not a slave to status and wealth," he said. Well, he got the status and wealth part right.

So how do I let go? The idea is once I publish a novel, the whole world will look different. I'll be a real writer then. The caretaking gig will be the cool way I made it happen. Some people will be envious. The menial work will have been worth it. I will slay the Dragon Lady.

Meanwhile, I'll keep wanting to let go, and I'll continue to squirm. If I don't publish, will my life be misspent? I honestly don't know.

Terry Purinton writes noir crime thrillers set in New York City and its suburbs. When not chasing after murder and mayhem, he likes to grow flowers, walk in the woods and fish. He grew up in a rusting industrial town on the Ohio River, where he learned not to take unspoiled nature for granted.

His nonfiction writing credits include: treatments for true crime and social issues documentaries; Columbia University Teacher's College publications; National Wildlife Federation Field Guide to Trees of North America *(Sterling);* The Art of Fiction Writing or How to Fall Down the Rabbit Hole Without Really Trying *(Labyrinth Press).*

He wrote his first novel when twelve years old, but says it paled in comparison to winning first prize in eighth grade for the essay, "My Country 'Tis of Thee," for the Northeastern Ohio League of Women Voters. It has been a hard act to follow.

The "Perfect" Man

María Stellatelli

Dear Sebastian,
You used to ask me what was wrong, why I looked so sad. I don't know if it makes any difference to you now; it's already been four years, but I still come back to that stage of my life, looking for a missing piece of the puzzle I haven't yet solved.

After my relationship with John ended, I haven't been able to establish a lasting relationship. I've never trusted anyone enough to fall in love again. That doesn't sound like me some years ago, right? But something broke during those months with John, and sadly, I am no longer the romantic innocent I once was.

Still, I did learn something during the past four years. Adult life doesn't necessarily begin at a specific age or time in life. For some, a moment comes when suddenly, your innocent eyes open to another, bigger world, possibly a meaner world, definitely one more realistic. That moment arrived when I was twenty. I didn't understand what was wrong. Why I was so sad at the time. I had always felt being John's girlfriend was close to being in paradise, but in reality, I was in hell.

I met John just after you had broken up with me. Miserable after our breakup, I promised myself the next relationship would be different. I'd find my perfect someone, a man who couldn't live without me. And soon, I found him.

John looked perfect—handsome, a modern-day "Prince Charming" with blond hair, big hands and captivating green eyes. He filled every void you had left. He had many friends, as he was so much fun. Most important, the way he looked at me made me feel I was the most special person in his life. He would never break up with me, never want another as he wanted me.

After the first date, I was sure he was the guy I would marry. I asked him once where he had been all my life. "With the wrong girls," he said. I knew I was rushing into a new relationship, but I didn't care. Nor did I care what my friends thought. I believed the train only stops once at your station. You either get on or let it go forever. I got on.

A few months after we met, John and I were having dinner one evening, when he announced his plan to drop out of university, quit his job and curtail his social activities. He and his dad were going through a tough time. He wanted time to think.

"Nothing gets solved by stopping everything just to think," I said, and suddenly, he was yelling—I only cared what people would think if he dropped out. I was acting selfish and stupid, just like his mom. Something broke during that conversation. I remember that day and my feeling of dread as if it were yesterday.

I knew this signaled trouble ahead, but as many young women who believe there is a "perfect man" for them, I didn't want to see it. I couldn't let go of my beautiful dream. So, I ignored the warning signs, which was easy, given what he did soon after.

A few days later, I felt unwell and stayed home. I was looking for a romantic movie on TV, when my mom suddenly entered my room and announced a visitor. There John stood, a big smile on his face, saying, "Breakfast surprise!" He had brought everything I like to eat: Sweet pudding, toast with ham and cheese, yogurt, cake, orange juice. It was like a hotel breakfast, which we ate together, before watching the movie—an ideal surprise for a rainy day in pajamas. It was such a sweet, thoughtful surprise that I forgot how angrily he had yelled only a few days before.

I felt the breakfast was his way of apologizing and showing his love for me. And sure enough, after each blowup, there were always surprises. The surprises made me forget completely the angry, abusive shouting.

During the following weeks he dropped out of university and cut back work to a couple of hours a day. He became super-sensitive, even irritable. Every time I asked how he was doing, he assumed I was judging him and became violently angry. Then suddenly, he would switch and say I was the most important thing in his life.

After one such blowup, he asked me to save a night for a surprise. I was so excited. He picked me up at home at 8:00 p.m., and we drove until we arrived at the River Plate. He parked and retrieved a backpack hidden under the backseat. He opened my car door—he always opened my door—and led me by the hand to the river bank, where he laid out dinner on a beautiful, red tablecloth. I couldn't believe my eyes.

The night was beautiful. Shinning stars spread above us, making the water sparkle. Big stars, tiny ones, millions and millions of endless stars over a black curtain. There's a funny thing about nature´s beauty, which makes you more sensitive and opens your heart, and under that amazing sky, I fell in love with the guy who had planned this magical evening and those big green eyes that looked at me adoringly.

A short time after we were formally a couple, John came for dinner. While setting the table together, Mom asked what he was doing during the summer. "I'm going to the Lake Tahoe Work & Travel program in the US for four months," he answered. I couldn't believe my ears. Why was I finding out like this? That was not my vision of a loving relationship. I couldn't stop thinking about it, so the next day I phoned and demanded an explanation. He yelled at me and hung up without even saying good-bye.

This time, the "surprise" was a table for two at a popular venue in Palermo Soho, the chic part of Buenos Aires. I hadn't been ready when he arrived, so as I came downstairs, I heard him telling my brother about his trip. "He'll have to make it up to me," I joked, "because he didn't tell me he was going away for such a long time."

As we traveled along the freeway to the city, he remained silent, steered into the fast lane and speeded up. When I asked if he was pissed off, he let go of the steering wheel and started yelling: I made him feel awful in front of my brother. I was selfish, uncomprehending. We were going very fast. And he wasn't looking at the road. All I was able to say was, "Please put your hands back on the steering wheel and look at the road. We'll be killed."

While he parked, I got out without waiting for him and walked inside the bar. I couldn't look at him. Tears ran down my cheeks. I pressed my arms around myself. We could have crashed. And we would have died. There was no doubt. But as always, I managed to rationalize his behavior by blaming it mostly on myself. So it was forgotten.

Every year, I saved a weekend for a religious retreat; the silence helps me reflect on my life. That year, the organizers asked friends and relatives to write letters to those going on retreat for a Saturday evening surprise. The letters were all affectionate, wishing me the best. But his letter wasn't like theirs. His was a rehash of the arguments we had been having, arguments that ended with his yelling: I wasn't supportive. I reflected our mechanized society. I didn't understand the real meaning of life. The letter ended, "Although you make lots of mistakes and are very limited, you still have some good qualities. Even if we break up soon, I enjoyed this time with you. . . ."

When he picked me up at the end of the retreat, I told him I didn't like his letter, but he blamed me for what he had written, because of my constant questions about his life and his upcoming trip. He hammered the steering wheel violently and shouted. I pressed myself against the car door and stayed as far as possible from him. When we arrived at my house, he grabbed my hand and pulled me to him. He begged me not to leave him; he would die without me; I was the only good thing in his life, but please, don't ask any more questions. So I decided to drop those topics for good. I loved him, and he couldn't live without me. That was all that mattered.

Do you remember, Sebastian, that day at the university when you asked me what was wrong? No one had asked that in a long time. My friends never asked, nor did my parents. Nobody but you noticed something was breaking me apart. Was I disguising it so well that no one noticed? Or were they avoiding the topic, afraid of what the answer would be? But you looked directly into my eyes, saw my pain and noticed the tears I held back.

You said I had been looking sad for some time now, and you wanted to know why. You asked if everything was okay with John. I didn't answer. "Then break up. Make a pause. Take some time to reflect upon yourself—you're not okay. You're not supposed to be this way if you're in love," you said.

"I can't do that," I answered. "John says I'm the only good thing in his life, and he'll die without me." What I did not say was that I wasn't sure how to solve things without John. He always had an answer for what troubled me. I depended on him for everything by then.

Don't get me wrong; it would be a mistake to think I was miserable. When things were good, John and I were magical together, which made up for his passing, angry moments. Our friends reinforced the impression of our being a happy couple, which allayed any lingering doubt of my having found *the perfect man* and let me hide from the truth of his abusive nature. At a party we attended shortly before he left for the US, an acquaintance from high school came up and said she was so happy for me; I looked radiant with John. She thought we were such a fun couple, always laughing and dancing. And he was so handsome. We were perfect together.

Finally, a few days before he left for Lake Tahoe, we had dinner at his family's home and then went upstairs to watch TV. His mom and dad went to bed next door. We remained silent, watching TV. I couldn't think of anything but his leaving and the immense emptiness I felt. He asked why I was so silent. When I told him I would miss him, he stood up and started walking out of the room.

I called him back. I said we were having a conversation. He shouldn't just walk away. He turned around, eyes soaked in anger, grabbed a chair and threw it at me. "This is no conversation! Understand? It's not a conversation! I can't stand your crying. You don't understand anything. Don't ever again say you are going to miss me," he yelled.

I don't remember ever feeling so scared in my life. I just wanted to get out of that house and never go back. I grabbed my phone and looked for the number of a cab. Suddenly, he was hugging me, crying, telling me his life was miserable. Nothing in his life made any sense. He said he had nothing worthy but me. I hugged him. I told him what an amazing person he was. I told him his trip would be great fun and not to cry, because I loved him. Everything would be all right.

When he calmed down, I texted a friend to pick me up. As I waited for her to arrive, he came downstairs with his guitar and started playing a song about love, smiling as he sang. There was something strange about his gaze; he seemed not to be there anymore. Then he put down his guitar and started kissing my lips, then my cheeks and down to my neck. I froze. So he kissed me harder. I wouldn't react. His arms were completely around me; his big hands on my back. He held me against him and looked for a response. But there was none. He kept moving his hands around my body, touching me. He wouldn't stop, so I finally moved my head to one side as if I were enjoying it. "I knew you wouldn´t be able to resist yourself," he said and smiled triumphantly. I felt repugnance. But I couldn't move. I didn't have the guts to push him away.

The bell rang. When I got into my girlfriend's car, I realized he had never said he was sorry for what had happened. His mother and father never came out of their room to see what was going on. They just let him shout and throw things at me, as though he did this every day.

Ten days after he left Argentina, a friend handed me a letter John had left for me. When I got home that night, I read it over and over. It was the most beautiful letter I had ever received.

It wasn't addressed to me. It seemed to be something he was telling someone else about me. It was supposed to be my description. But instead, it was a detailed description of perfection. This description of a goddess was not me; I was not like that. I was a lonely girl who didn't know how she would find the way to live without him, so dependent that she couldn't decide anything for herself. I felt like a little ant, defenseless and alone in a mean, big world. After all that had happened, I was lost without him. I hadn't been good enough for him, so he had left.

Four years have gone by, but those memories still hurt. It took me a long time to realize what I'd gone through. But the feelings I described about his letter are true: I felt unworthy.

Manipulation completely tears down your self-esteem, and it takes a long time to recover.

I still haven't overcome fully what happened. I'm still scared, Sebastian. Scared to be shouted at again, scared not to realize I'm being manipulated. Every new date is a challenge, a challenge to realize and react to the slightest hint of aggression from my date. I guess it's not fair to look at men that way, but I can't help it.

I'm learning now to take care of myself. I'm beginning to see that not every guy is John. I know I'll be able to do it. I'm prepared now. I won't be manipulated without noticing as easily as last time. I've lost innocence, that's true. What I went through has made me stronger. I'm an adult now. I've let go of the girlish "Prince Charming" myth. Hopefully, that will keep me safe from now on. One day, I will be able to believe in love again, the true kind.

With love and gratitude,

María

María Stellatelli, twenty-five, lives and works in Buenos Aires near her family and is an editor of a magazine specializing in human and social topics. Last year, she had the chance to travel to New York City for three months, where she took creative writing classes at New York University, which rekindled her passion for telling stories.

In her free time, she's a singing student and a novice chef. She enjoys every activity that can stimulate senses and motivate creativity. She writes, "I've always been very observant of what happens around me. I'm a believer of the importance in giving a voice to those who have stories that can help others. I'm convinced stories must be told in order to inspire people, and I hope to hold the pen that narrates many of them."

. . . OF FRIENDS
AND LOVED ONES

Commencing Being Fearless

Roz Kuehn

I spent the months after my divorce on autopilot. In my peripheral vision, the world looked shiny—like a newly-minted coin or a switchblade. I had lost my bearings; I couldn't tell when to hold on, nor when to let go. So it was providence when Raquel Squelch and Cookie Monstrosity rumbled past my craft stall on Wilmington's Brandywine Boulevard.

My sister, my dad, and I had scored the perfect spot, across from the Bellefonte Café, our community's friendly watering hole. To our left, the caramel corn machine popped happily and emitted a hot sugar scent. Sonja's knitted handbags sold well, as did the wallets Daddy had fashioned from used orange juice cartons. My enormous, gold spray-painted Birthday Thrones offered respite to tired people walking by.

"Orientation's on Thursday," Cookie said, gracefully stopping short on her skates, despite her downhill trajectory, and handing me a flyer. Her arm was sleeved in tattoos; she wore a tattered tutu. I thanked her and looked at the ad for Diamond State Rollergirls' upcoming "bout" against the Fall-Out Femmes. The Femmes' logo—a nuclear reactor and a nod to the contaminated western Pennsylvania terrain that spawned them—puffed on one side of the flyer, while Delaware's own Trixie Trauma leered, her traumatic butt punching its way out of ravaged fishnets, hinting at what awaited the Femmes.

I wanted to tell the gals I hadn't roller skated since the 1970s when I was twelve, and my bones were getting more brittle by the day, but they had already whipped onward. A secretary in a law firm, when I wasn't typing pleadings, I was staring into space, planning my exit from the corporate world as a best-selling maker of Birthday Thrones. I liked fine wine, reading literary fiction and flower gardening. Beside me, in the shade of our awning, Daddy munched away on his bartered-for snack while the caramel corn guy opened and closed his juice box wallet. Sonja made change for another handbag sale. My six thrones sparkled unsold in the sun.

Thursday evening, I entered through metal doors and followed a glossy cinderblock maze into the echoing arena, which the derby league rented for practice after hours. To my right, the daffodil-yellow booths of a shuttered snack bar glowed eerily.

Corpses Christy welcomed me rink-side. "Hey, there. Follow me. So! Camaraderie and trust are two lessons you'll learn," she said. In my street shoes I was invited onto the track to meet my future teammates. "I'm Slip Me a Mickey," said a tall, crazy-eyed woman with skin so black the shadows were lavender. "I'm Lotsa Moxie," said a slender blonde.

"I'm Dee Capitate."

"I'm Lip Bomb."

"I'm Miss Fortune."

There were about fifteen women in all.

Corpses Christie and I sat on the divider wall, legs dangling, and watched the women push through exercises. Their wheels thundered as they fearlessly charged around the rink. Nimbly, they stopped as one. When Lip Bomb tumbled, she hollered in pain. But up she clambered, laughing.

"I want to try this," I said.

That Saturday morning, I stood at the *Kill Pads* display in the sporting goods store. No way would I break my calcium-deprived bones with these Goth potholders strapped to my knees. I added a shiny black helmet and hobbled to a full-length mirror. I looked badass. Mistaking me for a league member, the boy at the counter gave me a ten percent discount. I rushed home to commence practicing being fearless.

Berber carpeting was a non-traditional roller skating surface. That much I knew. Yet the bedroom was where my TV was, and Sandra Rinomato, the host of the show "Property Virgins," calmed me. With a babysitter's serenity and sense of fun, she asked a pair of newlyweds what they thought of a condo in East End-Danforth, Toronto. I waded past my dresser and nightstand on my eight-wheeled "quads." Since my ex, Luke, had taken the highboy, there was room to move about. Soon I'd worked up a sweat. Resting on my bottom, I thumped down the wooden steps for a glass of water. The living room had carpet of a different texture, but I adjusted like a pro and glided past the sofa where my cat, Tin Cup, snoozed.

I know exactly what people mean when they say, "The accident happened so fast, I couldn't react." My brazen stride onto the kitchen tiles was followed by a sudden departure from terra firma. In a moment of bowel-loosening dread, I hung parallel to the floor. Then I crashed down, ricocheted off the old wooden chest that served as a side table, into the filigreed metal of an art nouveau lamp. Then there was silence, broken only by the squeaky swinging of the glass lampshade that had come loose, exposing old, frayed wires. I lay there, half on the carpet, half on the tile, as gravity rushed in and jiggled my fat back into place.

I stayed put, listening to the lampshade until it quieted. "I'm alive," I said finally. Channeling Sandra Rinomato, I prompted cheerfully, "Well? What do you think?" Tin Cup sat up and looked at me.

☙❦❧

The next day, Luke came over to cut the grass. "I'm joining the roller derby," I said. My paraphernalia lay strewn across the living room floor. My quads, resting on their sides, looked like snoring monsters, wheels gaping. Luke was moving in slo-mo, like he'd been up all night, playing guitar, smoking pot. His languid gestures drove me nuts when we were married. Now I didn't mind.

"I heard something about that," he said slowly, setting his keys on the coffee table. His T-shirt and shorts looked like they'd been bunched up in a drawer since our split. He smelled like curry and dust. I said nothing. He sat in my favorite Pier One arm chair, which he said I could keep when the house sold, and watched me gear up.

"I'm concerned," he said, rubbing his face.

"It's against the rules for them to hit me. It's a penalty."

"What if . . . someone gets a penalty . . . and you get a broken orbital bone?"

I hesitated. I hadn't bought leather skates like Corpses Christy had recommended, and my toes went numb if I tied the laces too tightly. I backtracked a few holes. "I just hope they don't break my nose. I decided I love my profile."

Luke's chest buckled as he tried to suppress laughter at the size of the kneepads I strapped on. "Where's your helmet?"

Shyly, I put it on, clasped it securely beneath my chin. I wasn't really shy; I was play-acting. Luke knew me, through and through. I wasn't embarrassed in front of him, like I'd be in front of a new beau.

"That's cool," he said, regaining control. He was looking at me with kindness, like I was a child.

Suddenly I felt his love. And then I did feel shy. I said quietly, "This is what the experts wear. So they don't get hurt."

"What?" Luke asked gently. He leaned closer; he hadn't heard.

"It's what the experts wear," I repeated, blushing now.

He smiled. "Well, I think you're very wise."

Cradling my skates in the crook of my arm like pit bull puppies, I climbed into my VW and drove around the corner from our house to the nature center parking lot. It was sunny and peaceful. I opened the driver's side door, removed my Dansko sandals, pulled on my colourful, striped, derby-girl socks and wrangled into my skates. It was like stepping into someone's mouth, wiggling your heel to fit into his chin. It truly wasn't natural. I took a deep breath. The recycling dumpsters were a good forty feet away. It occurred to me I didn't know how to stop, save by banging into a barrier. A woodpecker knocked; the smell of clove-scented phlox and syrupy honeysuckle permeated. I clambered up. My feet immediately tried racing away from me. I clutched the door of my Jetta, the metal edge searing my palm. I held fast, my fingertips turning white. I grimaced in concentration, willing myself not to feel. In the distance, our riding mower started up. I strained to hear as the sound grew closer, then moved far away again, then grew close again, as Luke rode in a circle. Holding on while letting go, I broke and began to bawl.

Roz Kuehn received her bachelor of fine arts from the Corcoran School of Art in Washington, DC. She is the author of a novel, Various Stages of Undress, *loosely based on six years as an exotic dancer in Washington, DC, which was runner-up for the Faulkner-Wisdom Competition, and a finalist for both the Breadloaf Bakeless Prize and Bellwether Prize. She has also received numerous Delaware State Arts Council fellowships, including a $10,000 Master of Fiction fellowship, as well as a Barbara Deming Memorial Award for feminist writing. Her memoir,* Losing Glynis, *is about a coterie of well-meaning girlfriends who swoop in and make a royal mess of a close friend's dying days. She acted as fiction editor for* The Washington Review *for four years and currently works as a legal secretary in a New York City firm.*

No Longer
George Schofield's Wife

Norma Nixon Schofield

When my husband died, I began to understand those cultures in which the wife throws herself on her husband's funeral pyre. In one short second as George drew his last breath, I went from being George Schofield's wife to being nobody.

George and I had been very close. I had long thought of us as one connected soul living in two bodies. When his body died, I felt mine should, too, so the soul could be whole and free. But I didn't die.

Then I began to feel his half of the soul was living with my half in the one body we had remaining. I crept about hugging the walls like a shadow, desperate not to be seen, not wanting to speak or be spoken to, feeling like a chimera. (I had seen such a man on a TV episode of, *House*. One-half the man's body was hostile to his doctor, while the other half was not. The left hand slapped things out of the doctor's hand, while the right hand tried to hug him. House figured it out, of course. I kind of liked that idea.)

George and I were best friends for thirty-three years, an *item* for thirty-one and married for twenty-seven. We met in a writers' group in 1976. There followed two years of arguing tooth and nail about who should write what and for whom, until one day we looked into each other's eyes across a table we'd been pounding to emphasize our points and realized we were in love.

The sun shone down on the tinkling waterfall as we sat in a park in Caracas, and he read to me from Paul's letters to the Ephesians from a small Bible awarded to George in Sunday school when he was a child. 'Now Heaven walks on Earth,' I said to myself, thinking Shakespeare. I would have followed him anywhere.

But we'd both been married before and wanted to be certain. Besides, the marriage wouldn't have been legal in a foreign country. I also wanted my mother there and my brother to give me away. We were finally ready four years later, and I became George Schofield's wife in Connecticut.

George was a sandy-haired Englishman with beautiful hazel eyes flecked with green. He grew up in London and survived the Blitz of the Second World War. I was an African-American who grew up in park-and-bridge-laden Pittsburgh, Pennsylvania, the steel center of the United States. Together George and I had the world sewn up: I was the outgoing American with *know how*. George was the polished Brit with *savoir faire*. Together, we could, and did, go anywhere.

Our life in the tropics was one long party. As Lifestyle pages editor of *The Daily Journal*, Caracas's English language daily, I received invitations to receptions and dinner parties every evening. Every diplomat and foreign businessman in Venezuela wanted his activities reported in the English newspaper, so the folks back home could read what he had been up to. There were many other parties as well, given by the ex-pat community of Americans, Brits and assorted English-speakers. We were out every night.

And then there were our yearly trips to England.

"He who is tired of London is tired of life," George would quote Samuel Johnson annually, as we stepped off the plane at Heathrow. The question was whether it would be more fun to live in London full-time or whether one would feel more zest with occasional visits. My George loved the zest of London, exploring the city anew while looking for the favorite haunts of his youth.

A few years ago, when George was lying on a gurney on his way in for an angioplasty, and I was massaging his feet, a medical attendant looked at me and said, "He's high maintenance, isn't he?"

"Yes," I admitted although I hadn't realized it before. George was high maintenance, but I loved it.

Retired, he was working on his second book, a novel set in South America. He started at nine in the morning, broke for lunch and stopped writing in time for cocktails in the library, "Jeopardy," followed by dinner.

Then one day he casually said, "I give you permission to finish the novel in case I don't." That should have been a warning. But he wasn't even sick.

"I'm not sure you want me to. I'd probably turn it into a love story," I said.

George frowned but said nothing. About a week before he died, he came down to dinner and said, "I finished the book. The surprise ending is brilliant and far from a love story ending."

In every room of our house, I keep lots of framed pictures of George and me together. Here we are leading Girl Scouts up a mountainside, snakebite kits in hand. There we are arriving at the Tamanaco Hotel in Caracas, George in black tie, me in long dress and lots of gold, for one of the British Commonwealth Association's annual balls. In the last photo taken of us, we are posing with a friend from Ghana and his bride on their wedding day in New York.

The photo I carry with me always, though, is of me sitting on George's lap and smiling. It was taken on the beach in 1978, on the day I realized we would be together for the rest of our lives. It turned out to be for the rest of his life but not of mine.

George and I had a chance to talk during moments of lucidity between painkillers during his last illness. We spoke of the accomplishments of our life together and what was still on our collective 'to do' list. Looking over our lives together, we agreed we had enjoyed every moment. He admitted to worrying sometimes in silence during times when we had little money. I do like to live well, but I had never minded living modestly. It's rare to find love.

We also discovered that instead of lingering for years, no longer able-bodied, no longer lucid or able to play our nightly Scrabble, we'd rather be, "Here today. Gone tomorrow." But that seemed a moot point. Although he was sometimes in excruciating pain, we weren't worried. We thought modern medicine had it covered; he'd soon be better.

When his illness didn't go away, I became frightened and told him not to let himself die because he thought I didn't want to take care of him. "I'll be happy to have you in whatever shape you are. I need you," I told him.

"I stood before God and man and swore to look after you, and now I can't," he lamented.

"You've given me enough knowledge to take care of us both," I said, still in denial about the seriousness of his illness.

When George died I opted out of the affairs of the planet. I didn't listen to the news or follow the stock market. I didn't want to see or be seen. I wore nothing but black. I couldn't stand to walk by a mirror and see myself in colors.

After my husband died, people gave me many suggestions about coping with his loss. The advice I most treasure was to wear some of his clothes. I put on his watch, his socks and his jackets and found this deeply comforting.

A close friend, whose husband died a year before I lost George, told me if I listened long and hard, he would still be there to look after me. And this I did and do. But it's hard to think I will never hear again his, "Hello, Mate!" in answer to my, "Hi, Sweetie."

Eventually, the deep pain of George's loss began to lessen, but as the grief lifted, I ran right into guilt. I couldn't help feeling guilty for letting George go. I almost expected the police to show up at the door, saying I'd failed in my duty, poisoned him by allowing him to take the meds his doctors prescribed. Perhaps if I'd hired a private nurse to be on vigil twenty-four-seven, he wouldn't have died. Or perhaps if I'd taken up a crusade 'round the clock and demanded his four to five specialists coordinate with each other, the GP, and the ER resident the last night, he wouldn't have died. They didn't love him; he was my responsibility; and I had failed him.

Then came the thought: Why me? Why did my husband die? I have lots of friends, whose husbands are old and failing. Their husbands are tottering about on canes, being pushed about in wheelchairs, making weekly visits to emergency rooms, but they are still alive. Why had I not been trusted to take care of George in his old age?

Finally, I reasoned it out: George died at seventy-seven after a two-month illness. But he might have been ill from seventy-four to seventy-seven. He might have been in a wheelchair for three or four years with me spoon feeding him, injecting him and all sorts of things, like our friends' husbands. Instead, we lived like a pair of forty-year-olds until his last two months.

Perhaps we'd been blessed, I reasoned. It had actually played out the way George wanted it. He was here today, gone tomorrow.

George had definitely beaten the odds. He'd survived through the London Blitz in the early 1940s, the upheaval and disorder of the Caracas earthquake of 1966, and the shock and horror of the terrorist New York bombing of 9/11. He had seen 28,299 sunrises while the average is only 25,000. What more could I ask?

Finally, I could begin to let go of the guilt that went with being George Schofield's wife and not being strong enough to keep him alive. I began to think back to the beginning of our marriage. I had just read *The Gods Themselves* by Isaac Asimov. This novel has a three-member 'couple' or triad with two men and one woman. I liked that—two Georges to look after me instead of just one.

It has a Rational (male), a Parental (male), and an Emotional (female). The female is beautiful and spends her time dancing on rooftops in the twilight. She's fun for the two males who are serious-minded (the Rational) and full of homemaking responsibilities (the Parental). But it takes all three of them to mate or melt, as they call it, which she enjoys superbly.

I can do that, I thought at the time. I can be a super lithe female who has fun and dances on the rooftop in the moonlight. And my George was both Rational and Parental. He was serious-minded, knew all the answers and looked after me, the Emotional. Continuing the parallel, my mate always looked to me for fun, because my favorite word was joy, and I made sure we lived surrounded by it.

When I first met George his idea of fun was for us just to *be* together. I told him I saw him as a comfortable and welcoming easy chair covered in faded chintz, sitting in a corner by the window in the library in a country home. Myself, I saw as a crystal and silver table in the foyer of a beautiful, modern New York apartment, holding champagne and glasses to welcome guests.

"I plan to live on one side of the forest this season, and the other side of the forest next like some of my ancestors," I told him. "I want a pad in London, a mansion just outside New York with a pied-à-terre in the city, and a place in the south of France." The list went on and on. "A place for respite in Ghana, West Africa. An apartment by the sea. A cabin in the mountains." I wanted to flit about from season to season.

George listened, then said, "I'm not some old faded chair in the corner. That's not what I am at all. I'm just like you. I want to travel the world. We can go together."

And so it came to be. With George at my back, supporting and taking care of me, I, the Emotional, held everything together and made it all fun.

In *The Gods Themselves* the three members of the triad eventually melt together permanently and become a new being, a leader called a Super Rational, who has the characteristics of all three triad members, the Rational, the Parental, and the Emotional and is part of the establishment and sought out for counsel.

So what's left for me now, five years later, as I learn that I do have the strength to give up being George Schofield's wife? I like to think my next step is the Super Rational phase—to take on the characteristics of the Rational and Parental sides of George along with my Emotional side and become a Super Rational. Now, starting to let go of being George Schofield's wife, I shall have to become George Schofield's widow, or as they used to say in the cowboy movies, The Widow Schofield. I shall have to start reading *Barron's* and *The Wall Street Journal* again, so I can make intelligent decisions about my place in the world. I'll have to cook my own meals, make my own cups of tea and watch my health. I have to make sure my grown children are where they're supposed to be and help them get there if they're not. I have to continue working on the to do list George and I made up together. And I have to keep my spirit alive by occasionally dancing in the moonlight.

Norma Nixon Schofield—The Widow Schofield—loves "faraway places with strange-sounding names" and travels every chance she gets. Originally from Pittsburgh, PA, she lived ten years in South America. Although she studied in Irvine, California and lived in rural Connecticut until the awful school shooting, in her heart she's a New Yorker and never far away from the big city from which she can easily hop to London, her late husband's big city.

Schofield writes about murder in exotic places and is currently finishing the novel her husband left her when he died. Yes, it's taken her that long to let go. "We always planned to write a novel together just never got around to it. This'll be it," she says. Her second novel, set in Kumasi, Ghana, the seat of the ancient Ashanti nation, is in progress. She can be reached at normageorge82@gmail.com.

How to Send
Your Husband to a War

Beejay Silcox

You will put on a dress to wear to the airport. You will put on lipstick and eyeliner and perfume, too. Then in the end, you will wipe your red mouth clean and wear jeans and sneakers, but you won't be able to shake the scent of lily. He will wear a new uniform with his blood type stitched across the breast pocket.

You will pretend this good-bye is the same as the others. You will stand at the departure gate and step though the small rituals of your marriage. You will say 'enjoy your war,' and he will say 'enjoy your peace,' and you will both laugh, because it's a terrible joke.

Your friends will ask polite questions about impolite subjects. They will ask if you regret not changing your name. They will ask about triage and phone sex. And without asking, they will only take you to films where everybody lives happily-ever-after. They will send money to widows and mutilated children in your name and wait for your gratitude, because they have bought it.

You will learn to taste pity in the air.

At parties, you will be introduced to strangers as His wife, and the strangers will think they already know the most important thing about you. They will empathize at you, get political for you. They will put their hands on you and call you brave and never ask your name. You will stop going. You will stop being invited.

You will write love letters you never send. You will flirt with prayer. You will flirt with strangers. Some of them will flirt back. One of them won't take no for an answer. He is the only person who will see how angry you are.

In the mornings you will dress for work. You will wear headphones at your desk so that nobody speaks to you. You won't play music, just listen to the quiet waiting in your ears like the private sounds of a seashell. You will stay late and be praised for your dedication. You will spend money on shit you don't need, which you buy late at night on the Internet: an ice-cream maker, oversized pillows, an art deco lampshade with a repeating pattern of foxes and hunters. You will fill your freezer. You will fill your bed. When you sleep, you will dream of the fox.

The women at the post office will weigh your letters and lick your stamps and reach across the counter to smooth down your hair as you write your husband's ID number from memory across the address label. You will send books he won't have time to read, with inscriptions he won't find. You will send hard-shelled chocolates that can't melt. You will send soft soap and strong coffee. You will send an engraved teaspoon, so that he must think of you every morning as he stirs in his sugars. You will fill your envelopes with the raw and bloody hope that he will want to come home.

And once a week, you will talk to him. The connection will be thin, and you will have no choice but to shout at each other. And you will shout. Your heart will beat its fists, and you will shout like you are kids stretching a tin can string across the fat curve of the world.

Beejay Silcox, an Australian writer currently completing her MFA at Virginia Tech, came to writing circuitously. She has degrees in law and psychology and has worked as agony aunt, a government strategist and a criminologist. Above all, she is a seeker of adventure, having been kicked in the head by a mountain gorilla, blessed by a voodoo priest and stuck in quicksand. She is married to a diplomat, and they live a strange and nomadic kind of life— they eloped to Las Vegas and drove to Timbuktu in a car held together with a bra strap. When she grows up, she wants to be a storyteller.

Out with the Old

M.S. Turchin

Maddie knew it was time for a new bed. One year had gone by since her husband Al had died, and it was time, she felt to her very bones, to be free to spread out over any side of the bed she liked. In the bed they bought thirty-odd years before, she simply couldn't. The mattress was indented on "his side" with a trough so deep from his long, heavy body that when she lay down, she fell into a deep canyon with such jagged lumps, it was a struggle to climb out. Maddie once tried sleeping there, but she awoke in the middle of the night feeling the bed had her in its grip, and Al was pulling her down. She was sure she was having a heart attack. Her chest contracted so hard, she couldn't breathe.

"You've seen too many horror movies," her son Josh kept saying, patting her hand and stroking her still-brown hair, while she panted for him to call 911. The ambulance took her, gasping and sweating, an oxygen mask strapped to her face, to a strange hospital, where she found herself surrounded by crazy drunks and screaming, handcuffed criminals in the emergency room. It turned out she was having a panic attack. After that, she avoided sleeping on Al's side. Even so, when she made the bed mornings with Grandma Paulie's deep blue spread crocheted with beautiful, perfect rosettes, she saw Al outlined there, something like the Shroud of Turin. That, she never told Josh.

A few months ago, Maddie knelt down on Al's side of the bed and drove her nose deep into the mattress, searching for some evidence of him. She had thrown out his pillows and covers almost immediately after his death, even though the sheer waste violated her hausfrau sense of frugality, and she had wept, miserable over having to make that decision.

"Should I? Shouldn't I? Should I? Shouldn't I?" Maddie polled friends and family. She was incapable of making a decision without a majority consensus, something Al had hated in her. "Just make up your mind," he'd bellow from the living room couch, while watching some sport on TV—football, baseball—somehow hearing her, even though she was whispering into the telephone, hand cupped over mouth. She'd instantly shut up. She didn't want yet another loud, unending confrontation, from which she would back off eventually anyway. She'd continue polling later, more quietly, out of his hearing, so he couldn't interfere.

Things weren't that easy for her. She didn't make snap judgments, come what may, like Al. She liked hearing other opinions, nodding, gathering facts, collecting ideas, taking what might be the best of the bunch, but lining up others in case she had to change tacks quickly. It was how she learned to operate where she had grown up in a bay-side neighborhood cut off by a sand-strewn toll bridge, so strangers turned around and went back, sure the bridge ended nowhere. You looked out your kitchen window to the boat tied up to the dock behind your home, and what neighbors said mattered: "It's a good day for a sail," or "Snapper's running; going out?" "The weather's turning. Better stay home." They had been, after all, the ones you expected to come to your rescue. No such expectation had ever existed in the Brooklyn neighborhood of her adult, married life.

Maddie tried washing his bedclothes—twice—on the washing

machine's hottest setting with a cup of bleach thrown in, as her sister-in-law suggested, but to Maddie's eyes the pillows and covers were still stained and sour with sickness and death. So, on Friday following his death, Al's covers and pillows were neatly tied up in black plastic bags. She stood on the brownstone stoop, watching the garbage men heave the bags into their yawning truck, stinking refuse spilling out the sides, and she continued to watch, until the bags were devoured and gone. Surprised to feel no regrets, she folded her thin, age-spotted hands into the pockets of the black sweat pants she customarily wore at home and went inside. It was too cold out, even if the moms and children passing on the sidewalk were still wearing light sweaters. She didn't have the meat on her bones those young people had.

But the mattress she kept after all; it was just too expensive to toss. Kneeling there, nose sunk deep into it, she was sure she detected the salty aroma she'd always associated with Al. Although she knew this was really just the strong, salty-sweat odor men exuded simply moving through their days, she imagined she caught the sea-spray from the old fishing boat, "Swept Away," they'd had when young. They always laughingly told in unison the story of its maiden voyage: how the engine had died somewhere out in the Sound, and they called the coast guard. "Boat's name, Captain?" the coast guard officer asked, and they had practically died of humiliation from the coast guard officer's deep, slow laugh when Al replied, "Swept Away."

Maddie had knelt there, breathing deeply, remembering the coast guard officer's belly laugh, their embarrassment at the time and their laughter ever after, until she decided she was an idiot and smelled nothing.

Still, she never again slept on Al's side of the bed, never even sat on it. His side became a repository for bedtime books and magazines and the clothes she set out neatly for work the next day.

At first, she couldn't imagine what kind of bed could ever replace this one. She loved its burnished, wrought iron metal bars, as well as the style she and Al had picked out. And then, it had been made by Joe Porque, the metal worker, her father's hunting buddy since she could remember. Once when she was little, her dad took her to Joe's shop to see the deer they'd bagged, the animal spread across a jig-saw table in a still-life of death.

"See how big its antlers are?" Joe had said. "Want to touch?" Maddie was frozen by the decision: She would have liked to get so close to the deer that she could run her fingers down a long, ridged antler, but she could already smell the dank odor of blood and the wet-wool smell of hair.

When Al and she had gone to Joe's all those years ago to have the bed made, he had walked them around his shop, slowly pointing out the different finishes and styles. They'd chosen a campaign type, no-nonsense, like Al, with strong, straight bars, built to the exact, right height for him. It was a little high for her; she had to slide out of bed, swinging one leg down to the floor first, but she didn't mind. She was always careful in the middle of the night. Her father's friend had delivered it himself, slowly carrying the heavy bed to the second floor with his teenage son's help, setting it up carefully, so they wouldn't scratch the bedroom floor and then admiring his handiwork. Yes, she told him. I love it.

Many years later, when Al got sick and shrank, the bed became too high for him, too. This time, Joe's son came alone, his father being too sick to work, and cut down the legs right in the house, so Al could get in and out without falling. That was better for Maddie, too.

Crazy that such a massive thing turned out so versatile. When Al couldn't work anymore, and they had to move to a smaller home, the king-sized frame didn't fit through the front door. Joe's son swung by in his truck, picked up the frame and returned it the next day, hinged down the middle, with extra, supporting legs. Maddie offered a tip, but he shook his head, saying, "It's on me. We all go back so far." So Maddie ended up living with the bed for thirty-four years, a lifetime.

"I'm getting a new bed," she announced to Josh at breakfast, clutching her large, morning mug of black coffee.

Maddie held her breath, shrinking further into her small self, waiting for the explosions she somehow now set off in Josh. Hulking over his newspaper before running off to work, Josh didn't raise his eyes.

"You hear me, Josh? I'm getting a new bed."

"I'm not deaf. What do you need a new bed for? Yours is perfectly fine." Josh wiggled his large, soft body a few inches off the chair, as though to get up, before he fell back into it and made himself comfortable. He'd require more effort than that to get his twenty-five-year-old, overweight self out of that chair, Maddie thought. He'd gained a good fifteen pounds, since coming home to be with them for Al's final illness. Then, he never left. He liked not having to hold himself in check, as he had to when sharing an apartment with friends.

A couple of dark hairs wiggled through a gap between the buttons on the shirt stretching across Josh's enlarging stomach. Ugh, she thought. She didn't remember Josh that way. To her, he would always be the little boy, who snuggled close to her in that enormous bed. Now, he was a large, hairy, sloppy man—another large, loud man. What was she supposed to do with him?

"I can't sleep there anymore, Josh," Maddie said. "I just think of Daddy."

"What'll you do with this one?"

"Put it in the cellar."

"What! With all the rest of the junk you don't need and keep collecting? You're expecting me to get rid of it eventually, aren't you?" Breathing hard, like a bull who's seen red, Josh returned to his paper; he had even begun to speak like his father.

"You know, Josh, not everything has to be a fight."

"Yes, it does, when you do ridiculous things." Josh glared at her.

At first, it had been nice having Josh back, joining her for morning coffee before he went off to work, cooking with her when home at night. But as Al faded, Josh grew larger, filling the spaces Al gave up. And, Josh left his things all over the house, a Joshua trail, marking his territory.

Maddie looked at him, wondering whether she should poke the bear. "See you tonight, Josh," she said. Later, when she came out of her bedroom dressed for the day, Josh was gone to work, and the house was quiet. Maddie went to the kitchen drawer, where she hid anything she didn't want touched—Al had never helped in the kitchen, let alone looked in a drawer, his sole function being there to eat—and took out the decorating magazines her sister Janet suggested and a thick folder of photographs. Maddie had carefully cut out and organized by style and color the photos she liked best. She sat at the table studying them. When Janet came over, they went through the photographs one-by-one.

"I won't be able to clean under this; the sides come almost down to the floor," Maddie said, holding up one photograph for her sister to see.

"Won't this one be too heavy to move, like your old bed?" her sister asked, pausing over a photograph of a large bed with an imposing, mahogany headboard.

"I don't think I'm getting a king-sized bed again. What do you think?"

"Queen-sized takes up less room."

"The enamel would chip off on this one," Maddie said, examining a photo of a sleek, modern bed.

"This finish will scratch," Janet said.

There were a million considerations: Leather beds, metal beds, plain mattresses on frames, beds with headboards affixed to the wall. Platform beds, day beds, four-poster beds, beds with canopies. Then colors!

As brown-haired as Janet, although older by six years, Maddie leaned into Janet's shoulder, while they studied the photos spread across the kitchen table. From a distance, it was hard to tell who was who. More coffee percolated, filling the room with warm comfort. The sisters took off their shoes and put their feet up on the chairs. The day wore on.

"What color do you get, when you've had a dull silver practically all your life? Can you see me in red?" Maddie laughed. "Maybe purple. How 'bout hot pink?"

Well, why not? she thought. It was overwhelming, really, and the sad thought gnawed away at her that Al would have hated every bed, any bed she would choose.

"What difference does it make what Al would like?" her sister prodded.

"No difference. It makes no difference whatsoever. Let's put this away. It's too much to think about," she said and stopped thinking. It would come to her one day, the exact right new bed, the height perfect for her with no accommodation for any other person. She'd be shopping downtown, and it would be in a store window. She could see herself walking in and saying to the salesperson, "That's the bed. I want that one." It would magically appear in her bedroom, which would glisten with freshness and light.

She imagined Josh coming home and finding the new bed, as bold as day, there in her bedroom, and him stomping and shouting in and around the house, slamming doors, hating the bed, yelling at her, loudly, insistently, unendingly just like Al would have done. Well, not this time, Maddie thought. Maybe Josh would just have to go, too.

M.S. Turchin is a lifelong Brooklyn resident, previously from a small, obscure waterfront community. Her oeuvre includes poetry, short stories and memoirs. She now has a new bed.

A May-December Valentine

Myra Chanin

I am fifty-eight years old, happily married to a terrific guy, yet besotted with love for a man thirty-four years my junior. His wit and charm still enchant me, even though I know we are playing our end game. Lately, he prefers nubile bodies to the wisdom of the ages. When we first met, he sobbed whenever I had to leave, but now, only I sentimentally recall our lying side-by-side on his narrow bunk at dusk with him begging me to read *Goodnight, Moon* to him one last time. Obviously, the love of my life is the apple of my eye, my only child, Steven Bruce Chanin, a swell kid who's everything his father would have been, if he'd only had me for a mother.

To list his virtues may be vulgar, but I'm doing it anyway. He's intelligent, sociable, interesting, capable, disciplined and polite. He has even acquired a façade of modesty. I believe he takes no drugs. He has only one flaw: He prefers someone with younger skin. In the past, when women bewailed the coming of age of firstborn sons, I called them possessive, manipulative and mocked their callow psyches. Now the gods have punished me for my hubris by smiting me with the same irrational passion. My husband Alvin and I have been married twenty-five years, but I've always considered our alliance ephemeral. I've seen even closer bonds torn asunder by properly adoring Yuppies. Steven is our only mutual blood relative. Our love for him transforms us from cohabiting combatants into family. I never knew I could love anyone as much as I love that boy.

The night before Steve left for MIT, Alvin was sidetracked by a legal crisis, so Sonny and I went out on the town alone. I was all gussied up in a slinky black sheath with every wrinkle cream known to Bonwit Teller swathing my aging dermis. Steve looked suddenly manly in his double-breasted blazer and Alvin's only unstained Armani tie. As we walked down the street toward the car, I heard a neighbor, who normally sees me in scruffy jogging suits, ask his wife, "Who's that sharp chick with Steven?" What more could any Cougar Mom want? I was out on a dream date with the kind of boy who would have shunned me during my fat, hostile adolescence.

At the chicest pasta joint in town, my heir and I sipped vino and nibbled mousse-filled zucchini blossoms. He discussed advances in genetic research with me as though I had a logical brain, and he'd never laughed louder at my appraisal of the quirks of our near and dear. In the beveled mirrors facing our intimate corner table, I watched my reflection flirt with the lad. What a handsome couple we made! We looked even more radiant when I removed my glasses and viewed us though my 20/200 eyeballs.

The following morning I drove Steven to the airport and happily waved bye-bye as he boarded the iron bird before rushing home to explore empty nest sexuality. A few nights later, Alvin and I were committing unspeakable acts behind open doors when Steve called to announce he'd joined a fraternity. Instant brotherhood had proven irresistible to our only child. That weekend we drove up to his Boston digs with the back seat of our car stuffed with computer equipment, his most precious possessions.

I'd never seen the boy look happier. His "brothers" shared his passion for paramecia and threw terrific parties. Why, in only three days he already met four attractive young women who actually cared about transistor intestines. Boston was his Golden Medina! Any day now, he might even get to use both condoms that had been hopefully rotting in his wallet since puberty.

Alvin and I spent the afternoon at a presentation the Dean designed to temporarily distract parents from tuition payments. We took Steve to dinner at a swell restaurant where we ate great lobster while expensive champagne flowed. We affirmed our past, toasted our future and all loved each other very much. The years of concern had paid off for this Mom and Dad. We were replacing a dependent son with a fascinating friend.

By breakfast, Mr. Fascination had turned into a bored, squirming captive. We'd all run out of things to say, but I ran my mouth anyway like a blind date fearing her prospects for a return engagement were nil unless she amused. At home togetherness had been less tedious—we always ignored each other for hours, even bringing a book or newspaper to read at our individual breakfast and dinner tables. But now, I was exhausted. My facial fascia was pooped from perpetually smiling. It was time to say so long.

In silence, we drove our restless son back to Cambridge.

"This is fine! Stop here. The ATO back entrance is up this little street," he cried, bolted out of the car and raced across Massachusetts Avenue traffic. Halfway down the street, he suddenly seemed aware he hadn't formally taken leave of us. He looked back, waved, turned his back on Mom and Dad and went striding into his future.

He'd gone away many times before, but this departure was different. Our roads were diverging. He was rushing towards life's unlimited possibilities, as I reluctantly hobbled towards decline. I have always hated being left out of anything. As I watched him walk into his own life, I was shocked to find myself sobbing.

Alvin comforted me. He was less bereft. I had lost my fantasy lover. He had finally outfoxed his rival.

For the next month, I mooned like a lovesick schoolgirl. Steven called often enough, reported he was doing well, but the special intimacy he and I had shared was gone. Over the telephone my observations, which once would have made him roar, now sounded like the nasty gossip it was. He was totally disinclined to answer normal, motherly questions, although he and Alvin chatted at length, obviously sharing manly perceptions. It would have been bad enough to lose my sweetheart to another woman, but to lose him to his father was unbearable.

At home during Thanksgiving weekend, Steve was pleasant but remote. His preferred companions, his fraternity brothers and *that girl,* were strangers to me. It was too much trouble to share the details of his existence with someone unfamiliar with both setting and players. I resented being evicted from his head, yet each time I gazed at him, love for him overwhelmed me. Because I couldn't express this love, it turned into melancholy and gradually encased my feelings like emotional cellulite.

I was somewhat relieved when he said he'd only be spending ten days of Christmas vacation with us. He'd been invited to Colorado to go skiing with friends and then would work on an independent research project most of January. In addition, my routine was disrupted by his post-MIT schedule. He now worked or read until 4:00 a.m. and had his first meal of the day when retired Floridians dined on early bird specials. Alvin and I talked things over and decided to spend our week with him in New York City.

He met us at our modest suite hotel, greeted us with smiles and real affection, which meant only one thing. Something was wrong. He was troubled. MIT had not lived up to his intellectual standards. Like most grown children, he had spared us his bliss but described his disenchantment in detail and at great length. Thank God for adversity. It had made us our son's trusted confidants again.

We listened, asked only essential, pithy questions but offered no suggestions that could be construed as either criticism or advice. We knew better than that! We expressed confidence that he'd find suitable methods of dealing with life's current disappointments before schlepping to Petrossian for caviar and beginning a week of theater going.

Before he flew back to Boston, he told us how lucky he felt to have parents who cared for him enough to allow him to unburden himself, yet treated him with the respect due a fellow adult, instead of taking advantage of his distress and using it as a means of continuing to dominate his life. Naturally, we were pleased to find ourselves in the 90th percentile of the parental bell-shaped curve, and it was nobody's business that we did the right thing for all the wrong reasons.

Steven shares his doubts and problems with us now, and our connection is deliberate and strong again, but I still can't watch him walk through the departure gates at the airport without feeling my eyes fill with tears.

I travel in sophisticated circles. My friends have exciting careers and/or whoopee sexual connections, but in the secret caverns of glitzy ladies rooms, just utter the words *my son* and find yourself in the lowest depths of whatever Gehenna is reserved for a mother whose beloved boys are grown and gone. A divorce lawyer who never cleaned her own house describes herself making hospital corners on her son's dormitory cot with silent sobs shaking her body; a vice-president of an ad agency amusingly documents her jealousy each time she meets another "flawless inamorata." We are proud we produced confident, secure, independent thinkers, but don't really understand why they take jobs in Jakarta when wonderful opportunities exist only a stone's throw from Mommy's house. We are prepared to let go, but not this week, not this year, not during this lifetime.

My own mother lived entirely through my accomplishments and never perceived me as a separate entity. I don't need my son to excel in order to supply me with *naches*—the reflected glory bestowed on a M*O*T*H*E*R by the success of her kid. My own accomplishments bring me plenty of satisfaction, which is why this mommy in midlife gives her son space without guilt. If I don't hear from him, and I want to talk to him, I call and I never berate him for not calling me four times a day to see if I've had a stroke. I invite him to join us on lavish vacations, which he seems to enjoy. He never suspected how much of his inheritance paid for that week at the Ritz in Madrid.

I am wholly rational if partially neglected and understand nature's lack of interest in anyone who's no longer able to reproduce. For Steven to feel about me as I feel about him would be perversely anti-life. I only hope he will nurture his own children with as much care and devotion as he received.

I sometimes find myself daydreaming about grandchildren. Perhaps they will let me love so unreservedly again, but first there is the matter of *mein schneer*—in Yiddish, my daughter-in-law. Have you ever heard a harsher, less euphonious sound? To date, none of Steven's dates have made my heart skip a beat, but he doesn't know that. I've learned from friends' mistakes never to imply that anyone he's hot for is less than perfect.

Like Sherlock Holmes, I deduce conclusions about his love life from acts of omission. When his young woman has no last name, I know she's not a Goldberg, Greenberg or Rozenveig. His first college amour was Vietnamese. She was followed by a Venezuelan, and then came a Scandinavian. Could he be working his way through the alphabet backwards? Hopefully when he's ready to stand under the *Huppah*—the Jewish wedding canopy—he'll be up to the J's. I would prefer he marry a Jewish woman, because our traditions have value; I'd like to see them continue. I would embrace a convert, and if worse comes to worse, would a brilliant Buddhist grandchild be such a terrible thing?

Compatriot mothers of married and lost sons tell me to pray that Steven marries an orphan, as the only good *machehtinnisteh*—mother of the bride—is a dead *machehtinnisteh*.

But why stress myself out unnecessarily when I can keep busy orchestrating the seduction of my only son's future wife, whoever and wherever she may be. I know she won't love me like a mother, but I hope she will consider me her comrade. A daughter-in-law who regards me as an ally, rather than her enemy, might just force my precious baby to visit me at The Home twice a week.

Myra Chanin is eighty-two years old and still remembers what it was like to be twenty-eight. She's stumbled into a life that ran the gamut from failure to various degrees of success and is not done yet. Her climb toward fame started with both kinds of cheesecake. She was the Mother Wonderful of Mother Wonderful's Cheesecakes, which led to her winning Philadelphia's Best Cheesecake awards, followed by publication of three cheesecake cookbooks with recipes tested to perfection. The second kind of cheese-cake in her life occurred when she posed naked for feminist photographer Becky Young and discovered her body, which she always thought third-rate, was actually second-rate. Other people agreed. Her photos appeared in magazines and were sent out in promotional material for her first book, The Secret Life of Mother Wonderful.

Between then and now she produced, love-slaved and side-kicked an all-night national radio show, The Joey Reynolds Show, *until 2010.*

When that went off air, she returned to writing and now blogs for The Huffington Post *and reviews for* Theaterpizzazz.com. *She's still married to Alvin, that long-suffering saint, and her son is happily married to Jessie Dotson, a woman who is truly his soul-mate. Their merry, musical daughter, Allison Louise, is a source of great joy to all.*

Marbles

Maureen Johnson-Laird

Last summer, I rented an apartment in Bloomsbury, just north of the British Museum. On the day after my arrival, I was relaxing on the sofa, when loud music came blaring into the living room. I looked out of the front window and saw a group of about thirty older people gathering in the square below. Some were carrying banners bearing the classic peace symbol of the Campaign for Nuclear Disarmament, a "ban the bomb" organization that I had been a member of in my youth, some fifty years ago. My heart thumped with excitement as I ran downstairs. I bumped into the landlord in the hallway who was busy polishing the curvy oak banister.

"What's going on out there?" I said, opening the front door to Pete Seeger's "Where Have All the Flowers Gone?" bellowing across the road.

"They're the peace people. They come to Tavistock Square every August," he said, focusing on rubbing the banisters to a highly-polished sheen.

I crossed the road to the square. A large statue of a muscular Gandhi, sitting cross-legged on a plinth, was in the middle of the lawn. A few tourists, some with expensive-looking cameras, were putting flowers in the hollow pedestal beneath the statue. A grizzled old man with rolled up sleeves and a bandana round his head limped across the grass to meet me.

"Welcome," he said, "I'm Bernard. I assume you're here for the ceremony? We'll be starting in a minute. We're having a bit of bother with the microphone."

"My name's Mo. I didn't know the Campaign for Nuclear Disarmament was still having rallies. I was active in the movement in the Fifties and Sixties, but I live in the USA now, so I'm completely out of touch."

"We meet here every year on August 6th, Hiroshima Day. Tourists just notice the Gandhi statue, but the square has other peace symbols. Let me show you," he said, setting off across the grass and stopping in front of a shapeless grey boulder.

"That was placed here to commemorate conscientious objectors all over the world," he said. He limped off, moving fast, and I followed him until he stopped under a large cherry tree.

"This tree was planted in memory of the victims of Hiroshima and Nagasaki who died in 1945."

"Who's that?" I asked, noticing a tiny bust of a woman on a pedestal half-hidden by bushes.

"That's Virginia Woolf. Her house was nearby, until it was destroyed by a bomb in 1940 during the war."

"I've seen a photo of the damage," I said. "Her studio was visible, because the outside wall of the house had been blown off."

"Yes. You can see why we, in CND, think of this place as *our* peace park. Many of the Bloomsbury Group—Lytton Strachey and the painter, Duncan Grant—were conscientious objectors. Do stay," he continued. "The program is short. We're all gray-haired now, but we can't give up. They still haven't banned the bomb."

I took a seat on a park bench and listened as Celia Hewitt, the widow of Adrian Mitchell, recited his poem "Fifteen Million Plastic Bags" about the aftermath of a nuclear war.

As Celia recited the poem, I was remembering the banner for the first march in 1958. It was a simple design with white lettering on a black background and CND signs on each side of the center. The CND symbol, which was to become a powerful international image, looked like a broken cross with its two arms hanging down but was the semaphore signs for "N" and "D." The banner was carried by two marchers, who stretched it from one side of the road to the other. That year, fifty thousand people lined up behind it to walk the fifty-three miles from London to Aldermaston, which was the government's establishment for nuclear weapons.

I met Sheila Morgan on that march. Her red hair stood out against the dark clothes and grungy appearance of the other marchers, but I didn't get to know her well until we met again at a CND meeting in Hampstead. She got my attention again when she shouted at the chairman of the organization, an Anglican Canon: "Of course we've got to break the law. Any movement worth its name has to take risks. Remember Gandhi—he led the salt march in 1930, and sixty thousand people were arrested for breaking the law. That event sparked the end of the British Raj. We can't have a polite revolution. We've got to break the law, too."

I went up to her after the meeting and introduced myself. "You probably don't remember me, but we met on the Aldermaston march."

"But, I do remember you," she said.

"I was impressed by the way you argued with the Canon," I said. "And I want to join any civil disobedience, but I'm a bit out of my depth."

"Meet me for coffee in the women's common room at University College tomorrow at noon," she said. "Don't let them keep you out. Tell them I invited you. I'm a lecturer in physics there. Maybe I can help you get the hang of things."

When I turned up the next day, Sheila was sitting in one of those comfortable leather armchairs that are a feature of so many London clubs. Her curly red hair and her slim frame contrasted with the faded, shapeless beige dress she was wearing. Off the rack in a thrift shop, I supposed: Women lecturers didn't make much money.

"How do you like our women's common room?" she said. "We haven't had it long. The men have one just for them, so we lobbied for this separate space. I told them: 'University College first admitted women on an equal basis in 1828, but some of you still don't get it.' "

"You're so uninhibited about speaking up at meetings." I settled into an identical chair opposite her.

"Trained myself when I was a young woman at Oxford," she said. "Only two other women in my year were reading physics. To overcome my shyness, I always asked the first question in lectures. Do that, and it allays your anxiety about speaking in public. Did *you* go to university?"

"Yes, I've just finished a degree in librarianship. Now, I'm working in a medical library, but it's not very exciting. I'm more interested in women's rights."

"You're eager and you're active, but don't waste your energy while you've got so much of it. Work for a cause you believe in, before you get saddled with a family. Never think that a husband and children are enough to fulfill you in life. You need to make your own mark."

"I'm very keen to be involved in the peace movement. I'm happy to go on marches, but I'm nervous about being arrested for breaking the law."

"Everyone is at first, but don't be. Not many people are prepared to admit it, but everyone is vulnerable. The real worry when you're arrested is what will happen next. You don't know whether they'll let you go, or take you to court. And then, if you appear in court, you don't know what you're going to be charged with. They make it up as they go along."

"Were you ever scared?"

"Yes, one time, in a large group of protesters. We were on a march to the Prime Minister's house in Downing Street. A line of mounted police with batons barred the road. Someone gave us all a handful of marbles to throw under the horses' hooves, so they'd slip and fall if they charged us.

"Horses frighten me, but I didn't want to harm them. I lost my nerve and ran away from the demonstration down a side street."

Sheila was about to say more, but a waiter interrupted to ask if we wanted tea or coffee. Sheila sighed and said, "I have to leave shortly to give a lecture, but why don't you come to the next sit-down demo? We're protesting in Whitehall on Saturday against the arrival of American nuclear weapons in Britain."

On Saturday, I took the tube to Westminster, but the walk to Whitehall took longer than I'd expected. When I arrived, hundreds of people were already sitting, blocking one side of the street. It was an impressive sight. I had to search for Sheila in the crowd and finally found her lecturing to a well-dressed old man wearing a trilby hat, sitting like her, crossed-legged in the road.

"Don't you think," she was saying to him, "that we ought to block the door to the Ministry so people can't get in and out?"

"It's an interesting idea, but I shouldn't want the policemen to drag us all away to prison before the journalists arrive."

I realized the old man was Bertrand Russell, who was sitting next to his wife, Evelyn. Sheila turned to welcome me, and I sat down next to her. The road was hard—much harder than I'd imagined.

"I was worried that I wouldn't find you. There are hundreds of people here." I lowered my voice to a whisper, "It was impressive to find you talking to Russell. I wouldn't have the nerve. How did you get talking to him?"

"Told him that our inspiration was his example of going to prison in the First World War. He said, 'I'd do it again.'"

"How amazing," I whispered. "He's still going strong, and he's in his eighties."

"His *late* eighties," Sheila whispered back.

We sat and sat, and the police, who were arriving in numbers, took no notice of us. Perhaps, I thought, they won't arrest us. An hour went by. At length I said to Sheila, "What's going to happen?"

"The police are playing a waiting game," she said. "They're angry because their leaves have been cancelled in order to be on hand for this demo. They're hoping we'll all get bored and disperse. That way, there's no need to arrest us. It's hard work to carry away eight hundred non-violent demonstrators."

"I never expected to hear you express sympathy for the police."

"If you *are* arrested, get them to prove which paving slab you were sitting on," Sheila said.

"I'm not sure that they'd be amused by that argument."

Just then a voice came over a bullhorn. "You're welcome to leave any time. If you stay, we will arrest you. You will be charged with offences against the Public Order Act of 1936."

Nothing happened for two more hours. The protestors passed the time in different ways. I noticed someone knitting. Two elderly sisters offered us some dainty-looking cucumber sandwiches and then quietly buried their heads back in their books.

Once again the police bellowed at us to leave. Then when no one stirred, they started to make arrests. Two policemen came for each demonstrator, one at the head and one at the tail. The first one put his arms under the demonstrator's shoulders, and the second one grabbed his legs. In rough synchrony, they hoisted the limp bodies into the air and bundled them away into waiting vans. When the vans were full with a dozen or more protestors, they drove off. The road gradually emptied. They took Russell and his wife with extra care. Soon only Sheila and I and the two sisters who'd given us sandwiches were left sitting in the road. How odd it is, I thought, to be sitting down in the middle of Whitehall, empty of traffic, on a Saturday morning. I felt a combination of excitement and fear. When a young policeman and his slightly older colleague came for me, I went limp.

"Come along, dearie," the older one said, "you're the last of the Mohicans. Now, we can all go home."

It was a relief that something was finally happening. I kept myself limp as they carried me the short distance to the waiting van. I was grateful that I was wearing trousers and not a skirt. I heard a horrible crunchy sound as one of the policeman trod on a guitar abandoned on the sidewalk. I was the last one they could squeeze in. The van smelt of stale cigarette smoke. Handcuffs hung down the side. No sign of Sheila or the Russells, but I counted a dozen of us in the van.

The driver turned around and grinned at us with yellow teeth. He spoke through the metal grille dividing us from him.

"Hold on tight. You're in for a rough ride."

"Give us a break," I shouted back at him, feigning bravado. I'm beginning to sound like Sheila, I thought.

As the vehicle tore off down the street, I waved to the remaining onlookers through the small window in the back of the van.

We were taken to Bow Street police station. The men were separated from the women, and I was relieved to find myself in the same cell as Sheila. It was the last cell down a long corridor, and I didn't know the other women already installed in the tiny space.

"Are you all right?" Sheila said.

"I'm feeling nervous; it was hard to be among the last to be arrested. How about you?"

"I told them to bring us all a cup of tea."

The cell was far too small for eight people. Sheila and I sat down on the dirty floor. Others were squashed together on the single bench. In one corner, there was a tiny barred window and when the policeman closed the heavy cell door, I understood the full meaning of confinement. The white walls were dense with graffiti, recent messages scrawled on top of the earlier scribbling. A woman in the next cell shouted, "Has anyone seen my backpack?"

A tall, well-dressed woman sitting beside us stood up and handed out books of crossword puzzles. I noticed her expensive silk suit and matching shoes. She seemed an unlikely protester. The cell was not much higher than the top of her head and lit by a single light bulb. We'll be falling over each other when it gets dark, I thought.

"My name is Zenobia. Maybe these will help us pass the time. I devise crossword puzzles for *The Kensington Post.*"

"How did you land a job like that?" I said.

"My father. He passed the job on to me when he retired."

"Why did he name you Zenobia? Did he call you after a crossword puzzle clue?" Sheila said.

"No, he named me after a third century queen."

I turned to Sheila: "Do *you* ever do puzzles?"

"Every day. They help to stave off dementia. I don't want to end up like my mother. She left home one day and couldn't find her way back. Had to start wearing a name tag like a dog."

"Were you ever married?" I asked.

"Yes, but it didn't work out," she said. "Politics! When he left, he said, 'I'll leave storming the barricades to you.' He was a big classical music buff and ran off with a professional violinist. He died after a heart attack during Stravinsky's 'Rite of Spring.' I always say that piece could induce a heart attack in anyone."

"You don't sound very sorry," I said. "Did you have children?"

"Two daughters. Jane, the eldest, was in love with a married man. He wouldn't leave his wife, and she became a hypochondriac. Stays in bed a lot. Karen, my younger daughter, dropped out of university to follow the Maharishi Ji. Now, she does primal scream therapy in California. A pity, because she's smart."

Sheila took off a sweater. "I should have worn fewer layers. Cells are either stifling hot or freezing cold. At least I didn't have bacon for breakfast. I did that once, and it was salty. I got a terrible thirst, and then we ran out of drinking water."

"You're always harping on about salt," I said.

"It's Gandhi's influence," she said.

As though on cue, a policeman appeared with mugs of tea and stale cheese rolls.

"Even the police feed people," Sheila said, as he handed us the food.

We spent a sleepless night on the floor. The next morning, tired and hungry, we had a brief glimpse of sunlight as we were escorted from the cell to the courtroom in the adjacent building. We were charged in groups of six, and a policeman whom we'd never seen before, read his "evidence" against us, from a notebook. The magistrate asked whether we were prepared to keep the peace for a year. Sheila and I agreed and were released. We found out later that some protestors, including Russell and his wife, refused to be "bound over to keep the peace," and so they were sentenced to one week in prison. For the second time in his life, Russell was imprisoned.

After the arrest, my life became one long round of meetings, door-to-door canvassing, and demonstrating. Sheila taught me to ignore our doorstep critics.

"Go away, we don't want anything to do with Ban the Bombers."

"You should be locked up."

"Why don't you go back to Russia?"

In 1970, a university library in New Jersey offered me a job. Sheila was upset when I told her I'd decided to emigrate.

"Why go to live there? They've got the bomb."

"I know. But the job is to catalogue an important feminist collection for a university library."

I didn't tell Sheila, but it was now clear to me that no British government, whether right or left wing, would ever abandon nuclear weapons. I'd stopped believing demonstrating would make a difference.

"When are you coming back?"

As it turned out, I was not able to visit London for a long time. I tried to keep in touch with Sheila by phone, but she seemed less interested in me, now I was no longer in the peace movement. In one call she told me she'd retired from teaching and was working as a volunteer in the central office of CND. But, five years ago, my circumstances changed. I phoned Sheila to tell her.

"I'm coming to London and looking forward to seeing you."

She didn't sound excited to hear from me. The line was not clear, but I thought she said, "The doctor says I'm going batty. I'll see you this evening."

"No, I'm coming to see you next Friday afternoon at three o'clock," I said.

She seemed unable to get our arrangement straight.

I felt uneasy, a week later, as I climbed the steep hill to her house on a street bordering Hampstead Heath clutching a small pot of lilies. It was a wet day, and the heath never looked inviting in the rain. When I reached the house, the front gate was hard to open; it was off its hinges and dragged on the ground. The garden was overgrown, and the neat outlines of flowerbeds had disappeared. As I walked to the front door, wet fronds of privets brushed my face. I rapped hard with the lion-shaped knocker and waited with the rain from a broken gutter dripping on my head.

Sheila opened the door. She had never looked neat, but now she was unkempt. Her bright red hair was gray and tangled, her face deeply-lined. She did not look at me. Her eyes were vacant.

"Hello," she said. She didn't use my name. I gave her a quick hug.

The living room was dark, the shutters half-opened. The place was grubby. Her kitchen was at the far end of the room, and the sink was piled with dirty dishes. I put the pot of lilies on the draining board.

As I sat down opposite her I noticed my boots had left damp marks on the scruffy rug that was peppered with crumbs.

"How are you?" I asked.

"Low energy. Don't get out much," she said.

"Do you have any help?"

"I've rented the basement to a nurse who works in the local hospital. She keeps an eye on me."

"Maybe you need more help?"

Sheila didn't reply. She had always hated being told what to do.

I offered to make tea. I could see she wasn't up to it. As I washed the cups, she pressed a chocolate biscuit covered in silver paper into my hand.

"That's all I've got," she said.

"Don't worry, I had a big lunch," I said.

"What about the girls? Do they keep in touch?" I asked.

"Karen is doing her screaming therapy in California. She visits once a year. Jane lives nearby, but I never see her. We had a big fallout."

Sheila's eyes closed. She seemed to find my visit tiring, though I had only just arrived. She noticed me looking up at the dusty shelves, pointed upwards with her cane and said, "Take any books you want. I'm leaving everything to the peace movement."

I reached up to the shelves and selected Adrian Mitchell's *Collected Poems*. "I'll just have this," I said, "I haven't much room in my luggage. Life's very different in America. It's been quite a difficult adjustment for me."

"CND moved its offices," she said.

Sheila wasn't interested in America. I nearly asked, "Do you know who I am?" But I bit my tongue. Uncomfortable in her presence, I left the house soon after, confused and despondent.

❧

The singing woke me from my reverie. Bernard, who had welcomed me, was now sitting beside me on the wooden bench in the square.

"You nodded off," he said.

"It must be the sun," I said "It's not usually so hot here in August. How long have you been a peace activist?"

"Oh, forever. Since the beginning."

"Did you know Sheila Morgan? She's about your age and was very active in CND."

"No, but I know her name. Was she a friend of yours?"

"Yes. When I met Sheila, my mind was asleep. She fired a rocket into my brain that woke me up about real politics. She made me an activist."

"Why don't you ask Donald over there if he knew her?" He pointed to a man in a wheelchair, sitting behind a table. "He's the one selling peace buttons and placards. He knows everyone."

I didn't ask Donald or anyone else if they knew Sheila. She had let go of me. And I had to let go of her, but not her fearlessness

The annual gathering was coming to an end, and I joined in the chorus of the theme song, "The H-Bomb's Thunder." Everyone knew John Brunner's lyrics by heart.

Men and women stand together, do not heed the men of war.
Make your mind up, now or never, ban the bomb for evermore.

The sun was not shining quite so brightly as the group moved away from the shade of the cherry blossom tree. Bernard opened his plastic sandwich box and took a slug from his thermos.

"You know you're old when you can no longer sit on the grass to eat your lunch," he said. "I've come all the way from Stoke Newington. Do you live nearby?"

"As I said, I live in America now. I haven't visited London for five years. This time I'm here for the summer." I pointed to the terrace of my rented flat on the west side of the Georgian square.

I wandered back across the road to the flat. When I opened the front door, the landlord was in the hall again.

"Have they stopped singing?" he said. "It's time for my nap."

Mo Johnson-Laird was born in London but has lived in America for twenty-five years. New Yorkers on buses still ask if she knows where she's going, and she still doesn't know how to order breakfast eggs. When she arrived in America, she started to write and is now working on a series of stories about a comic character called Barry.

Editor's Note: The 1958 Aldermaston March, organized by the Campaign for Nuclear Disarmament in response to the USA's first hydrogen bomb test, followed the next year by 60,000 marching the fifty-three miles, is Britain's equivalent in size and importance, to the March on Washington for Jobs and Freedom in 1963.

...OF HAUNTING
MEMORIES AND PLACES

The Holy Ghost Bird

Sue Parman

Through the small window in the wall that curves above my bed, I hear a bird chirping. I imagine the mother bird putting the baby to bed, just like I've been put to bed, even though it's still light. I have a hard time going to sleep. I lie awake imagining the bird tucked in its nest, cozy like I'm cozy, although I'm careful not to touch the curving wall over my head, because it's aluminum. We live in a Quonset hut (a word I've learned to say recently) in Iowa City, where my father is a graduate student at the university. I love the Quonset hut because I can hear the rain, which makes me feel even cozier. Tonight there is no rain, just light going away very slowly and the sound of birds whose lives I imagine. There's a Mama Bird, a Papa Bird, and two baby birds (one, like me, older than the other). The Mama Bird loves to tuck the baby birds into the nest. I imagine the soft feathers, the warm, beating hearts.

Now the birds are quiet. I imagine them asleep. Through the small window I can see a star, and somewhere far away, I hear a car. Light shines through the window, moving across the opposite wall and closed door, beyond which violins and a piano are playing on a record. Someone is moving around in the kitchen splashing water, scraping bowls. Footsteps are coming down the hall, and I close my eyes as the door opens. "Suzie?" my mother says softly. "Are you asleep?"

I can't resist smiling, even though my eyes are closed. She sees me smile and wraps her arms around me. "Silly Billy," she says, kissing my forehead. I smell fresh flour, chocolate. "I've been making cookies. I came to see if you wanted to lick the bowl."

Perhaps the evening doesn't go quite this way. The bird noises, the long twilight, star, sweep of headlights and the classical music are all there. And I am awake long after I know I should be asleep. But I don't notice my mother coming in my room, because I'm under the covers with a flashlight and a comic book about Johnny Thunder. When she says, "Suzie, are you asleep?" I feel guilty that I'm not asleep, even though the mother bird tucked me in. I wrap the blankets around me like feathers and turn my head away from her, saying, "I'm cold!"

I hear, thrum, thrum, boom, boom, the sound of a heart beating. It is mine. I want to turn around, but I don't want her to find the flashlight and the comic book, which I know I shouldn't have in the bed. I should be asleep.

Birds, unlike people, have no interest in being looked at. I know that now. Baby birds go about their business unaware of whether they need a little or a lot of sleep, whether their IQ is high or low, or if they've been skipped a grade. When they're ready to fly, their mothers kick them out of the nest. No one feels guilty.

"I was making cookies," I hear my mother say through the boom, boom of my heart. Her eyes can see me, my flashlight and comic book even though the room is dark, and I'm facing the wall in a tight ball. "I came to ask if you wanted to lick the bowl."

I turn around, but it is too late. She has already slammed the door. I sit up in bed, startled. Did I do this? What did I do? I did a bad thing. I was in a nest, and now I'm no longer there. I'm in a cold, aluminum room with lights roving across the wall. I stuff the flashlight and comic book under the mattress and wait for my mother to return. I imagine her smiling, kissing my fore-head, smelling of flour and chocolate, inviting me to come lick the bowl. But she doesn't come, and I start to cry.

The next day my skin feels as though thinned—not my outer skin, but some inner skin like a drum capable of vibrating if a butterfly dies on the other side of the world. It's not tuned to but-terflies, though; it's tuned to my mother. When she moves on the other side of the Quonset hut, even to apply a file to her nails (she wears them short and painted with clear polish), I hear her. I wait for her to speak, but she is silent. Her silence is very loud.

As the days pass, I notice for the first time that my mother cries often. I wonder if this is my fault. Does she think I don't love her? I turned away from her. I refused to lick her bowl. This is my fault. I must show her that I love her. I must not make noise when I get up in the early morning and build a tent of chairs and blankets. I must go to sleep when she tucks me in. I must make good grades, be perfect. Above all, I must listen to her stories about how unhappy she is, how she fought with her sister Alice, envied her sister Ginny and loved her sister Echo, and the stories about the romantic meeting with my father, the Conscientious Objector in the Camp, who sang and wrote her many letters when she was sick in bed with TB, and she turned down the rich boy's proposal and married my father instead. But now he is spending too long on his PhD, and she has to type theses until late at night, and she is so tired that she sleeps late in the morning, leaving me to build a tent of chairs and blankets and eat half a jar of peanut butter.

It was once an established and widely practiced custom for American men to venture out after their heavy mid-day meal on Christmas Day and compete in teams to see who could shoot the most birds and small mammals. Beginning Christmas Day in 1900, as if to issue a challenge to the previous century's colonial pillaging and man's biblically-endorsed dominion over all the beasts of field and forest, a small handful of ornithologists decided to count rather than shoot all the birds they saw within a twenty-four-hour period, thus giving rise to a citizen-based conservation practice known as the Annual Audubon Bird Counting. No longer limited to Christmas Day, the Christmas Bird Count now occurs during any twenty-four-hour window between mid-December and early January.

Although my parents' room in the Quonset hut is small, it is lined with bookshelves, which only go up so far because of the curved walls of the hut, and I can reach all the books. I am allowed to look at them as long as my hands are clean, and I'm careful. One of the most beautiful books has paintings of birds. The word Audubon is on the cover, and for a long time I think Audubon is a thing (a museum, a type of art, a compendium of bird pictures) rather than a person. I love the birds that have sharply contrasting colors like red and black, yellow and green. I draw the birds on discarded typing paper (my father's thesis must be retyped many times). I copy the long, sharp beaks and tail feathers, their black eyes with little highlights. I color them in with crayons, colored pencils, watercolors. Because they please my mother, I do more of them, numbering the pages. I have done less than half by the time the book disappears from the bookshelf. As I have been borrowing bikes from other children in the neighborhood, my parents finally buy me one.

"We don't have that book anymore," my mother later tells me about the Audubon book. "We sold it to buy your bike."

One night I dream the books are slaves who were sold. "I'll buy you back," I promise them. "Someday you'll be free." I wake up crying.

I bike up and down the hills in Iowa City. I bike down to the river and bring back a dead fish. I find a dead bird lying in the grass and poke it with a stick to see the rainbow color on its wings. When I find a live bird hopping on the ground, I bring it home, and my mother makes a nest for it in a shoebox. It is dead the next morning, and we bury it beside the Quonset hut. A few days later, I see a dead mouse with blood running out of its mouth. My mother is angry with my father for showing it to me. I am pleased he thinks I'm old enough to see it. My mother cries, and I go into the room I share with my sister and write a story about a teacher who hit me in school. I don't show this to my mother. Instead, I show her the story about Johnny Thunder who lived alone in a valley filled with mist. She tells me it is beautiful, whereas my father points out my spelling errors and asks what the point of the story is. I trust my father's judgment more than my mother's. I feel torn between writing more stories to show my mother and rewriting my existing stories to show my father how much I've improved.

My father finally gives up trying to finish his thesis and takes a job at Sandia Corporation as a technical writer in Albuquerque, New Mexico. He drives the old Crosley across the country while my sister and I travel with our mother on the train. She gives us each a plaid plastic briefcase covered with pockets, and we are allowed to open one pocket a day while we are on the train. One pocket contains Nutty Putty, which we bounce on the floor and then use to lift pictures from our comic books. The big pocket contains a comic book, *Johnny Thunder* for me, *Little Lulu* for my sister. Years later I will find my old comics stored in the briefcase.

When we arrive in Albuquerque, my mother is very unhappy. She tells me that my father has bought the wrong house. "I told him that the only thing I wanted was a fireplace," she says, although she asks me not to repeat this complaint to him. For three years after the house is built, it sits in the desert beside a huge red arrow that is stuck in the sand. I love the open desert, where I catch horny toads (I love to touch their soft bellies), dig pits in the sand and cover them with boards to make a house, and run barefoot through desert lilies that spring up after the rain. When development creeps closer to us, I prowl through the rubble of construction, at one point hanging twenty feet in the air from rafters of the new Safeway being built. I walk along the tops of concrete walls that separate the new houses beginning to crop up near ours. During the day I rarely stay in the house, and when I do, I close my door and write stories about lonely cowboys. I lie awake at night listening to classical music and the sound of my parents arguing. The arguing stops when my mother begins to cry. I have also learned to cry. There is a rhythm to the crying, like a volcano that wells up, explodes and then settles down. If we go for over a week without crying, the atmosphere thickens. My drum skin stretches, begins to vibrate. I learn to see it coming. I try to stop it by asking my mother questions about her family, or reading her my stories, or showing her my artwork. I feel responsible for her happiness. I can tell that my mother misses her family. She talks a lot about her father and the competition among the eight children for his affection. Who did he love the best? The oldest daughter Ginny was given gowns, cotillions and a college education in Virginia, and after being courted by an Indian Prince ended up marrying a minister whom all the sisters were in love with. The oldest son was sent to good schools and became an economist. The Depression meant no more cotillions or college for the younger children. My mother, the fifth child, worked to pay for two years of college before she caught TB, met my father and quit. Her father became ill and died soon after we moved to New Mexico, and years later I read one of her letters written just before he died. "Please tell Daddy I love him. Mommy, should I come home?"

I call my parents Mommy and Daddy until I leave for college, then my mother says I should call them Edie and Lee. My father is unhappy. "I want you to call me Daddy," he says.

"It's too late," I say.

My father has two weeks of vacation a year, and we spend it driving and camping. I like to put my sleeping bag outside the tent under the stars. By now I am wearing glasses and sometimes go to sleep wearing them, because I like to look at the stars. "As thick as fleas on a blanket," my father says about the stars.

My mother says, "Lee!" but I understand he is trying to avoid a cliché. He wants me to see the world slant. We have started to give each other Christmas presents like chocolate-covered bumblebees and canned rattlesnake, and I understand that we are avoiding the cliché of meatloaf and baked potatoes, a meal my mother frequently prepares. My father's efforts to spice up the meatloaf with tarragon meets with tears ("You don't like my cooking!") and an increasing tendency to precede the meal with double martinis. I am writing strange stories that weave unexpected themes. My mother continues to give her unqualified support (while telling me stories of how she used to write but no longer does, giving me the feeling that I am writing for her, fulfilling her dream). My father reads my stories with the same critical eye but with greater interest.

Early in the morning on a camping trip in the Four Corners area, I wake up on stony ground and look up at the pine trees black against the turquoise glow of dawn. A bird flies overhead, and I feel a splat on my eyelid. I am struck with an epiphany. "It's not what you don't do," I say to the bird. "It's what you do do."

This strikes me as both hilarious and profound.

When my father is promoted to head of the technical library, my mother tells me that he is now making twelve thousand dollars a year. She says this is a very good salary. The house at 5212 Arvilla NE is now part of the urban tide flowing toward the base of the Sandias and sits on the corner by a gas station. It has grass in the front and sand and tumbleweeds in the back. My mother decides we can now afford a house with a fireplace, and we begin to look for one. I don't miss the house, but I miss the friends I've made in the neighborhood, especially a girl named Phyllis with whom I make up stories, songs, and plays. She tells me, during one of our sleepovers, that her stepfather is having sex with her, and she is in love with him. I tell my parents, who allow me to continue to spend the night with her. She is five years older than I. She likes to write soppy love stories, whereas I'm still roving the untamed West. I have my first crush that year: Wild Bill Hickok, played by Guy Madison.

We move to a house twenty miles out of town behind Sandia Crest. Our address is a box in a post office seven miles away. The house is a custom-built, ranch-style hideaway nestled among pinions, juniper, and Indian paintbrush on half an acre of land. The living room is thirty feet long, with a fireplace at one end and plate glass windows looking up the mountain on the other. The ceiling has exposed redwood beams. Although beautiful, the house is very cold. We are now at an elevation of seven thousand feet, and the inside of the house rarely reaches a temperature of more than sixty degrees. The only other source of heating in the house is a floor furnace at the back, and since it usually isn't working, the fireplace becomes the literal hearth of the house.

Sometimes we sleep around it in sleeping bags, because the bedrooms are so cold. We fight over who gets to sleep with the dogs.

Soon after we move in, my mother tells us we can no longer use the front door because a bird has built a nest there. So as not to disturb the bird, we go around to the back door near the woodpile that leads into the kitchen.

Because my eyes are so bad, I have difficulty seeing birds—never mind identifying them. Unlike the Audubon book, in which birds pose with the seeds, berries or other food that typifies their survival strategy, real birds are to me nothing more than tiny bits of evidence that must be interpreted—a wing tip here, a shadow there, a flash of color. Except when a fat bird holding a worm hops within five feet of me with a red breast like a T-shirt emblazoned with the words I AM A ROBIN, IDIOT, birds to me are no more than assumptions.

I try to figure out what kind of bird is nesting on our front porch, but because I can't see enough of it, I can't use the new bird book my mother has bought—-not another Audubon book, but a paperback called *Birds of America*, which she and a new friend of hers are using when they go on walks. Her friend Barbara tells me that the bird on our porch is a Phoebe. The picture in the book makes the bird look small and dull. According to the book, the bird catches insects and sometimes builds nests on man-made structures. During the five years I live in the house, the bird never becomes more than a flutter of movement at the corner of my eye. My mother, however, insists that the same bird returns year after year, and my sister and I compete to be the first to say, "Look! Our Phoebe is back again!" as one of our many rituals of continuity.

We have many rituals: traveling down to Juarez to bring back bottles of cheap gin (two gallons per person, including children, allowed); camping along the Pecos River where it always rains as soon as we set up camp; gathering at the kitchen table for coffee and gossip (I am fourteen when my mother hands me my first cup of coffee and invites me to join her and my father, or her and Barbara, or her and many other people she gathers into the cold kitchen where the coffee is always perking). My sister develops her own rituals: going down to the post office to catch up on news; walking over the hill to the Palomino ranch to watch the horses. She joins 4-H, tries out for cheerleading and accuses us of being culturally deprived for not appreciating sports. I skip a grade, learn to drive as soon as I'm fifteen years and eight months, and take up archery, but when I finally manage to hit a rabbit, I feel sick. I keep up my archery, because I've got a crush on my high school history teacher, who not only appreciates my writing but invites me to join him and his wife (who has polio and prefers to sit and watch) at their after-school archery practice. I learn that his first name is Brainard, but he prefers to be called Ben, and I nickname him Ben Bow. A few years after I leave for college, he quits teaching at the high school and enrolls in a PhD program at the University of New Mexico and dies a few years later of heart failure. When I learn this, I think immediately of his wife, whom he treated as a delicate bird hovering on the edge of death. I wonder if both of them had always assumed she would die first.

My creative writing teacher, Mr. Ness, gives us a reading list we can take home to our parents but also gives us an unofficial reading list, which he dictates while walking around the room, looking like a prize fighter emulating Byron, his dark hair flopping over his broad forehead. I find *Lady Chatterley's Lover* and *Madame Bovary* dull and prefer reading folk tales about Huginn and Muninn (thought and memory), two ravens that sit on the shoulders of the one-eyed Norse god, Odin, and fly off in search of stories to tell him about the sorrows of the world. I read that ravens can mimic the sounds of cursing sailors and flushing toilets, and that King Arthur's soul flew from his body in the form of a raven when he died. I am also reading Camus's *The Stranger*, Thomas Mann's *Death in Venice*, and Dylan Thomas's "Do Not Go Gentle into That Good Night."

I apply to Antioch College, the small liberal arts college in Ohio where my mother spent two years, and am sixteen when I lug my trunk and suitcases onto the train headed east. I write in my journal, "No more tears," and recall my epiphany with the do-do bird. I write detailed letters to my mother, telling her all my adventures, sharing my successes (rarely my failures, except if they are heroic). I feel I have a conscientious duty to live my mother's life better than she was able to live it.

When I come home for Christmas, I have cut my long hair. At the party my mother organizes, to which she invites a few of my high school friends along with Ben Bow, Mr. Ness, and my art teacher, I wear a black sleeveless dress that makes me feel like one of the sophisticated New Yorkers attending Antioch. One of the guests is a friend of my mother's, a woman I have never met. She knows where the glasses are in the cupboards, the gin under the sink. "You're not the way your mother described you," she tells me.

"How do you mean?"

"You're nicer."

I picture my mother sitting on the patio drinking martinis with this woman, talking about me. I have heard my mother talk about others, but somehow had never imagined that she would include me in that list. "She's sweet," my mother will say about someone, "but a little on the naïve side." Or: "She seems like such a happy person that I sense some underlying conflict." The pavement shifts under my feet. The bird flying over my head has dropped some elephantine do-do. *Suzie is so X* . . . (Creative? Loving? Generous? This is how I have always felt she sees me) . . . *but lately I feel that she is Y.* (What is this Y? Cold? Neglectful? A bad person? Perhaps I've been this Y person all along.)

When I return to Antioch I continue to write letters full of details and affection, "Dearest Edie" letters, which contain shades of anxiety I later find embarrassing. I bring my first college boyfriend home for a visit, although I'm having second thoughts. My mother flirts with him. When I tell her that we've broken up, she is angry. "Why don't you marry him then?" I tell her. I am finding there is a limit to vicarious living. I feel the need to explain and do so in long letters, which leave me feeling drained and guilty.

When I tell my father that I'm not going to marry Paul, he says, "That's all right. You would have had to be like his mother." The image of myself not being a small, fat woman always cooking and talking fills me with relief. I am even more relieved when I learn through college friends that he has married, divorced and been institutionalized. "I was right!" I'm tempted to write to my mother, but by this time we are not speaking, and when I find the photograph of him with his arm around my mother, his parents sitting nearby, I wonder if he went to visit her before or after his breakdown. My mother has always collected wounded birds, and at this moment I suspect that she has probably had a hand in manufacturing them.

In graduate school at Rice University, I am supporting myself with a teaching fellowship, like my father did at the University of Iowa, and I find myself staying up late at night drawing detailed ink pictures of a falling Icarus. Wax drips; feathers wilt. During my second year, I apply for and am awarded a National Science Foundation grant that gives me more time to sleep and read. I have switched from psychology to anthropology. I read about the Dani of New Guinea, who compare men to birds. They believe that people, because they are like birds, must die.

When I come home for a visit, I tell my parents that the Freudian psychology with which they have been beating each other is culture-bound. Later I will write a book called *Dream and Culture* that points to the cultural underpinnings of dream interpretations over a two-thousand-year period, but now my voice is small and irrelevant and is received by them with the same self-righteous humour with which they received my sister's statement that we were culturally deprived. Their fights have escalated, fueled by double martinis.

"You want me to be like your mother," my mother tells my father. "You're in love with your father," says my father. I have decided I will never marry.

During my second year of graduate school, I come home for Christmas with a man named Jake. He is from India, and my mother tells him about the Indian Prince who courted her sister Ginny. My father asks me what in the world I'm doing. "He's not like me at all," he says.

"That's true," I say.

As my friendship with Jake deepens over the next year, I realize that the two men share more in common than either is likely to admit. They are both rationalists, widely-read and committed to universal themes of justice. But what intrigues me most is that, for the first time in my life, I no longer cry. When I go off to Scotland and he to India to do research for our respective dissertations, I write to him rather than to my mother. Just before I return, I receive a letter from my mother saying that she hopes I won't marry Jake because he is the wrong person for me. I read the letter several times and am filled with anxiety. Should I call? Should I write one of my long letters? *I don't have to explain*, I suddenly realize and feel as though I have let go of something heavy. I feel suddenly lighter, as if my bones have filled with air.

We move in together. When we receive our PhDs at the end of the year, we go to California to teach. We get married in front of a judge in Hayward, California, with a janitor and clerk as witnesses. When I see my mother's oldest brother, the economist, at a conference in San Francisco several years later, he is cold. "How can you treat your mother like this?" he asks.

If he feels that way, then I know the gossip is rippling through the large clan of my mother's siblings and all my cousins. I am no longer St. Augustine's shining city on a hill but have been relegated to the ninth level of Hell, right there alongside Judas the Betrayer. Inside I say to myself with amazement, *I don't have to explain*.

My daughter is four years old when my parents' divorce comes through, and while Jake drives to North Carolina to find a place for us to stay during his NSF-funded sabbatical, my daughter and I fly to New Mexico to spend a week with my mother to help her prepare the mountain house for sale. When we arrive she doesn't have any food in the house, except for some frozen Fruit Loops with which I feed my daughter before driving back into town to get groceries. I give up on meeting old friends, because my mother does not want to babysit. I tell myself that I am being selfish; that she is going through a very difficult time. I did, after all, come to help her.

All the books we have collected as a family have been moved to the attic, a half-finished room my father had always been planning to turn into a study. Only half the floorboards have been laid, and books are stacked along the wall, leaving only a narrow pathway between the books and open space to the floor fifteen feet below. Leaving my daughter sleeping (she also needs very little sleep, so I have little time), I begin to pack up books. My mother has told me to take what I want. I feel as though I'm rescuing my friends, the community that raised me. But as soon as she hears me moving around, my mother gets up, fixes coffee, and calls me back to the cold kitchen where we sit as we once did. Rituals of continuity. She wants to talk about Lee, about how awful he is being. I fix meals; I listen; I drink double martinis on the patio. When she tells me that the Phoebe stopped coming a long time ago, I start to cry.

After Jake and I retired from teaching, we moved to Oregon. I joined the Audubon Society and attended a class for beginning birdwatchers. As I looked at the other people in the room who were busy making notes about the Northern Flicker that drums on metal and the Red-breasted Sapsucker that creates a cribbage-board pattern to release sap and attract insects, I felt guilty. I knew I would never be able to see any birds. I asked the young man showing us the slides why he enjoyed watching birds. I must have sounded irritated because he looked at me with surprise. Everyone else in the room was a convert. "Because of the Holy Ghost Bird," he said. Several people sitting nearby overheard him and asked if he was talking about the ivory-billed woodpecker.

"What is that?" I asked.

I learned that the ivory-billed woodpecker, a black and white bird with a three-foot wingspan, was believed to have become extinct in the 1940s until 2004, when a lone kayaker in an Arkansas swamp claimed to have seen one. The claim set off a gold rush of birders who invaded Arkansas, triggering skeptical views that it was a plot to infuse the backwater area with tourist dollars.

The young birder shook his head. "A true birdwatcher would never do a thing like that," he insisted. "At the worst, the sighting would have been a matter of wishful thinking." He explained that to birdwatchers, a Holy Ghost Bird is the bird you most want to see in your lifetime. For some it might be a Whitehill Crane or a Snowy Egret, a Condor or a Golden Eagle. I tried to remember all the birds I'd seen in my life. If I were to compile a list, what would be the bird I most wanted to see? The only birds I could think of were common ones, like robin, sparrow and blue jay. Then I remembered the Phoebe.

"How did you get interested in watching birds?" I asked him.

He said his father got him involved in the Annual Audubon Bird Count when he was a boy, and he started making lists of birds he had seen. His most exciting moment was when, as a child, he thought he had spotted a rare bird. Everyone told him he couldn't have, that it was not found in that part of the country, but he was convinced he had seen it.

"For the first time I felt really close to my father. Even though the other birders didn't believe me, he supported me, accepted me as someone with sound judgment who could make grownup choices. It was the most important moment of my life. I thought I had achieved something truly extraordinary. As I became a better birder, I began to have doubts about whether I'd actually seen it. I ended up taking it off my list. It didn't meet the standards. And that's what bird watching is all about—meeting standards, compiling an accurate list. Birders never cheat. They never say they saw a bird when they really didn't."

"Really?" I was skeptical.

"A list like that would be hollow."

"And did you ever find that bird?"

"No. All my life I've been searching for that bird. I have the feeling that when I find it, I'll find the secret place of closeness to my father. It's my Holy Ghost Bird."

After my father died, I returned to New Mexico to scatter his ashes from the top of the Sandia Mountains. On impulse, I took a detour over the back road via Madrid to look at the house that had once been my parents' dream house. For a long time I couldn't find it. The road to the crest had been widened, and the turnoff to the little circle of quarter-acre properties called Linea del Cielo had been spliced with a feeder road that exited the highway some distance away. But even when I found the road, I couldn't find the house. I drove around the circle several times and finally parked at the bottom of the drive that had once led to our redwood-beamed hideaway. In its place stood an industrial-gray, two-storied monstrosity around which the trees had been cleared to make way for trucks, campers and mountain bikes. I suddenly remembered hearing that the original house had burned down long after my mother moved out, but I had forgotten, or maybe I assumed that my memory was metaphorical—the conflagration of a relationship that had crashed and burned.

What bothered me most, as I stood at the bottom of the driveway looking up, was that the architect, who had designed this tank-colored hulk of a base camp for urban mountaineers, had left out the nooks and crannies in which birds could build their nests. There was no front porch, no lintel, no chimney. I stood beneath the blazing New Mexico sky with its uncompromising blue and listened. I heard the dry rustle of wind in sagebrush and pinion, like whispers in an empty room. Somewhere out there was a bird. I strained to see it, to find the transcendent closeness, the full identification of knowing that perfect bird, so rare, so seldom found. I had glimpsed it once in childhood and for a second, standing beside a house that had disappeared, like a bird returning to a nest that was no longer there, I caught a glimpse of its wing tip and shadow, and my eyes were blinded by the flash of its incandescent feathers.

Sue Parman, a retired professor of anthropology, is the author of numerous academic books (including Scottish Crofters, *now in its second edition). She has also won numerous awards for poetry, plays, essays, short stories and art. Her most recent book combines poetry and art (*The Carnivorous Gaze, Turnstone Press, 2014*). Her most recent article is a memoir based on her correspondence with Tolkien ("A Song for J.R.R. Tolkien," The Antioch Review, 2015). She is currently completing, The Death Flower, a biomedical mystery set in the Amazon. For further information please visit www.sueparman.com. She lives in Oregon.*

Hoarding Memories

George P. Farrell

It's a fact: People hoard things from the past. Hoarded items are not puzzling specimens from Mars but recognizable artefacts of tiny civilizations known as families. Take a child's rocking chair passed from generation to generation, preserved at Grandma's house for the latest grandchild to use on sunny Sunday afternoons. At day's end when the grandchild goes home, the little chair is put away till next time. Grandma eventually dies, and her children fight over custody of the tiny rocker. Finally, the loudest and orneriest wins out, and the chair continues its slow passage into the future as a thing that must not be destroyed. Into the winning sibling's attic it goes, occasionally re-discovered and brought down for the latest family newcomer to try out. But the chair tips over, cracking the child's head on the hardwood floor. My god! It's the twenty-first century; that chair is abusive to children. Back into the attic is goes.

Other things accrete as well, such as photos of solemn, overdressed people from a simpler time struggling to have fun at a picnic. Didn't they laugh back then? The black and white photos have been carefully dated on the back with a fine-nib pen, fitted with matte-black corners and stuck in an album of pre-acid paper. They will never turn yellow and rot away. Never.

Who the hell are those people anyway? Open the album. In a flash you're up to your knees in pudding-like nostalgia. Who needs to look at this crap? Why not throw it out? No! You don't just freakin' throw family in a landfill. Put the album in the attic with the rocker.

Accretion is a process driven by guilt. Guilt is a crushingly wonderful motivator.

But what if a person collected things not in an attic but in the woeful corners of the mind? Disturbing things from the beginning of a person's time on earth. Such a hoarder might occasionally, while lying in bed staring at the stained ceiling, take a peek at these mystifying things that vibrate with the menace of a pit full of rattle snakes. If he moved closer he might be able to see these mystifying memories and be enlightened. But they are simply too frightening to approach. What then? What kind of hoarding is this? It's not the same as accumulating photo albums or tiny rocking chairs. It's more akin to zoo keeping. These mystifying things are so dangerous that to gaze fully upon them could lead to mental destabilization. They could drive you crazy. Why not just let them be? A dark, rattling pit is best left unexplored, right?

When I was a little boy, we lived in a small bungalow on the waterfront, in a quaint little community of bungalows atmospherically alive with wandering alcoholics, flea-scratching dogs and spraying tomcats. My mom grew up there. My dad discovered and fell in love with it, finding it far superior to the Harlem railroad flats of his youth. They married at the time Hitler was perfecting his blitzkrieg. I arrived at the peak of the Führer's success.

The war in Europe scooped up my father and took him out of our life while he was still just a blur to me. He was gone for two years and returned as a large, semi-stranger from a far-off land whose presence filled the bungalow and wedged uncomfortably between my mom and me.

Spitting distance from our house was a little brown sand beach. In the summer time, if the tide was high and the day warm, I went swimming with Mom and Dad in the tepid and semi-polluted saltwater. After splashing around in the languid seaweed, baking under the hot sun, we all went back into the little house and showered to rid ourselves of the salt and god knows what else. The house had a cubicle of a bathroom, subway-tiled walls, tiny hex-tiled floor, a toilet, sink and, of course, an enamelled, iron bathtub, which was to play a major role in my young life.

I loved my mom. She was very beautiful. Even as a toddler I knew this as I hugged my arm 'round her leg, rested my cheek against her smooth thigh and looked upward at the delightful rest of her. After swimming, she took me into the shower with her and rinsed me off. I loved it—the intimacy of our bathing together, the warm water, my wonderful young mom with the golden blond hair standing over me naked. I watched her rinsing the salt from her hair, the water flowing over the pure white skin, which her bathing suit hid from the sun and the calm tan the sun's rays had lavished upon her glistening legs. Her sweet image mesmerized me. It was a period of calm life, a good time for a sprout to grow.

There it is. A memory. An artefact to hoard and cherish. Not to be launched into the attic dust but carefully stored within the mind as experience. We all hoard experiences. You really cannot throw them away, even if desperate to do so. You'd have to throw yourself away. And of course, that's been done, many times over, always with the same, sad ending.

But when did that lovely showering experience turn into a nostalgic artefact? That happened when the experience ended. There came a time when my mother noticed something.

Something in the manner in which I gazed up at her firm, sculpted body. She noticed the degree of curiosity, the lingering aspect of my gazing. I was considered a little too nosey, too precocious. That ended our showers together.

From that point on, I was handed over to my father. He took care of my showers. I loved him, too, this large, semi-stranger returned from a long war in a far-off land. I gazed up at him, too. I rested my cheek against the toughness of his hairy thigh, the shower water catching and beading on the prickly hairs. Dad's body was very different. It was muscular, hard, rough and with familiar appendages my mother did not have. Not at all like Mom, none of her soft, encompassing sweetness, but I loved him. My mother craved his attention; therefore, I craved it, too.

Love? What does a very little boy know of love? Both the tender and the animal expressions of love. He knows only that within his little body there is a need to express affection. A need to be close, to feel contact. To reach out. To touch. To be playful within the innocent purity of childhood. It's why we have bodies. So that we may touch, which I did, as little boys tend to do. And what proceeded from that curious touching was surprising, funny and seemed to be what Daddy wanted and needed. Here was something a little boy could do for his Dad to make him feel good, make him love you. A fun thing that made him chuckle. The chuckling modulating down to a frozen smile. Then a puzzling thing occurred that eventually made the smile fade into vacancy. Then something very odd indeed happened. Startling. Disturbing. Did I hurt him in some way?

There's another artefact to hoard. And cherish? Maybe not. Maybe too puzzling to cherish.

And so began a journey that brought me close to the terrifying cliffs of madness and that dangerous desire to extinguish experience. It isn't the simple artefacts of experience that push you over the edge. It took a few years, but eventually it happened. What did it for me—pushed me off the edge—was the sudden and very shocking realization that what happened in the shower, or over the toilet, or in the dead quiet of the crawl space under the house, or in the car filled with curling cigarette smoke and deadly silence, or while walking in the woodsy park with my muted father—these things did not happen in the lives of my young playmates. I must have had some doubts. I was curious. Ask your best little friend if his father does those monotonous, tedious things with him, and the chubby little fellow's face strikes you like a lightning bolt, paralyzing you with shame. The chubby little fellow has no idea what you're talking about, but still, he looks at you with puzzlement, even revulsion. That is when the veil is thrown over the collected artefacts, and they turn into menacing monsters. What to do with them? The monsters are carefully huddled and pushed deeply into the dim, reinforced concrete rooms of the mind never to be looked at or even recognized as existing. Never to be spoken of again to anyone. Just collect them, hide them and make believe they never happened. But how does a little boy stop this repetitive, mind-numbing collection process? The artefacts just keep coming, no end in sight, his mind running out of storage rooms, pressure building. His little, chubby friend looking at him strangely. Me, looking at myself in a dissociative manner. No longer me, but him, someone other than me. I don't do this. Someone else does.

And now, who do I turn to?

Mom, maybe?

Too late. Mom was already throwing suspicious, hurtful looks, her face a mask of rage, pain and despair. At Dad. Worse—at me, as if I were a co-conspirator. Something changed in her life, too. She must have wondered, did her faithful husband find another woman? Is that where Dad and I disappeared to with metronomic regularity? Was she now involved in some sort of love triangle? I noticed the change. The tone in her voice lost its musical sweetness. Her face lost its prettiness. Her body sagged. She no longer looked like a well-worshipped goddess. She cried a lot, and a doctor came and gave her shots. She was starting to hoard artefacts herself. Things she didn't want to look at. Things that enlightened but at the same destroyed hope, like my stained underpants, which dropped her to her knees as if she'd been pole-axed. Enlightened in some horrible way she never thought of. When I saw that, I felt pole-axed myself. It wasn't another woman. It was me. What had I done? What had I done to my beautiful, loving mother? I'd brought ruin upon her. And so I begot another collectible artefact to push into a dusty corner of my mind: guilt. What a wonderful possession.

How does one describe the cold-blooded atmosphere in our quaint little bungalow? Decades later, I filled notebooks with scenes distilled from the muffled, bitter badinage between my bewildered mother and self-assured father. In a cramped house with paper-thin walls no conversation goes unheard by the children. Parents seem to forget that a child can hear and be pummelled by the words he hears. I picked my brain for the tones I had heard, the bitterness and despair. In my notebooks appeared the following distillation of memory:

From the outside, the little bungalow appeared well cared for, its dark, stained cedar shingles in good shape. The yellow trim freshly painted. The surrounding hedge rows were neatly trimmed and spotted with tiny, sweet-smelling flowers. Gunner had installed one of those new Thermo-pane picture windows. It didn't open but presented a full view of the Bay, the moored boats and the spit of brown sand beach. It was one of the first improvement jobs he'd done upon returning from the war in Europe.

The pleasant summer day was coming to a close. The sun was setting behind the old cinder road and the marshes bordering the tidal creek, which ran off to the west. Melissa stood at the breakfast bar in the small kitchen at the back of the house. A warm southwest breeze billowing the gauzy curtains behind her, the humid air caressing her bare, tanned legs. Gunner made the bar himself out of plywood and blue Formica. She had wanted pale green Formica, but he couldn't find that color or didn't want to; she wasn't sure. He was such a steady Eddy. Got his old job back at the printing plant. They even promoted him to foreman. Every Friday he brought home that little manila envelope with its stapled end flap, small enough to fit in his shirt pocket and inside his week's take-home, eighty-nine dollars and fifty cents. The amount was printed on the outside of the envelope. The man didn't stop for a beer with the boys or buy a tool he needed. He just brought the pay home and gave it to her to run the house and put a little aside for improvements.

He was a good man. She was sure he was.

Her hands shook, and she had trouble pouring the shot of gin, mixing it with the Tom Collins soda and the ice. The house was very still, Jamie in for his nap, exhausted after swimming, playing on the beach, showering with his Dad. Hard to believe he was already three. She lit a Kent. Had trouble with the damn match, the flame seeming to jump all over the place. She turned toward the small window that peered out on the back alley between the rows of bungalows.

It was a tight little community. Your nosey neighbours never more than ten feet away either side. She wondered why the tightness bothered her. It never had in the past. She felt nauseous and wondered if she might be pregnant. She felt so many different things churning around inside. The Collins felt good, a long, soothing drink of it. Maybe that would do the trick. Maybe she worried too much. Maybe everything was really all right. The thought calmed her, but after a few moments the anxiety returned.

She picked up her drink, her cigarettes and matches and walked down the short, carpeted hallway. The carpet was threadbare, some sort of faded burgundy color with black border. That would be her next project as soon as she got a few extra dollars together. Get a new runner. Something a little brighter, beige maybe. A small house needed lighter colors otherwise it seemed to close in on you. She passed Jamie's closet-size room and took a look. A fresh little piece of life, he lay on his back breathing through his sweet mouth. So peaceful. Skin like an angel's. A perfectly-formed little boy. How cute he was, and how good he was at using that cuteness to manipulate, get what he wanted. She worried too much.

The boy loved his Dad. Away for the first two years of his life and then all of a sudden he was there, a large, interesting stranger that the boy needed to get to know. The nausea rose up in her belly. She took another long, icy drink. She needed the courage the alcohol delivered. She had to have this talk. Or should she just be quiet? Maybe she had imagined it?

No. She didn't think so. There was undeniable evidence.

The small living room was still bright with late afternoon sun flooding in the new picture window. She loved

*that window and had begged Gunner to put it in. It made
all the difference brightening the room that had been so
bleak. The flowered curtains helped. She was proud she
was able to sew them up herself from some fabric remnants
from Harry's Discount. She settled onto the sofa, curled
her shapely legs under her and set her cigarettes on the
end table. She'd found that at Harry's, too. Bamboo and
glass. Very modern-looking, she thought. It went well with
the Danish modern sofa and the web chairs. She'd worked
hard to turn what formerly was the grim home of an elderly
couple into something bright and happy and youthful. A
nice, cozy place to raise a family. She had missed Gunner
so much for those two long years he was at war. Thank
god she had Jamie. More than anything, she wanted to be
a good mother. She had to have this talk. She mashed out
the stub of her cigarette. She drained the last of her Collins,
hesitated a moment and then decided to mix another.*

*She came back with her fresh drink, a little stronger this
time, and again settled on the sofa. Gunner looked comfortable in the blond wood chair with the bright red webbing. He
was reading* Life *magazine and smoking a Camel. He wasn't
five feet away, and yet he seemed so remote. He didn't offer
to mix her drink. He didn't look up as she entered the room,
twice. There were times when he didn't seem to be there.
Times when she thought he didn't really care for her. Times
when she got so angry she wanted to scream at him: Look at
me! Will you please just look at me. But she never did.*

*"He's three years old," she said. Her hands shook and
she had to put down the frosted Tom Collins on the glass
and bamboo end table. She unfolded her legs from the sofa,
leaned forward and fumbled to light another filter-tip Kent.*

He looked so comfortable in that chair, the peculiar chair made of fabric webbing pulled tight across the blond wood frame, fastened with little brass tacks. She loved the modernity of it, how well it fit into the tiny living room. A comfy dollhouse for her family.

She tried again. "He's a charmer. He knows he's cute. Children use their cuteness. It's the only power they possess. He's looking for affection. He wants to play with you."

He struck a match and leaned toward her to touch the tip of her trembling cigarette. It was the gentlemanly thing to do, an outward show of normality toward a distressed woman.

"He wants it. He wants to do it," he said. His voice was calm, his hand steady.

She tried again, her voice wavering.

"My god, he's a baby. He wants attention. He wants love."

"Melissa, it's Nature. A few months ago he was sucking your tits." His face was again directed at the glossy pages of Life magazine, a bald-headed, grandfather-like army general on the cover. He wet his thumb and turned the page. He picked his cigarette off the imitation crystal ashtray, took a drag, flicked off the ash and returned it. He reached behind him and pulled the flowery curtain she'd made. Pulled it just enough to stop a streamer of sunlight coming over his shoulder onto the glossy magazine.

She'd made the window treatments herself. She'd picked out the inexpensive furniture. She loved building her little nest on the waterfront, making it cozy and happy for her family.

"He was at my breasts for nourishment, for god's sake. There was nothing sexual about it. Are you out of your mind? He needs a father. That's what he wants. You were away for *two years in that fucking war. You come back, he's no longer an infant, and he wants to know you, love you. He wants to be a little boy with his daddy."* Tears distorted her face.

"Listen, Melissa. When I was a boy, it was a form of birth control. You had a boy, he took care of a man's needs, or what you got was a house full of kids you couldn't feed. It does no harm. Kids forget. They grow up, they leave it behind. For Christ's sake, you're making a mountain out of a mole hill."

It took her breath away. She sucked air as if having an asthma attack.

"You're fucking insane. You're a lunatic."

"Watch your language. What kind of mother are you? You want to be pregnant every nine months? The Church condemns birth control. You can't use a condom, a diaphragm. It's mortal sin, whatever the hell that is. What am I supposed to do? What about my needs? It's Nature. You have to be practical." He never raised his voice. He wasn't angry.

"I'm your wife. I'll take care of your needs. Your son is not your wife. You'll ruin him."

"I'm not ruining anything. You're drunk. Go to bed. Sleep it off."

"I'm your fucking wife, and I'm not drunk." She fought to keep some minimal composure.

"Look, if it bothers the kid, troubles him, there's ways to make him forget. He won't remember any of it. Either way, he'll be fine."

She looked at him and he met her gaze; her face crumbled.

"What do you mean?" She searched his gray eyes, this predictable man of habits, who wooed and won her over many other suitors. She'd thought he looked a bit like

Humphrey Bogart. Of all the horny men sniffing around her lush body she chose this one. Now she wasn't sure who he was. He was so cold. Was he even human? What did he mean, ways to erase a child's memory? His words came as if through a scrim. Mysterious, vague, ominous, evil.

"You'll see when the time comes. If it ever does." He glanced up at her, mashed out his cigarette and returned his gaze to the magazine with the grinning general.

She felt stunned. He might as well be beating her with a two-by-four, this man who never laid an angry hand on her. What do you say? How do you reason? Her mind became cloudy, muddled, unsure. It was a problem like no other. Did it have a solution? She felt torsion in her brain as if its stem was being twisted by a mighty, illogical wrench.

"Gunner, what about me? What about our marriage? Doesn't that mean anything to you?"

"You can have as many babies as we can afford."

"I'm not talking about more babies. What are we doing here? Is this a love triangle?"

He ignored her and concentrated on his reading.

It's a nightmare, she thought. It can't be real. Surely, she'll wake up and find out nothing of the kind is happening. It can't be happening. It's impossible. It was a terrible feeling of being trapped. She was a frail mouse with one leg stuck in the trap, trying to claw forward, dragging the trap like a large, misshapen tumour. Her mind raced back and forth, going over and over the same terrain. What did he say? What can I do? Her mind succumbing, sinking down, down, down. Clear thoughts became impossible. There was no way out. Round and round her thoughts whirled. This awful thing was going to ingest her. Dissolve her. Till she was no more.

How could the flowering of a young, fresh life be twisted into sexual seductiveness? How could a man do that or even think such a thought? Or believe it? The boy wants it? She wanted to fling the frosted glass at him. She stood up, a sudden motion. The room became dimmer and dimmer until she collapsed, unconscious, on the gray shag rug.

While she slept, silent gnomes within dug dark pits in which to hide this terrible thing. Cover it up. Tamp down the earth. Maybe, just maybe it wasn't really happening. Just a nightmare dangling in the dismal ether of the mind. Never happened. Never happened at all.

He finished the article about the bald, grandfatherly general, tossed the magazine on the floor and lit another cigarette. The blue-gray smoke curled around him and in his silence, one might believe he was pondering the war from which he had so recently returned and the power of repetition. How one could say anything, no matter how startling. History was replete with powerful leaders who knew you could say anything, and if said with conviction and persistence, it eventually became real, palatable if not tasty, slowly nudging its way into ordinary life, transformed and softened until people just settled down and lived with it.

He got up, stepped over his wife, went to the side window, closed the blinds, then crouched over her limp body. That's the ticket, he thought. Nothing is as bad as you think it is. She'll come around. He picked her up. She didn't weigh much. One-ten maybe. He carried her into the bedroom and placed her on the bed. She looked beautiful when she was at peace. Her blond hair billowed onto the pillow framing her face. He pulled a light quilt over her. All she need do is accept. Once you accept it, it's not so bad, really.

He went back to the living room and took his seat, a captain's chair by that big square window overlooking the sparkling bay. He smoked another cigarette and watched the boats bobbing at their moorings. He wondered if one day, they'd be able to afford a sailboat. They could sail together. He and the boy. He'd like that. After all, they both liked the same things, didn't they?

In my opinion, the pursuit of meaningless pleasure can become nightmarish. St. Thomas Aquinas, in the thirteenth century, wrote that venereal pleasures ". . . more than anything else work the greatest havoc in a man's mind." Although I agree in part, a world without pleasure is pale, gray and not much fun. That kind of world led me to want nothing more than to escape the cold night air of sick compulsion, lock myself inside myself and have nothing further to do with the human race, thereby exchanging one sickness for another.

The clutter in my mental back rooms was fast becoming a hoard the weight of which was intimidating. It was crushingly heavy. Especially the guilt. Yes, especially the guilt. Something had to be done. But I was nowhere near big enough to stop this collection process. I couldn't reach out to my little friends. I avoided them, avoided everyone, retreating into stony, silent, shyness. I was the little boy who liked to sit at the back of the classroom hoping no one would notice me. I felt shamed into diminishment. The collection of artefacts was simply too heavy even to leave the house with. I couldn't carry the spine-bending weight. How could I get out of this?

Why, the Church of course. There was my Saviour, nailed solidly to that cross behind the altar. I'd pray to Him, beseech Him.

I'd faithfully study my Baltimore Catechism, prepare for my first confession and my first Holy Communion. To the nuns and priests I'd go. But Holy Jesus! A realization hit me. This whole stinking mess was a mortal sin. At least, I was pretty sure it was. Venereal pleasure, an abstraction, had been bandied about in religion class. The very words oozed the sound of slime. Thou shalt not commit adultery, warned the Ten Commandments. Another mysterious word with some sort of sticky, runny meaning. Adultery was a mortal sin, a capital offense against god. I had to be stopped. I wasn't going to start collecting mortal sins. I'd burn in Hell. We all would. Dad would understand that, wouldn't he? Of course he would. I might have been eight or nine years old, but a man-to-man was required here. I'd have a talk with Dad. I'd tell him I needed to confess what we did. Tell the priest everything, do penance, otherwise we were all going to Hell.

Oddly enough, he did understand when I said I wasn't going to do it anymore. He wanted out, too. But the path he chose was strange. Strange and ahead of his time by over half a century. When I told him I wasn't doing it anymore, he agreed: he wasn't going to either. Not only was it coming to a screeching halt, he intended to make it seem it had never happened.

There was a way to do that. A way, I believe, he learned when he was a boy living in the crowded railroad flats of Harlem or out in the Dongan Hills wilds of Staten Island. He'd seen, I believe, his alcoholic uncles do it to his female siblings. He knew it worked. It tamed those wild, lustful girls and dimmed their pre-pubescent memories of their uncles' hard bodies. And he was determined to carry it out, not only on me but on Mom as well.

Similar to the CIA's method of torturing prisoners into confessing their sins, the way it worked on my mom and me was the opposite. My father's idea, I believe, was to suppress any possibility of confessing anything coherent to anyone, anytime. His idea was to make that veiled collection in my mind scatter and dissipate: water-boarding without the board. A simple procedure, all you need is a big, old, iron bathtub. He drowned me in the tub while my mother screamed, jumped on his back, pulled his hair, pummelled his broad shoulders—until her turn came—and I, pumping air wildly into my depleted lungs, watched. We watched each other being drowned. Over and over again to exhaustion. Let me assure you, repetitive drowning isn't any fun at all. It produced an extremely camouflaged memory that took decades to unveil and required the saintly patience of a devoted mentor. The difficulty with an obscure, buried memory like that is: You cannot recall it until you re-live it. That wasn't any fun either. In fact it was the most terrifying experience of my adult life and very nearly permanently buckled my mind.

Decades later, to reach down into that dark pit, pull off the veil, and tug that monster of a memory out and into the light of day was more than I was capable of doing alone. Luckily, I had help. Isn't it funny how help often turns up when you desperately need it? A friend appears to help you through your terror and despair. Is it possible that beseeching works?

So what's the payoff? What did I get out of this hoarding of memories? I became a writer. What the hell else could I do? I filled filing cabinets with all sorts of mental vomit. Intellectual bulimia. Brain masturbation. I loved it. I loved the relief writing brought me, that wonderful release of up-welling pressure. Beseeching the Universe.

Writing became my religion, my way of praying, a way of forgiving my Self. Writing brought understanding, as well as the ability to forgive the seemingly uncontrollable, frightening compulsions of others.

And of course, I hoarded every scrap, every word. Didn't throw out so much as a sticky note; it might have value, such as Uncle Albert's tarnished bronze medals in the attic. (Uncle Albert never won a race. He always finished third, apparently.) The hoard of memories never goes away. You can't throw them away or disown them. They have a fierce, unending life of their own and bubble to the surface at will. They are the ultimate, driving force of my life. The source of every word I have ever written. They are hateful beyond words. And yet I dearly love every bit of their bone and gristle. It is this compulsive hoarding of memories that has made me—ME.

George P. Farrell was born, raised, housed, clothed and well-fed in the Bronx, NY. Generally puzzled and baffled by life but always hopeful.

"In my early twenties I discovered writing as a cheaper and better alternative to psychological counselling. Discovered the Catskills was a good place to pursue a writing career and inspecting boats, a reasonable way to put food on the table. I have written six novels and a bunch of short stories, as I traveled along my learning curve, and so far have produced a literary income of forty dollars plus numerous, very-appreciated pats-on-the-back. I am looking forward, with some trepidation, to more of the same."

Throwing Out the Trash

Evalyn Lee

"Who would take a picture of her mother throwing out trash?" asks Joyce Maynard, the writer.

Maynard is running a memoir class on the Amalfi Coast of Italy. In my diary the class is dated Monday, July 18, 2011. The group is looking at a black and white photograph taken in 1982 of my mother throwing out the trash. Her back was to the camera when I took the picture.

Prior to arriving in Italy, we had been asked to bring a picture from our lives. To do this, I had climbed over five boxes of children's art, six dining room chairs and a mattress in our basement storage room under the back garden to retrieve the box of photos I keep, the ones that don't go in albums or frames. I don't throw these "reject" pictures out, because I always hope one day to understand why I took them. The picture in front of the class was one of those.

In this photograph every kitchen cabinet door is opened. The label of every single condiment bottle is facing forward. My mom's left arm and hand are outstretched as she reaches past the swinging top of the white plastic garbage can. The gesture is beautiful like my mother.

What you need to know to understand the picture is that my mother's mother died when she was ten, and when my mother was eleven, her father remarried. His new wife threw out every single one of my mom's toys and even gave away her bed. You also need to know that one side of my mother's family is Mormon. Mormons never throw anything out. Mormon-style, my mother stored food for Armageddon, even on the seventh floor of a Park Avenue apartment in New York City. You also need to know that Armageddon arrived early for us on a Friday, the first night of spring break in 1979.

"Take care of your mother," says my father. "I know I can't."

"Thanks," I say to a front door slamming shut.

It was a hard job looking after my mother.

She didn't get out of bed for six months. I shopped, cooked, cleaned and took care of my brother. I did my father's jobs of walking the dog, taking out the garbage and adding up the bills. I didn't do my old job of changing the kitty litter. I left that for my mother. She didn't do it. Finally to cook dinner for my brother without vomiting, I had to change the kitty litter. When my mother met Paul, the man she will marry a week after I take this picture, she got out of bed and changed the kitty litter.

In the picture, Mom is wearing a floral skirt. It has an elastic waist. Mom has gained twenty-five pounds as she planned her wedding, sold our Park Avenue apartment and got ready to move to Argentina with my soon-to-be stepfather, Paul. None of her clothes fit. Even her wedding dress had to be let out. She was on a very strange and desperate diet.

Even now I remember what is in the refrigerator.

There are four bottles of club soda, fifty carrot sticks in water, a beef tongue in a clear glass bowl, a head of foxy lettuce and a square of tofu floating in murky water in a green plastic net box. That's it.

My fourteen-year old brother is screaming on the phone to my father: "You will be downstairs. You will pay for my taxi. You will take me out for steak. I am starving. There is no food in this apartment."

My brother leaves without saying good-bye. He is not in the apartment when I take the picture, and Mom is too busy packing to care.

When my grandmother died in 1978, Dad could finally afford to get a divorce. But he never stopped complaining about my mother. Neither did my stepmother, who called her a spoiled Park Avenue bitch. My response to this remark was not polite or politic, so I, unlike my brother, was unwelcomed in their apartment, which is why I was in the kitchen helping my mother sort through our kitchen cupboards.

When I take this picture, my mother is throwing out the food she can't take with her when she moves to Argentina. When I take this picture, I know my father is a liar and a cheat because two years before I take this picture, and one year and three months after a very bad fight with my mother, my Dad handed me an address in London. I was to stay with his friend before I headed to Greece on a trip with high school classmates.

In London it takes me one whole day to figure out what's been going on.

I pick up a set of keys to the flat from my father's friend's office in Barclay Square. The girl who gives me the keys, an assistant, gives me a stare that is so strange, so intense, so out of order, that I am left feeling like road kill. The way that girl looked at me said something was very wrong.

At the flat that goes with the set of keys in Putney, I am trying to figure out where to put my empty suitcase, when I walk into my father's friend's bedroom. There beside the bed is a picture of my father. I recognize it, a headshot taken when he was made editor-in-chief of the Reader's Digest Press. Why is his so much younger face smiling out of an expensive leather frame in Putney? What was this old picture doing by the bed?

Four hours later I burst into tears at the National Gallery in Trafalgar Square. What am I going to tell my mother?

From the office phone I call my father: "I know."

"I am asking you not to judge me," he said.

"You have to tell Mom. I am not going to tell her."

I hang up the phone.

My father does not tell my mother.

Neither do I.

So when I take this picture of my mother throwing out the trash, I know my father has not loved her since I was nine years old. I know that he has been unfaithful to her for many years. What I don't know is that by not telling my mother about the woman who is now my stepmother, he gets to keep most of his family's money in the divorce settlement.

My father had mocked my mother all my life, ridiculed her interests, her appearance, her passion for dance and music, her intellect. Then he treated her like garbage and threw his life with her and us away.

I am forty-five, the same age as my mother in the picture, when I say to my mom on Kensington High Street in London, where I now live, "I am so sorry I did not tell you about Janetta."

Like my mother, I have had to move to a foreign country because of my husband's job. We stop at *Prêt-a-Manger* for a coffee. She pats my hand and looks right at me. My mom stopped being able to look me in the face in 1979, the week before spring break my senior year, after my first suicide attempt. It is only because I have kept a diary all my life that I know my suicide attempt happened exactly seven days before my father left the building.

My mother is slapping my face over and over and over. She has pulled me back from the open window, thrown my body across the bathroom, and my skull has hit the porcelain, pre-war bathtub. My mom leaves me on the bathroom floor, pours a whisky and goes to bed. Dad returns from walking the dog.

I don't remember crying. I do remember nothing was said. Now I doubt my mother even told my father what I'd attempted to do.

Years later my brother says, "You were so far out that window, I don't know how Mom caught you. It was terrifying."

My mother saved my life but never said a word about it. Not one word.

Even now, thirty years later, after my apology, when Mom and I can talk, now that she can look me in the face, we're not ready to discuss my recent attempt, but at least we are talking.

She says to me: "There is no need to be sorry. You weren't the only one who didn't tell me."

Today, people talk about all sorts of "personal" garbage but still not so much about suicide. In 2011, looking down at the picture of my mother on the table top in Italy as the sun skipped off the sea below us, I realized I still did not understand the person who would take a picture of her mother throwing out garbage. But I did begin to see a need to tell the truth about who I had become.

Some words in this essay were the beginning of that truth.

I'm not proud of the truth, but I will own it.

Twice in my life I have reached a point where it seemed the right idea to treat myself like a piece of garbage. Twice.

Once, seven days before the man I loved best in the world walked out to be with the woman he loved best in the world. The second time, when I was forty-four, my career had crashed to an end, and I had fallen deeper into an undiagnosed postnatal depression.

I'm writing this now at fifty-three. I look pretty normal. I have a husband, two kids and a house with no mortgage, a dog and a kitten. But I also still have that box of photos. I still have a story that is hard to tell, and I know that if I do tell it, most people will look away, never to look towards me again.

I wrote part of this essay on a porch at our hotel in Italy. But it wasn't working. I took it to one workshop, in an attempt to get it to work, but for writers who had overcome much more than I ever suffered, the need to look away from my face after hearing this story was strong. So I put the story away for four more years. Until Martha sent out a request for this collection of essays based on the topic of letting go.

Now I've had four more years of writing, of meeting writers, like Amy Ferris, who say, "Letting go is not the same as giving up. Let go."

Now I know that every single person in the world carries his own secret box of memories he doesn't understand. Now I know, well not all the time, but most of the time, how to ask for and to receive help. I didn't have to tell a soul about my second suicide attempt. I survived it with no one the wiser. But I did tell. I decided to tell the truth. Own my own unhappiness and confusion. I got help. Now I know that when I feel like garbage, I am not alone. And neither are you.

But I also know that some people, reading these words, like my mom, will struggle to look me in the face. For my mom suicide is not just a sin, it is a crime. What I can't get her to understand is how the garbage thinking of depression can make the idea of throwing yourself away make total sense.

That's how depression kills you. It creates a pain loop so deep that you can't imagine how it will end unless you end. You decide you will do anything to stop the pain.

I grew up in a family where it made more sense to kill yourself than to talk. That's crazy? Not to me. In my family, to tell someone what you were feeling was the ultimate taboo; it was easier to contemplate suicide.

But still I wrote, took pictures and kept journals, which proves I must have known from a very young age that I needed to keep a record, provide evidence and leave vital clues for a future self to find. Clues that I hope will help me to forgive myself, clues I hope will make me a better parent, wife, daughter, friend.

My kids know what I've attempted. It hurts me every day that they know. I didn't mean for them to find out, but I was fighting with my husband late one night and shouted too loudly about my life.

"Mom," said my daughter, "don't you know we hear everything you say?"

It hurts me that they know. But I have to believe it is better to speak openly about my sadness and my mistakes. Even if it was a mistake and a fight that brought my suicide attempts out into the open with my immediate family, I still pray every day for God's forgiveness for attempting to take my life.

Still it takes four more years. It's 2015, and I'm typing on a computer in the dark, stretched out on the sofa in our living room in London, redrafting the words I first wrote sitting on a balcony in a hotel on the Amalfi Coast in 2011. It takes four more years to find an answer to the question Joyce Maynard asked me: "Who would take a picture of their mother throwing out trash?"

A girl. A nineteen-year-old girl who knew with every day she lived that what you don't talk about can kill you, even if no one is listening. The girl who took that picture was a girl who didn't want to die. A girl who wanted to tell her story, a girl who needed permission to speak, and that girl was me. That girl is over fifty now, and she wants to say that you aren't alone. Even in the darkest place. She wants to tell you that you are worth it. That letting go is not the same as giving up. So let it go. And don't give up. Because no one knows how your story will end, not even you.

———

Evalyn Lee attended graduate studies at Oxford University, where she studied with the Joyce Scholar, Richard Ellman, and the literary critic, John Bayley. A former CBS producer, she has written on a wide range of topics, including the Gulf Wars and many investigative pieces for the likes of Dan Rather, Mike Wallace and Lesley Stahl. Her television broadcast work won an Emmy and numerous Writers Guild Awards. Her short stories have appeared or are forthcoming in Amarillo Bay, Diverse Arts Project *and* Willow Review. *She is working on her first novel, living in London with two kids, one husband and Hugo the dog and writes: "This is my first personal essay. I mean every word I have written—if depression strikes, try to let go of shame and blame. Aristotle got it right: 'It is during our darkest moments that we must focus to see the light.' You are the light of your own life. If you can't see it, reach out and find others who can."*

Album for a Poem

Jhon Sanchez

How I would like to be perpetual tears of ice on a tree branch, but life is like a thaw: In time, the ice melts and becomes thousands of melted tears. If only time would not run out, if only weather would not change.

At this age, I feel melted; tears are leaving me. Each second or each moment is melting my being. Life is like ice cream. The most delicious ice cream is the fastest to melt.

A poem gave birth to this essay. I wrote "Immortality," thinking about the lights of houses seen at night from a hill. The poem, as my professor told me, needs more work; for that reason I did not include it in my master's thesis in English and creative writing. I do not know what to do with it. I almost wrote, "I do not know what to do with him." (Poem is masculine in Spanish.) I know I should give him appearance, aroma and voice like a character.

While writing a poem, I try to transmit each moment, moments that I always want to remember, and moments that I would like to forget. A moment links your whole remaining life in one single color. It is like painting a pond by throwing in a dye-based stone. Don't paint the water with a brush, rather throw in the stone, and its expansive ripples will ink the whole lake, your life. With each stone, however, I need to remember that I not only live, but I also leave. I would like for this poem to be a journey of insignificant, sporadic moments. Those moments are the stones.

Should I start my poem with the image of hugging my mother's belly? It was after my twenty-sixth birthday celebration, in Medellin, Colombia. She was watching TV in bed. My niece, Carolina, was with us. I enjoyed listening to my mother's heart. Bun, bun, bun. My right arm stretched over her big belly like a road ascending a hill. This stomach has hosted eight children and two miscarriages.

If I were one of the two miscarriages, I would not like that word *miscarriage*, I thought. Her soft skin sagged like layers of clouds seen from an airplane window. People are like dresses; there are those who shrink with time and those who stretch. My mom's body was stretched. My left ear was near her navel. I placed my fist on the left side of her stomach. A couple of knocks on her belly, and my mother wondered what I was doing.

"I am your baby, Jhon, who wants to go out."

She smiled.

My niece took her headband and tied it to a thread and put it on my mother's chest. It was her stethoscope.

"Well, your baby is coming," my niece said.

All of us started to play the hospital game. My niece, the doctor, took my head in her hands, pulled it away from my mother and gave me a slap on my buttocks. I hugged my mother's belly again. We were all dying of laughter (a big cliché but in this case, I was being born of laughter). We hugged each other, and I thought that I still fit in her belly. This person called Jhon, with all his problems and mistakes, fits there any time and any moment.

Here in New York, how much I would give to hug her again. She died eight years ago; my immigration status in the US did not allow me to see her again. I stapled the scene of my twenty-sixth birthday to my mind; a mind soon called to die.

As I swallowed my night pill with the forlorn hope it wouldn't damage my liver, I asked myself, when is my niece going to appear in the poem? My niece is now an engineer in Medellin, my hometown. I was ten when she was born. We had the same dog, *Garoto*. An old dog that one day disappeared from my house. I helped my niece learn how to ride a bike, but I never learned how to ride one. She was my first guest invited to taste the first dinner I ever made; she survived because she did not eat it. We laughed and laughed. Her love break-ups never stopped us from laughing.

What moment is the right one for my poem? Our vacations in Panama? Reading *The Odyssey* to her in a childish voice? Maybe, the day she was ironing the clothes, and I was sitting on my bed . . . more than twenty years ago. That day between warm folded shirts and wrinkled pants, she learned that I was homosexual. She was the first person to know it. I gave her that secret like a Christmas gift, one more allocation of myself in her life as fellow passengers in the same vessel. If I could live my life in confession, each word, each sentence, each deed of my life would be a confession, not because it is secret, but because it is sacred.

I still call my niece. When we talk on the phone, I do not want to worry her with my doctor's warnings, my pains and payment of my health care.

"Tears and smiles are sisters, my sisters," sounds like a good mantra for my poem. The statement also reminds me of my sister. Nine years ago, I was living in Queens, New York. At that time,

I did not have a phone, and that day I had only five dollars in my pocket. While checking my e-mail, I saw a message from my niece. The subject said, *"None."* The message was short: Maritza, my niece's younger sister, had died two days before. I went to the store and spent my five dollars to buy a phone card. Instead of my niece answering, my sister picked up the phone and began to cry. I cried with her, but I also felt so happy to be speaking with her again: the girl who watched cartoons with me under blankets with a cup of chocolate; the mother who lay her two babies in my arms; the one who was my first secretary when I practiced law in Colombia. That mother was crying because she had not been able to endure listening to her daughter's breathing difficulties. I heard her voice cracking, telling and retelling about her daughter's death. The hospital, her impatience, her guilt. An hour was not enough to remember my niece's first steps and songs. We listened to the buzzer that announced the fifty-ninth minute, indicating I had to say good-bye. I hated with all my force that buzzer. When I hung up and walked on the street, I only remember darkness. I was blind walking on the streets of Queens. Each street was blurry on a sunny day. "Tears and smiles are sisters, my sisters."

Does that line make any sense for my poem?

Sadness and joy are two branches from the same willow. Happiness is the transpiration of tears and smiles. As the autumn wind plays with the willow's weeping leaves, the willow laughs and giggles. Every straight line is a part of a circle whose diameter is undetermined. This line of emotion, this mixture of the emotions would, finally, meet in the same origin point, like a circle. If only I could trace that line to return to the same point, but I can't in the short time of living.

"I do not know if you are going to publish one of your poems. But if so, for sure you might need to publish in the book an explanation of the poems," said my friend, Dennis. My poem hopes to recount a moment I shared with Dennis a couple of years ago. When I was living in Sunnyside, NY, a friend gave me a couch. My friends Dennis and Shinichi went with me to help move the couch to my house two or three blocks down the hill. Since we had neither cars nor trucks and six hands seemed insufficient, I asked the people in the store if I could borrow their platform palette pushcart. Then three friends, one Japanese, one American, one Colombian, me, performed an acrobatic show going down the hill on the speeding pushcart. It was a collective skateboarding on a summer day in New York. I wished we could continue at the risk of not stopping and hitting a car coming from the opposite direction. I yelled, "I want to remember this moment forever!" The poem started to be written that day with the desire to remember that we felt like trapeze artists, acrobats and clowns at the same time. A moment with my bubbling friends' smiles in a concert against the wind.

Sunrise sounds like *sonrisa* in Spanish. *Sonrisa* is a kind of smile. It is a soft smile, the kind that you have only for yourself. In my mind *sunrise* appears like a blue wind that blows up a red star. My poem could have a sunrise because on Columbus Day, 2003, the day *sunrised* and *sonrio* for me. My friend, Hiromi, came to visit me at Southampton. Without paying for a single ride, we took the bus to Sag Harbor, then another bus to East Hampton, and from there we went via bus to Montauk. On our way to Montauk, we sat in the first row of the bus. Down the hill, the ocean lay like a curtain circled by an auditorium of small houses. It was a couple of seconds full of blue, sky and sea. Later, we got a ride to the lighthouse. On the way back, I called a cab that never came, so a guy gave us a ride to Montauk. We ate ice cream and we took a bus to Southampton again. We walked five or six miles to an Italian restaurant, then went to Southampton College to go to bed. In fact that day, the whole day, was like those seconds on the bus, like a heap of good luck when we did not have to pay for any rides. We had good luck like a day when a bullet crosses near your chest. One more movement of your body and you would be dead. One minute late and we would have to pay. The day is now over and from now on I will need to pay for my rides and perhaps a bullet will go straight to my heart.

One spring day, on my birthday, a person was waiting for me at the door of my house in Queens. A tablecloth with a candle and a vase with a flower sat on the sidewalk. After the wind blew out the candle, the night became skin, sweat and silence, finishing with sunrays on the cups of coffee. Magic had a common border with madness. Where madness finished, the land of magic started or *stared* like the verb *star*, not *stare*, but maybe. Nothing more ridiculous than a candle, a vase, and a flower on the sidewalk, but nothing was more appropriate for my poem. If I felt magic every day, I would be confined in an asylum.

Recently, a friend invited me to her house for dinner. We walked her dog and the sky was full of stars. Julie talked about the stars, Sirius, Procyon and Vega. Behind the stars the dark sky seemed like a broken glass, with a white scratch along the whole celestial sphere. I hoped the sky would not fall in pieces on my head; this scratch was only the Milky Way. Wondering about the stars that night came from my ignorance. This person, I, who did not know anything, always tried to answer all questions. Under those stars, astronomy meant to me a cracking glass, the passage of time. Time will pass until the sky will fall; until then, my own terror will remind me of the moment I felt the falling sky.

These are random memories of joy, good luck, happiness, confession, affection, ignorance, magic. Sparking moments in my memory's life. Sometimes, I concentrate and try to fix one of those moments inside me. I want to have at least one moment marked on my brain. I write poems with the hope of printing them in my mind; I also write poems to forget, with the hope of being liberated from the past. But I cannot forget even a horrible experience, for now. These indelible moments cause a worse sensation, as I know I will forget them anyway. I have to let them go. I am going to die, and my brain is going to turn into mud. Beyond my will, beyond my remarkable moments, it is a fact that all of them will remain buried in the ground.

Immortality is the aspiration to continue remembering after death. If I could snatch one of those moments with me, at the *very least* the most terrible moment in my life, then beyond death I could be sure that I have lived: "I lit up myself," as I said in my poem.

Jhon Sanchez is a Colombian-born writer who came to the United States seeking political asylum in 1998. Through the process of learning English as his second language, he discovered his voice as a writer. His poetry and fiction have been featured in The Overpass Magazine, The Brooklyn Paramount, *and* The Bronx Memoir Project. *His short story, "The Japanese Rice Cooker," selected by New Lit Salon for the anthology,* Startling Sci-Fi, New Tales of the Beyond, *edited by Casey Ellis, was recently nominated for a Pushcart Prize. In addition to his writing career, he is also an attorney.*

He is proud to claim that he is board certified for his mother's plantain pie recipe, "Unique in the world." He holds an MFA in creative writing from Long Island University, JD and LLM from Indiana University, and BLL from his native country and sometimes thinks that making the plantain pie is more important than all of that. Awarded the Edward Albee Foundation residence and the New York Mills Art Cultural Center residence, his email address is Jhon.attorney@gmail.com.

Haunting Dreams

Millie Kerr

For the third night in a row, I awake in a tangled mess of sweat and sheets, my sea-blue bedding clutching me like Saran Wrap. Flashes of the farm, which my grandparents once owned on the outskirts of San Antonio, have returned like lightning bolts, even though its rolling hills are now home to McMansions and other superfluous, man-made things.

Bolting upright, I fumble for the lamp and slide open the bottom drawer of the bedside table. Inside are fragrance and beauty samples, dried up bottles of nail polish, and the Klonopin my doctor begrudgingly prescribed. I twist open the plastic bottle, preparing to swallow an oval yellow pill, grab my leatherbound diary and scribble what I recall from the dream:

I'm sitting at the green piano like a dutiful pupil while my parents' laughter reverberates up the stairs and into the sunroom. Outside, our dog Lucy is barking, while black and white kittens nap beneath the wooden deck stairs. Suddenly, my brother calls, "Millie!"

I rise, heave the screen door open and run towards the maypole. We run in circles before tumbling to the ground, then grab our bikes and begin pedaling down the gravel drive. Crickets buzz in the underbrush; cows moo in the distance. I pedal faster, my brother's striped T-shirt dipping beneath the hill's crescent, but I can't catch up. As I approach the final cattle guard, the white façade of the farmhouse fades into a grainy apparition.

The following morning I awake with a crystal clear image of our farm still intact. There's a brief period of ecstasy—a moment when I think my dream is real—before I recalibrate to reality.

I remember the first time my brain tricked me in this way. I was six years old. I woke up, bounded out of bed and dug through my jewellery box looking for a charm bracelet my parents had given me. I couldn't find it, when it suddenly occurred to me there was no occasion to warrant a present. It was only then that I realized the bracelet had been a figment of my nighttime imagination.

The recurring dreams of our family farm are different yet the same as the bracelet dream. I'm old enough to distinguish memory from fantasy, but unlike the charm bracelet my parents never bought me, the family farm still exists.

Of course, not the way it used to.

As my grandparents got older, they increasingly worried about their financial situation and began selling pieces of the farm to San Antonio real estate developers eager to capitalize on the city's growth. First went the peripheral pastures. In their place sprang early residences of an elite suburban community called The Dominion.

My brother and I rode our bikes to our farm's edges, quietly peering into square, neatly trimmed backyards. We built fires on "picnic hill"—our farm's lone high point—and wondered whether the cedar-drenched smoke would reach those homes insistently encroaching upon our wild playground.

Years later, after my grandparents sold all but seventy acres, we stopped climbing up picnic hill, which had become nothing more than a suburban look-out point. My grandparents passed away, leaving the farm's future in the hands of my mother and her brothers, all of whom felt the development's aggressive growth stripped our property of any real value.

I was eighteen—on the verge of adulthood but not yet taken seriously by my parents' generation. They dismissed my proposal to convert the farmhouse into a restaurant or bed-and-breakfast.

The farm was sold after the extended family convened on its lush lawn for one last Easter brunch. I must have wandered its quirky hallways and walked to the base of picnic hill and spun on the maypole one last time, but I don't remember; it happened so fast.

My dreams—or are they nightmares?—began soon after the property sold. At first the dreams took the form of time travel: I was a kid again, back on the farm as it used to be. My subconscious was validating my desire to turn back time and undo the mistakes made by my grandparents and their children. During waking hours, I began imagining the farmhouse untouched, gathering dust, still housing years of family memories.

Several years into college, while visiting my parents in San Antonio, Mom and I went to shop at a newly constructed mall west of The Dominion near the old farm. I couldn't believe how much the city had changed in my years away. The formerly remote area had morphed into one of San Antonio's wealthiest districts, and there I was participating as a consumer on the very land I'd hoped to protect.

After a few laps around the shopping center, I begged Mom to drive through The Dominion's gates. She gave me a pleading look. "Let bygones be bygones," it seemed to say, but I've always picked at scabs.

We turned onto the main drive and navigated past the golf course on the right and the pool and spa on the left. In the years that we shared our farm with the residential club, we accessed our property from a hidden gravel road near the entrance. To my great surprise, it was still there—still unmarked.

My mom and I exchanged hopeful glances and slowly drove down it.

When we reached the place where our entry gate used to be, we came upon a newly-built stucco structure flanked by parking spaces and half-finished fences demarcating the site from what lay beyond. We parked towards the back, made sure no one was watching and inched through a gap in the fence. Now moving fast, we bounded through a dense patch of cedar trees until we arrived at the circular road that led to the old farmhouse. The area was untouched, the road clear. Further up the slope, we finally reached the cattle guard leading to the house, the one I'd cycled over countless times in my dreams, and there stood the house—fully intact.

If I'd been alone, I would have taken this for another dream, but with Mom in tow, her face as stoically optimistic as mine, I knew the house had to be real.

The house was locked, and we were reduced to walking around the outside, peering through dusty windowpanes for a dim glimpse of the rooms, but I tugged on one knob after the other, ever hopeful. Finally, our persistence paid off. We cracked open a sticky wooden door and entered the old sunroom, at first with the trepidation of trespassers, but growing bolder as we went from room to room. Here was the master bedroom and parlour to the left, where I used to sit with my grandparents on chilly, winter days. Above it—flanking the master bathroom— was the large closet where my parents placed my crib during the first year of my life, which was spent at the farm. Down another corridor was the small bedroom where my Dad sang me to sleep when I graduated from the crib, and the "choo-choo room"—named for its wallpaper—where my brother, cousins, and I crammed into twin beds one New Year's Eve, all waking with the chicken pox the following morning.

Farther on were the rickety wooden stairs leading to a strange, two-story bedroom, whose screened porch always housed hornets' nests. Below it was the old dining room, its white walls no longer adorned with the antlers of deer my grandfather shot on weekend hunts.

We continued walking in silence and reached out to touch the painted dining room wall that depicted birds and their nests in delicate, interwoven branches. The paint was still there, but our long, oak table was long gone.

Upstairs, in the bathroom, I could practically smell the scent of Dove soap, a farm staple. Then we entered another sunroom, where I stared at the site of the old green piano. Closing my eyes, I stood for a long moment imagining my younger self practicing on its bench, but the visual slipped through my fingers when my mother touched me on the arm and said softly, "We should go."

We slowly walked back to the opened door, gently closed it behind us, and made our way to the car, knowing we'd probably never see this special, family place again.

It's been ten years since I trespassed into my past. I've considered returning more times than I can count, but I can't risk losing the farm once more.

My nightmares are another story. They're frequent—unrelentingly delving into a chapter I should close—but the form has changed: I now dream of the farm's future rather than its past.

I'm in the house—it always starts this way—entertaining friends and family. The farm's vibe is different now. Sofas, walls and light fixtures have been updated to a modern design. We've expanded the structure—added small guesthouses where picnic hill used to be. In a narrow corridor behind the kitchen, where we formerly tacked print photos to the walls, are framed portraits of our modern-day family.

I step closer, studying them: What milestones have we celebrated here? Did I marry on the green lawn like my parents decades ago? Has Mom continued her mother's tradition of plotting epic Easter egg hunts for her grandchildren?

The photos begin to fade.

I inch closer.

Then—darkness.

Millie Kerr is a freelance writer, wildlife conservation advocate and former attorney. Although she predominantly writes about travel and wildlife conservation, she is a generalist with a diverse portfolio; her work ranges from satirical essays to reported pieces on environmental and cultural developments. She's written for a broad range of digital and print outlets, among them The Atlantic, The Economist, National Geographic Traveler, The New York Times, *and* The Wall Street Journal. *A Texas native, Millie has spent most of her adult life on the East Coast and in England. She's currently studying for a master's of philosophy in wildlife conservation leadership in England at the University of Cambridge. Her website is milliekerr.com.*

... OF WHO YOU THOUGHT YOU WERE OR MIGHT BE

The Wooden Spoon

Mina Samuels

When I was growing up, there was always an antique pottery jar filled with wooden spoons sitting on the counter
beside the stove. When at last I owned my own kitchen and my
own French country tiled counter, I searched for months, comb-
ing antique shops, for just the right pottery jar for my wooden
spoons. Nothing new would do. Nothing from Pottery Barn or
Williams Sonoma could ever fill my need for a used, grey or
dark brown, preferably with a chipped rim, kitchen spoon jar,
the kind a person in "olden times" might have stored flour in, or
received cream deliveries in. I finally found what I was looking
for, and it makes me happy each time I take out a spoon to stir
something I'm cooking. And yet, the wooden spoon, so gentle
for stirring, the best way to ensure no harm will come to your
non-stick pans, has another, darker connotation for me.

"Hello?" I said.

There was a pause, a deep breath. My brother R does that
when he's starting calls, so I know who it is before he even
speaks. He always says, "Y-ello," cheerfully, the deep bass of his
voice booming over the airwaves. The voice instinctively makes
you feel safe, like you want to confide in him. When he was a
teenager, a girl who dialed the wrong number was so taken by
his voice that she talked with him for more than two hours. This
time he didn't say y-ello; he paused and breathed deeply.

"Yeah, hi, Mina," he said at last, as if surprised I answered. He's right, too; I don't answer the phone much. Back then, I preferred to wait and hear who it was on the answering machine. I had answered the phone in the living room, so I stretched out on the couch, knowing my brother liked to talk for a while when he called.

"How are you?" I asked. How often do we say that and not really mean for the person to say anything substantive in response? I'm fine, is what we expect to hear. My grammar-stickler mother always says, "I'm well," because saying, "I'm fine," means something different from what we all think. It means fine, as in silk or wine, as in a person who is good, a fine person. I have always resisted this grammatical admonishment, which, like so much else my mother says to me, seems aimed at making me feel unworthy. I say I'm fine when asked, and my brother usually responds that he's fine, too. Not this time.

"I'm," R started. Then he began to cry. It gave me a prickly feeling. Had I missed something important? I could hear myself choking up. It's hard to be with someone crying and not want to cry, even on the phone.

"What's wrong?" I asked. Although he's a man who cries, he had never called me before and started crying, except maybe for joy, when his children were born. He wasn't even making a pretense of having a normal conversation. I felt sick. "Is it the kids? Did something happen to one of the kids?" I thought about my two nephews and my niece. I felt cold. R stammered out a no. And yes, his wife was fine. He was well, too. I stopped feeling sick. Those were the things I was most worried about, the life and limb things. It meant I could stop imagining some insidious cancer was eating away at someone in my family. I thought I could guess what was bothering him. It wasn't the first time he'd called me for a loan. This was something I could fix for him, at least in the short term. I owed it to him. My penance for the fact that talking to him, seeing him, made me tired and tense, all that history crushing us.

"It's Mum and Dad," he finally said. The words burbled between sobs. The prickly feeling started up again. I could feel it even in my shins. I hadn't thought of my parents. R lived in our hometown, a somewhat sleepy place just far enough away from Toronto not to be a suburb. I'd left at eighteen and never once in the sixteen years since had it ever crossed my mind to move back. I had options, choices in a way R never did.

"What? What happened?" I was imagining calling the airlines to get a ticket, canceling my plans for the next few days, or would it be weeks? Would I need to take care of them? What an irony.

"Why are they like that?" My brother's voice got shrill.

So my parents weren't injured or dead. It was a fight. He and my parents had always had friction; I had always had it, too. Only our much younger brother N had escaped my parents' displeasure.

N was six years younger than I, four younger than R. R is adopted. My mother wanted four children. My father thought two might be quite enough, thank you very much. After I was born, although not because of it as far as I know, my mother suffered from severe thyroid problems. She was told she would never be able to have more children. When I was two my parents adopted R. My parents are nothing if not planners; children were ideally spaced two years apart. R and I now filled my father's quota. Then, quite by surprise, my mother got pregnant four years later. Then we were three, or a family of five, in any event, at least one too many, however you counted. It wasn't our youngest brother who was the extraneous one. R and I alternated as the inconvenient extra. Although the age difference was not enormous, it was enough so that we had a different childhood from N.

I was an unwanted surprise, a birth control failure. My young parents were unprepared emotionally and financially for my arrival. I ruined their early plans—my father's budding diplomatic career, my mother having any career at all. R, the adopted one, ought to have been more wanted. After all, it took a year of effort, patience and being under an outsider's microscope to "get" him. Yet, they were in the end no more prepared for him, than they had been for me. I think they miscalculated the effect of a second child. It isn't half again as much work. It's more than double the work.

Then N came along; a surprise, like me, but a happy one this time. From the moment he was born, N was the favorite. R and I weren't even jealous of him. It was almost as if we understood why my parents would like our baby brother better. N was more like them—high achieving, uncomplicated and more traditional. He is the quintessential what-you-see-is-what-you-get person. He lives more on the surface of life, the way my parents do, not prone to introspection or self-doubt. And he was the youngest, predisposed to be spoiled and best-loved.

When we were grown, N and I became closer. We were much more alike than R and I had ever been, despite the differences in our childhood. We had innate (biological?) similarities—the kinds of books we read, the trips we took (sometimes together, driving madly all over South Africa, stopping for punishing hikes along the way), the sports we did. Yet there was always a gap in our sibling friendship. We did not share childhood memories, as R and I did.

"What happened?" I again said into the phone.

I could hear R gulp for air. My heart twisted. R is a kind, gentle, unexceptional middle child. He has always had legions of friends, because he could truly sympathize, but he wasn't good enough for my parents. He was slow to learn. I was smart as a whip but rebellious. I hated traditions that demanded girls do such and such, yet I doubted myself at every step, and my parents nourished those doubts with their constant disapproval. I was that lethal combination of wayward girl and the eldest. My intellect didn't make up for all the other things my parents found appalling in my behavior—the friends I chose, the clothes I wore, their rules I hated. I didn't benefit from the sunshine of their admiration any more than R. But my being smart did cause R to suffer, or at least I have always seen it that way. If I hadn't been smart, then he wouldn't have seemed behind in comparison.

"I don't know," he managed to get out. "I was there and Dad, and . . . I was telling him about C (his oldest son). And Dad said maybe C could use a tutor, because he was falling behind in his reading, and did I really want that to happen. And of course he had to say that I was in no position to help on that score, but I must know, given my own situation, what a problem it could be. That's what Dad said. Like I'm some kind of . . . I don't know what. And how can he say that? It's like he . . . Dad . . . C's my son. I'm a good father. I can help him. I didn't ask for advice. You know that way he has, like he knows just what everyone should do. And I got upset."

I let my brother talk. I didn't understand everything he was saying. His words were garbled, and he wasn't finishing his sentences. Even when he was not upset his sentences were often strangely ordered, hard to follow. I blamed my parents. Language was torture for my brother, while for me it is the tool of my work and a constant source of joy.

"C is fine. He's not stupid," R said.

I heard the words he did not say: I'm not stupid.

"Dad and Mum think they can . . . It's like I can see what they aren't saying. They think they tried to help me. They think they did nothing wrong. They think it was my fault. So I exploded." My brother laughed when he said this last, not a fun ha-ha laugh, but the kind so bitter it made my mouth pucker. "I said, 'Why can't you just say you're sorry to me?' They just looked at me in that way they have. Like, like they didn't even know what I was saying. Then Mum left. She just walked out of the room like I wasn't even there. And Dad was doing that thing. You know. He was pretending like he was all calm. And he said, 'Look, your Mum and I have left the past behind. We've moved on.' "

My brother sounded like he was hyperventilating. I was hip-deep in guilt. Why him? Why not me? Even when we were little, I could protect myself better. I should have protected him better, too. Worse. Maybe I didn't protect him at all.

"I'm sorry," I said, not knowing if I was saying it for my parents, or for the fight, or for myself. "You know how they are. They don't look inside. They are constitutionally unable to look at the past as something that requires examination. For them, the past is history in a book, or in Dad's photos, never something that has anything to do with today." I stopped. I didn't want to be an apologist for my parents. Worse still, I didn't want to be an apologist for me.

Their relationship to the past is something I don't understand about my parents. My father is not the type to traffic in regrets, at least not so we'd know. My mother is full of regrets, I think, but she has never known what to do with them, coming as she does from a Protestant ethic, a household where emotion was best kept to oneself, and the "why" of things was unimportant. Neither has ever been to a therapist, to my knowledge. Why wallow in the past, when the present is here to be lived now?

That's the philosophy that's been their guide. The psychological "why" of things seems not to hold their interest. As a consequence, they are loath to look back. Perhaps they fear Lot's wife's fate if they look too closely at the past.

I, on the other hand, perhaps to compensate for their propensities, look back often at things in my childhood, trying to understand why I am who I am. And then there's trying to understand R, our shared past. As we talked on the phone that day, the waves of guilt threatened to drown me.

"Do you remember the wooden spoon?" my brother asked suddenly.

My body went rigid.

"The wooden spoon?" R repeated. "I remember how you..."

"I remember some," I said and started crying. I excused myself and went into the bathroom to get some paper to blow my nose. I looked at myself in the mirror. I wanted to see how ugly I was. My face was red and wet and blotchy. I didn't want my brother to hear me crying. I remembered the wooden spoon, but I didn't remember enough. All my life since we were children, I had been haunted by this hole in my memory.

When R was a child he couldn't learn to read. I learned to read as early as a child can. By the time I was four, I was reading books, not Proust to be sure, but I could make out words, discern the patterns of sentences and understand the arc of a story. My parents simply couldn't understand why R couldn't do the same. They thought they could beat language into him through the palms of his hands.

I didn't remember if it was every day or just most days after school, but I do remember my mother or father sitting my brother down at the dining room table, putting pages filled with words in front of him and standing on the other side of the table as R struggled to make sense of the jumble of letters on the page. When he didn't get a word right, which happened every session, my mother, or my father—whichever was playing tutor at the time—would tell my brother to hold out his hands, and when he complied, crack him over the palms with the wooden spoon. Once, as the spoon landed on his hand, it broke. The bowl of the spoon flew out of my brother's palm and onto the floor. My mother was left holding the splintered handle.

I remembered the wooden spoon. Oh yes. I remembered it. And now, I began to remember the hunted look that came over my brother's face as he tried to sound out the word CAT, or BOY. C-C-CA . . . The word would stumble out in pieces, as if it had more than one syllable. Often he would say TAC. He would stutter when he was trying to get a word out. I remember the sound of wood against flesh, and the way his palms, which were normally pale, would have red, spoon-shaped marks on them. I remember that he cried, that my mother cried, too, when she held the spoon, but she didn't stop.

Why? What possessed my parents to do such a thing? Anger that we their children, or at least R and I, had robbed them of their early adult dreams? Was it their youth? My parents had not yet learned to love each other properly, how could they love us? Perhaps this violence was what they knew. My mother had grown up in farm country and attended a village school where corporal punishment was the norm. Her mother was made of iron, but I never knew if it extended to her fists. As for my father, I only knew his parents as my gentle, doting grandparents. He always described his parents in idyllic terms—never fighting, never raising their voices. So much the opposite of how my parents were together. I don't know where the violence came from. To me it was a natural part of growing up. But I have never wanted to hit a child. Perhaps that's one of the reasons I chose not to have them. When I was finally able to tell this story, it was a surprise to me to learn others were shocked by my parents' ferocity.

I went back to the living room and sat on the couch. My brother was crying into the phone. I was crying, too, silently. He couldn't get out the words he was trying to say. I was more terrified to hear them than I had ever been of hearing anything.

Oh yes, I remembered the wooden spoon. I was there. What I had never been able to remember was my part in it. Where was I in all of this? My brother N wasn't. He was too young and had no memory of any of this. And because he had no memory of these things, he hardly believed they happened. Like my parents, he believed things are best left in the past. I was like my parents, too, because I had left them in the past, when I might have confronted them, the way my brother had. But it was his fight; at least that was what I had told myself.

The real reason was that I didn't remember the bits with me in them, my role, and my, my what—my complicity? I saw these things with my own eyes. I heard the sounds. I felt the tension while we waited to see if R was going to get the word out. In my memory, I am looking at my brother from behind my parents. But what was I doing there? Not trying to stop it, I remembered that much. But then, how could I have? I was raised in an environment where children were only to speak when spoken to. I was not exempt from their corporal punishment. My parents used the wooden spoon on me, too. It usually befell me for reasons to do with my temper or my mouth. And it happened far less often. Still, it would have been enough to keep any thoughts of interfering far back in my mind. So what was I doing there?

I know that children are cruel. Everyone says it. It must be true. I remember a neighbor's son once executing a cat by hanging it from our backyard tree. Was I cruel to my brother? I wasn't always kind to him growing up. Frustrated by his slowness, I finished his sentences for him and bossed him around; I thought I was so much smarter. I sometimes hid from him when he wanted to play with me. But what I couldn't remember was something bigger. And because I couldn't remember, I had always assumed the worst. Did I taunt my brother as he struggled with words? Did I laugh in his face as the wooden spoon came crashing down? There, I've said it. Was I a party to my parents' beatings? All my life I have feared this was so.

As adults, when my brother spoke to me about "the troubles" in his relationship with my parents, I couldn't look him in the eye. If we were talking on the phone, I would breathe more shallowly, as if that way he might forget about my role in this painful part of his past.

"I remember you," my brother said. I crushed the phone to my ear. My hand and the phone covered in sweat. My ear throbbed.

Somewhere around when R was twelve or thirteen, we learned he had dyslexia. All the wooden spoons in the world would never have put back together the fractured message my brother's brain received when he looked at a page filled with letters. But it was too late. The damage was done. He hated reading. He hated words and language and pages and books. They were his mortal enemies.

"I remember you," my brother again said.

I thought I was going to throw up. Here at last was the accusation I had always feared. I remember you stood there and laughed at me. You made faces. You mouthed the word "stupid." And most damning of all, You did not protect me.

I waited for him to say those things. Unlike my parents, I would not be able to leave the past behind. I was the bad sister I had always feared I was, ugly inside and out.

"I remember you," my brother said again.

I lay on the couch, looked up at the curve where the wall arched into the ceiling and thought, I was my brother's keeper, and I had failed him. I closed my eyes and waited for him to continue. If I asked forgiveness, would he grant it? Would I deserve it?

"I remember you," my brother began again. "You used to stand there, hiding behind Mum or Dad, trying to mouth the correct word, so they wouldn't hit me with the spoon."

I rolled onto my side, my face pressed against the back of the couch, and curled into a ball. My mind raced like a computer trying to de-frag my whole past all at once. I had spent my life since childhood certain I had let him down, feeling guilty for not trying to protect him.

In time I was able to let go of my guilt toward my brother. Not all of it, of course. I am still torn by the feeling that I have been lucky, where he has not, that my life is easy in comparison to his. But I know now that whatever the sources of our differences, it's not my fault; at least, not in the way I used to think it was.

Mina Samuels is a full-time writer, editor and performance artist. In addition to many ghostwriting projects, her previous books include, Run Like a Girl: How Strong Women Make Happy Lives; a novel titled, The Queen of Cups; and The Think Big Manifesto, co-authored with Michael Port. She has written and performed two one-woman plays: "Do You Know Me?" and "Hazards." Samuels's website is www.minasamuels.com.

The Battle Within

Marione Malimba Namukuta

Some things we are always eager to let go of, like hair dye that has overstayed its time. More difficult to turn our backs on—a culture we despise but were born into, a marriage we know has been over for a while, a loved one who has battled an illness long after there is no hope for revitalization. Even after we have come to the decision to let go, the process is never easy.

In 1999, I lost my younger sister to pneumonia. Then at Christmas that same year, my mother died after suffering a chronic illness for two years. Having lost the last of my parents—my father died when I was six—I left behind my home, dignity and the familiar as I began to navigate the world from a new point of view. For four years, my two remaining sisters and I were separated, each tossed from one relative to another, all poor with little or nothing to give. Those who had the means to take care of us did not want to. Eventually, our maternal auntie, who drank a lot and was verbally abusive, took us in but made clear it was only for charity; she had no obligation towards any of us. We were to expect nothing from her and earn our stay at her house.

Being an orphan at an early age of thirteen is hard. Knowing you are not wanted is harder. That period of my life seemed to last for a very long time.

When you have been devastated by watching your dreams slip away, endured the betrayal of friends and family and lost

loved ones, you make a decision to either get stuck in disillusion-
ment or soar above your circumstances, for this will fundamen-
tally affect who you are and who you will become.

I chose to leave behind the down-trodden and helpless
orphan girl; I was determined never to return to that state of
being. I awakened to the need to take care of myself and be
self-sufficient materially. And, I have achieved this: I am hard-
working, responsible and strong-minded, but even so, life continues to bring with it a lot of uncertainty. Abandoning a label,
which the circumstances of life have dictated and placed on you,
is one of toughest things I have done and still have to do. I have
to keep looking over my shoulder to make sure the little girl is
not catching up with me. One would expect that after you have
been disappointed over and over again, letting go would spiral
into an automatic response, like a well-mastered art, instead of
every challenge bringing with it a new and unexpected conflict.

Each time as I let go of the challenges my life presents—
regardless of what they are—I face these questions: Could I
simply be running but in the wrong direction? Could there have
been part of the girl I gave up who might have been worth sav-
ing—like the sweet, wide-eyed, innocent and trusting girl I used
to be? Am I really capable of letting go or too bound by fear? Is
that perhaps who I am—a person who is incapable of letting go?
I question and scrutinize, hoping to find an explanation or find
out who is responsible for this particular fate, answers which are
not easily found.

Something I thought would take a day or two instead is taking a lifetime. Will I ever be free completely? I thought letting
go was how we made room for new opportunities or allowed
ourselves to grow and blossom to our full potential, but clearly, I
am nowhere close to that end. On occasion I have contemplated

packing up and moving to a new place, city or country, or losing myself in drinking and sex, in the hope I will end up oblivious to painful reality.

Lately, it seems as though the more I try to let go, the more my life slips away from me, and what is left is the burden of watching it, as if I am removed and on a pedestal. Every choice, every mistake, every failure stares me in the eye, and makes me afraid I am going back to being the thirteen-year-old, helpless orphan girl.

Three years ago I found myself reliving a pain I thought I had successfully buried at age six. When my dad died, for years I told myself he had gone on one of his trips. Over the years I missed him, but I never really grieved him, because in my mind he was never really dead. It took a man I thought I would spend the rest of my life with to break my heart for it to really hit home that my father had died. I had to be in a truly vulnerable state and without seeing what was about to happen, just like my father's death. Suddenly, there I was in the quietness of my bedroom, heartbroken and six years old again. While my pain was justifiable, it was odd; it took me away from the present heartache to a totally different place and time, when I was losing my daddy over again. I wonder what this says about me.

There have been times in my life when letting go was something that gradually unfolded without much pondering. It was not deliberate like it is now. It is in my most deliberate effort to let go, that I find myself most conflicted.

The hardest part of letting go comes from the conflict that lingers as I tentatively explore how and whether to let go. After all, when is it truly okay to abandon your beliefs, give up on a loved one or dissolve your marriage to find a new you and a new dream? If successful at letting go, will we not seem fickle?

Letting go too soon may be perceived as caring less or never having cared at all.

Persistence is painted as an admirable quality; in fact most success stories are punctuated with it. Can persistence also be a hindrance or clutter that suffocates progression? How and when is it truly right to let go, and when and what should we hold on to?

Marione Malimba Namukuta, twenty-eight, single, lives in Kampala, Uganda. She works as a researcher specializing increasingly in the fields of population and health, monitoring and evaluating both national and international projects.

Namukuta has keen interests in other cultures, a command of several languages and loves to write and travel. She writes children's short stories and is a member of the Uganda Children's Writers and Illustrators Association. Her e-mail address is marionmalimba@gmail.com.

A Prayer for Lost Things

Carolyn Wolf-Gould

My afternoon at the clinic was busy, as usual. I needed a nap by the time Mr. Midge arrived for his appointment. He looked bad. He always looks bad. He rolls his own butts and smokes with no filter. I don't know if the stains on his hands, beard and face would be lighter with store-bought smokes but suspect so. He smelled of soggy bonfire, like creosote caked inside a wood stove. He huffed himself into the exam room and collapsed into a chair, feet splayed. His friend Delilah walked in behind him.

"How are you, Axel?" I pressed his hand and sat on my stool. My exam rooms are small and windowless. They need a paint job—still the same industrial yellow they've been for twenty-five years, only now with more smudges. The exam tables have tan, vinyl tops, dented drawers.

"Not so good, Doc, if you really want to know."

Delilah seated herself in the extra chair. She's much younger than me—fresh and pretty—and she always comes in with Axel. It's unclear just how the two of them are related. Axel once called her his girlfriend, but I can't believe that. He is primeval; she, a spring bud. But something binds them together—something complex—and it puzzles me. Delilah wore a low-cut blouse that revealed shapely cleavage. Those breasts were constructed from silicone. Delilah developed breast cancer two years ago—bad cancer, both sides—and had a double mastectomy. She left more than

235

her breast tissue behind after that surgery. She'd quit her waitressing job at the Busy Bee Diner, as well as a surly man named Roy, whom I once treated for piles. Delilah had stopped drinking, too, and lost her flattened look. She used to resemble a violet that had been pressed between the pages of a dictionary, but she'd filled out and grown handfuls of love on her hips. She'd taken pains with her eyes that morning; her lids glowed with powder; her mouth glistened, a round rosy plum. She nodded hello. I nodded back.

"What's the matter, Axel?" I wheeled my stool to face him. My knee braces bulged under my slacks; my arthritis had flared.

"I'm tired all the time. I can't breathe. I can't do what I used to be able to do, and it's killing me."

"Are you worse than last time?"

"He's worse." Delilah set her shiny red purse on the exam table and rummaged inside until she found Axel's puffer.

"It's true." Axel held the puffer to his lips and inhaled twice. "She sees it and tries to help. She's not drinking either. She really sees."

"What's worse?" I put my hand on Axel's wrist, felt his pulse.

"It's because of the tractor." Delilah took back the puffer and stowed it in her purse. "He won't tell you about that. But it's driving him batty."

"The tractor is making you worse?" I concentrated on Axel's appearance. His face was pasty but no different from usual, and I'd checked his blood count numerous times. He was overweight, but that wasn't new either. His insulin was making that worse.

"I am having it repaired. It's taking a long time," Axel said.

"In the living room." Delilah flipped her lips to a pout. "The fixer guy said cold weather was coming, so he took the whole thing apart and spread it all around the living room. Big tractor pieces are everywhere, and we live in a small trailer."

"It's an old tractor. You might even say it's antique. I want it done right," Axel explained.

"How long is it taking?" I asked.

Axel nibbled a hangnail. "He started in April. It's still not done. It's all in pieces."

Delilah shook her head. "There's nowhere to sit. If you try to sit, there's always something metal to move, but we're afraid to mix up the parts."

"I see." I glanced at the calendar on the wall. It had been warm all week, but it was already mid-September. Just how big was this tractor? I wondered. I pictured a green John Deere with yellow hubcaps, a front loader. I imagined their TV perched on top of the tractor's bucket, chairs squeezed around in a room hazy with smoke.

The exam room filled with the tingling of chimes. Delilah pulled her cell phone from her cleavage and hit the silence button. "It's making him cranky. He has nowhere to sit and gets mad."

"How much are you smoking?" I knew for sure that a tractor had not caused Axel's health problems. If I hosed down his overalls and wrung them over a pot, I'd wind up with inches of thick, brown tobacco resin.

"Too much. More now, because of this. I can't do anything to make him move faster, so I just smoke."

Delilah made a face. "You should see this guy—the repair man. He sits on the couch with a part and his sandpaper, watching TV. He rubs a little, then stops, rubs a little, stops." She made sanding motions against the side of her cell phone. "He even falls asleep there in front of the TV."

Axel nodded. "He sleeps on the couch every night. Falls asleep sanding."

I looked in Axel's ear with my otoscope. "What's the matter with him? Why is it taking so long?"

Delilah pulled up her knees as I scooted to Axel's opposite side. "People say he's not right in the head. I think he's crazy. He doesn't say much, and what he does say doesn't make a whole lot of sense. But Axel had to hire him, and now we're stuck."

Axel took in a deep breath and exhaled while I listened to his back with my stethoscope. "If he'd put his mind to it, he could finish in two weeks. But he dawdles."

I thumped over Axel's kidneys. "Does he have somewhere else to sleep? Maybe he likes living with you."

"Yeah." Axel stretched his neck as I palpated his thyroid. "He has his own place. But he's always asleep on our couch in the morning. It exhausts me seeing him there all the time. I can't hardly sleep from the stress."

I chewed the inside of my cheek. This was not an illness I'd learned about in medical school. "Well, your sugar is off the chart. Maybe that's what's making you tired," I tried.

"No. It's been high forever. This is different."

"We know you have emphysema. How about trying some different puffers? And get rid of the smokes?" I listened to the front of his chest with my stethoscope.

"Nah. I don't want to quit. Don't want any more meds."

I moved my scope to the skin over his heart. Same old erratic beat. I wasn't sure why I bothered to listen. The slosh of blood through shredded valves was not reassuring and offered no hint of returning vigor. He'd been fending off my healthy suggestions for years.

"How about that sleep study? Last visit Delilah said you snore like a broken muffler. It could be sleep apnea troubling your rest."

"Nah. I could never sleep in some lab with wires attached to me."

I was out of suggestions. I couldn't fix Axel, couldn't mend a single one of his problems.

"It's the tractor." Delilah stood and picked up her coat. Apparently, she knew a stalemate when she saw one and was aware of the limits I had with my care. Axel stood up, too, and I followed.

"Well, I guess I'll see you in three months then?" I shook Axel's hand. Sometimes a handshake is all I can offer. It wasn't clear to me why he should come back in three months. Why would he bother?

Axel took the clipboard I handed him. "Thank you, Doc. I'll work on my blood sugars, I promise. I'll cut down on the smokes. See you next time."

I watched the two of them walk down the hall toward check-out. Axel wheezed, and Delilah tap-tapped along by his side in her pumps.

My next patient was Beryl Humphrey. Beryl has a million phobias, but the worst one is soap. Water, too. She's allergic to bathing. After she leaves the office, my nurse scours the exam table with bleach and sprays wintergreen scent in the air. Beryl refuses to have blood work or change her medications. She's had diabetes for years and declines any treatment. Recently she's developed renal carcinoma, which has probably spread. She doesn't let me explore that problem either, refuses the CAT scans and referrals to oncology. She shows up once a month, pees in a cup and asks, "Am I still pissing blood?" I wait for the cancer to show up somewhere else. It's only a matter of time.

"Something's really wrong today," Beryl clutched my hand and held it too long. "It feels like there's a jelly bean squashed under the skin on my ass. It hurts to sit."

Beryl's niece Gloria had brought her in. Gloria has an unusually small head. She crouched on the chair next to Beryl's wheelchair, wearing a T-shirt with BIODEGRADABLE printed in green block letters across the front. She never says much. Beryl isn't supposed to drive anymore, not since she lost most of her sight from macular degeneration, though I'm pretty sure she still does. She'd brought me a form to fill out last spring, for permission to hunt from her car.

"What! Don't tell me you're hunting," I'd said. "You're practically blind. How can you aim?"

"I bring Gloria. When she sees a turkey, she tells me which way to point my shotgun."

Gloria grinned at the sink and ducked her head. I had refused to sign that form.

"Can you stand up, Beryl? I'll take a look."

Beryl gripped the sides of her chair and hefted her bulk out of the seat. She smelled like urine, like sweat, like a house with old dogs. She pulled down her crusty sweat pants and stuck her filthy butt in the air. I suspected that butt hadn't been cleaned since Beryl was a child. She was over sixty now. An abscess bloomed on the right side of her anus, petals rich, red and hot. I touched it, and Beryl winced. I saw pus under the skin.

"You need a surgeon. This infection could track into the rectum. It's a bad one. It needs to be drained."

"You do it." Beryl spoke over her shoulder. "I don't see other doctors. You know that."

I do know that. Beryl has an insane terror of all doctors who aren't me. I palpated around and inside Beryl's rectum. Only dried feces there. No pus.

"It's up to you." I helped Beryl pull her sweatpants back up. "But you're not going to like me. You'll be telling your friends your doc gives you a pain in the ass."

Beryl blinked her warty eyelids. "I already tell them that. This won't be no different."

"I'll give it a try, Beryl. But there's no guarantee. You still may still need a surgeon after I finish."

"I know you can do it. You're my doctor." Beryl scooched her terrible body around on the exam table until she managed to balance on top of her spread abdomen. Gloria pulled down Beryl's pants again and stood next to Beryl's head. I gowned up and put on my gloves, then plunged my scalpel into the point of the abscess. Pus welled out onto the skin. Gloria stepped back. The room smelled like sewage.

Gloria plugged her nose with her fingers. "All that? How could all of that come out of there?"

I pushed on the skin around my incision to help the pus flow. There's nothing more satisfying than draining an abscess. All doctors know this, but don't say so because it's not nice. "This should do the trick, Beryl."

Beryl sighed. "I feel better already." But she yelped when I stuffed in the packing.

"You have to keep clean. I'd like you to soak in the tub twice a day," I said and taped a square bandage over the wound. Gloria looked at me and shook her head.

Beryl looked thoughtful. "How about I fill the lid of a garbage can with water? I could sit in there. I can't get in or out of the tub."

I tried to picture Beryl at home, sitting naked in her garbage can lid. I suspected her house was as filthy as her clothes. "That will have to do. Use hot water. If for some reason you miss your appointment tomorrow, you must pull the packing."

Beryl grabbed both of my hands and grinned. "I knew you could do it, Doc. You always fix me up good."

My last patient was Mercedes, a sixteen-year-old who came in with her mother. Mercedes had been adopted from Guatemala as an infant. She had a wide face, stocky curves, cinnamon skin and long black hair. She was physically healthy but in and out of the office every week with a myriad of complaints.

Mercedes leaned against the exam table and peered at me from a remote place behind her eyes. "I need a pre-op exam. I'm scheduled for breast reduction surgery next week."

"Why are you having breast reduction surgery?" I asked.

Mercedes folded her arms across the top of her baggy shirt. "I'm huge. My bra straps cut into my shoulders, and my back hurts all the time."

I looked at Mercedes's vital signs. Her weight was one hundred fifty-five pounds, height, five feet, four inches.

"How long have you felt your breasts were huge?" I thumbed through Mercedes's thick chart.

"Forever. Ever since I got them. They bounce all over when I run. At school they call me 'Turbo Tits.' It's embarrassing. I can't find bras that fit right."

"What's your bra size?"

Mercedes hunched her shoulders. "36 DD. They don't make bras that big."

"That's my size, too." I corrected my posture, stood straight. "And they certainly do make them that big. I bought one last month."

Mercedes's eyes dropped to my chest, then back up to my face. She was silent. I turned to Jaqueline, who perched in a chair. Jaqueline was fair and tall, almost gaunt and wore a cream cashmere sweater that accentuated her willowy torso. She's my patient, too. She's a marathon runner and has two biological daughters shaped just like her.

"What do you think about this?"

"It's Mercedes's decision. It's up to her," Jaqueline held up her hands. "I'll support whatever she does. I feel for her though.

I really do. I just took her bathing suit shopping, and nothing fit right. She bulged out of everything. It was awful." Jaqueline's breasts lifted the front of her sweater discreetly, like mangos. "She got huge boobs from the get go. It doesn't help that her sisters are twiggy. They're perfect. Mercedes got all the bad luck."

I stared at Jaqueline, unsure how to respond, then turned back to Mercedes. "The surgery causes permanent changes. It leaves scars on the breasts. It will make your nipples numb, and you may not be able to breast feed."

"I don't care about numbness or scars. Nobody sees my breasts anyways. And I'm not going to breast feed. That's disgusting."

"Are you sexually active?" I asked.

Mercedes blushed. I mentally kicked myself. I knew better than to ask such things in front of a parent.

"No. Who'd want a girlfriend who looks like me?"

"Lots of people. You have a beautiful body, and you might care about numbness and scars later. I'm not sure you can decide about breast feeding at your age," I said.

"I want the surgery. I hate my breasts. I don't care about any of that."

I turned to Jaqueline. "What about you? What do you think about scars and numbness and breast feeding for your daughter?"

Jaqueline shrugged. "I bottle fed all my babies. The numbness? She doesn't know what that's about."

I looked hard at Jaqueline, who turned her face to the floor. "It's up to her."

"Let me ask you something," said Mercedes. "You said you're the same size as me. Don't you ever think about getting a breast reduction?"

I had been a pert 32 C, until I started birth control pills in my thirties. Then I gained poundage, most of it into my cups. I wince when I look in the mirror or at photos from weddings.

"No," I lied. "I wouldn't want scars or numbness, and I breast fed my babies."

Mercedes stuck out her chin. "Oh, come on. Never?"

"Why fix something that isn't broken?" I avoided her eyes, paged through the chart. "You're healthy enough for surgery, but it's the wrong thing to do. You aren't old enough to decide how this procedure might affect you."

"Ohhh." Mercedes made an unhappy face at her mom. "But I'm already scheduled!"

"In the last two months, Mercedes has been seen in our office for headaches, stomach aches, chest pains, indigestion and cramps with her periods," I said to Jaqueline. "I worry about anxiety and depression. We need to focus on helping Mercedes learn to love her body the way it is."

Jaqueline's wrinkled her forehead. "Oh dear. This is a huge disappointment."

"Do you understand what I'm saying?" I asked her. "Breast reduction surgery doesn't cure angst."

"I know, but I just feel so sorry for her, having to deal with these enormous breasts. They weigh her down. I wouldn't want them either."

"You can't make a young woman love her body by cutting pieces of it off."

"You could say that about any cosmetic surgery. But people still do it," Jaqueline said.

I studied her. "You're right. But we are only talking about Mercedes."

Jaqueline shrugged again.

I handed Mercedes a gown. "Change into this, and I'll do your exam."

When I went back in the room, Mercedes slouched on the exam table in her gown. I asked her to drop the front so I could examine her breasts, which were round and full with dark nipples.

"You have beautiful breasts," I told her. "Stand up and look in the mirror on the door. You're just right."

Mercedes yanked the gown back over her chest. "No. I've seen them already. I don't want to look."

I listened to Mercedes's heart and lungs, checked her belly and the pulses in her feet. "You're healthy, but I won't approve this surgery. You're too young to decide."

Mercedes pouted, defiant. "I'm going to find a different doctor. One who will say it's okay. My mom said she'd help me."

I looked at Mom who appeared to be counting the floor tiles. "I'm sure you can find a doctor who will approve this. But I ask you to think first, Jacqueline. She can't proceed without your consent."

Neither of them spoke. Mercedes ran her nails over the paper on the exam table, and Mom packed up her purse. I said good-bye and left the room. I went into my office, closed the door and tried to lay my head on my desk, but there were too many charts with phone messages attached. My eyes ached as I sat in my chair, watching the lights on my telephone blink. I sighed, took the top chart off the pile, read the message and picked up the phone.

Hours later when I got home, I found the house empty. Chris had left me a note saying he'd taken the kids to baseball practice. Two small hamburgers congealed in a cast-iron fry pan next to a bowl of wilted broccoli. I spooned the food onto a plate and sat alone at the kitchen table. Kippy stood by the chair wagging her tail and looking expectantly at the burgers.

"Here, Kippy." I handed her one. She gulped it down, then looked at the other burger still on my plate.

When my cell phone rang, the caller ID said Bella. My heart flipped, and I cradled the phone to my ear.

"Hi, Aunt Carolyn! Glad I caught you home for once." Blaise's voice was deeper each time he called, but he still spoke with the same lilting inflections he'd had as a girl.

"Hi. I'm glad, too." I remembered seeing Bella for the first time after the midwife had laid her on Sophie's breast. She'd blinked at Sophie and sucked her own fist before she latched on. "Chris is off with the kids. I was just wishing for someone to talk to. How are you? How's everything going?" I asked.

"It's going fine. I changed the gender marker on my driver's license and social security card last week. Now they say male."

"Good for you." I lay my free hand on my shirt, over my breast.

"I know. I feel good, too. And I've saved enough to schedule my top surgery. I found a good doctor here in the city, a specialist in masculine chest reconstruction, which he'll do the same time as my mastectomy. I have a consultation this week."

"Oh?" I'd taken Bella shopping for training bras the summer she turned twelve and lived with us three months while her mom was in rehab. Bella refused to try them on; instead, she experimented at home with ace bandages and tight T-shirts for compression.

"I can't wait to get rid of these things. I want to teach yoga without bouncing, or getting squeezed by that frickin' binder. It hurts."

When Bella was fourteen, we jumped the fence one night to go skinny-dipping in the reservoir. I stood with my feet on the warm, sandy bottom and watched Bella leap from a downed tree into the water, her slim breasts etched with moonlight.

"Did you tell your mom yet?"

"No. She will freak. That's why I'm calling. I need some advice."

I pictured Sophie sitting alone at the Formica table in her studio apartment, sorting through the piles of mail-order catalogues and unpaid bills. She often didn't answer the phone.

"Are you sure about the surgery, Blaise? It will change everything."

"I *want* to change everything. I'm sure."

"What if you decide to have a child? You maybe still could, if you stopped the hormones for a while. It doesn't always shut everything down."

"I'm not having the kids. That's Cindy's job. I already told you that." I heard the edge to his voice, recalled how much it had pained him when he'd had to defend his position to Sophie. I fed the second burger to Kippy and brought the plate back to the sink, phone still to my ear.

"I know, Blaise. You're right. We have talked about this. It's just that I worry. Your breasts . . . . "

"For me, it's like having a birth defect—like a cleft lip. They don't belong. I want them gone."

I rubbed my left hand across the fullness of my own breasts. "I know. It's your body, Blaise, but it will be hard for your mom to understand. Do you want me to go with you when you talk to her?"

"Thanks, but it's okay. Cindy is coming. I love you, Auntie."

"Love you, too."

Kippy followed me to the kitchen and stood at attention, as she did when she wanted a walk. I scraped the cold broccoli into the compost pail and turned to the dog.

"You want to go to the park? My knees hurt, but I'll take you."

Kippy wagged her entire backside.

"Are you happy with your body, Kippy?" I scratched her head, then her back. Kippy flopped on the floor and turned belly up. I stroked the line of her doggy teats. Kippy had been spayed as a pup. She'd never had babies.

I tightened my knee braces around the outside of my pants, grabbed my book and the leash and walked Kippy down to the park by the school. I stood next to the creek in the spruce forest, where Kippy chased squirrels, and listened to the water coursing through rocks, trying to stop thinking, my mind buzzing like a chain saw.

I tied Kippy back on her leash and sat on the bench under a maple tree. A small cloud of gnats circled my head and a few landed near my eyes. I rubbed them away and opened my book. I had an hour to read before sunset. *Lorna Doone*. The book was ancient, yellowed pages, a red cover with gilt. I tried to make sense of the words on the page as the sun dipped behind the trees. My mother had read it to me as a child, while I leaned against her soft chest.

"May I pray for you?"

The bearded man had appeared suddenly. He seemed to be in his mid-twenties. He wore a grimy, loose tunic, but his eyes were clear. Too clear? Maybe even simple? It was hard to tell in the fading light. I'd have given him a diagnosis if we'd been in the office. People come into focus when they sit on exam tables. Here, there was too much grass, too many trees. His edges blurred into the green. For yanking me from my book, he deserved beheading, but I had a niggling thought—he could be Jesus. He looked like Jesus. It was that kind of day. What then? What if I said no?

"You want to pray for me?" I didn't scowl, slam my book shut, or jerk Kippy to standing.

"Why?"

"To ease your suffering." He nodded at the black braces wrapped around my knees. "I see you're afflicted."

In the past when upset, I would have gone for a run, but now my knees hurt. After telling so many patients they had arthritis,

I had developed it myself. My doctor looked sad when she said, "bone on bone" and rubbed her knuckles together. She hadn't prayed. She'd jabbed a long needle under my kneecap, which hadn't helped with the pain. It wasn't fair. I was too young to have arthritis, too active. I should be sprinting in loops around this playground, not sitting on a bench. I felt more afflicted in the heart but let the man think he knew where I hurt.

"You can pray for me," I said.

The man nodded and placed one hand on my head. The other hand rested by his side, and I saw that his nails were stained, the cuticles outlined in soot.

"Father, bless your tormented child. Heal her legs. You have restored the sight of the blind, the breath of the dying. Show us the miracle of your grace and take the suffering from this woman, your servant. Cure her lameness, allow her to cast aside her crutch and walk freely again. Amen."

He seemed to be done, but kept his hand on my head. I wiggled free and leaned to pat Kippy where she lay in the dirt panting, thirsty. "Thanks. But I don't have a crutch."

"I know, but that's how the prayer goes. The lame must cast away a crutch in order to walk free."

"Ah." I contemplated my braces, which were scratched and reeked of old sweat. I'd like to cast them away. But I'm a Unitarian. I don't believe in miracles.

"Do you know The Lord?" he asked.

"I do," I lied. This conversation was heading toward an argument I did not wish to have.

The man took off his backpack and sat beside me on the bench. "You're lucky, then. So lucky. I envy you, even with your terrible knees. I'm still searching. I have not found Him yet."

"Maybe you shouldn't be looking in playgrounds," I suggested.

He opened his backpack, took out an apple and offered it to me.

I shook my head.

"I'm afraid I don't have enough faith. Even here, I'm doubtful. I'm not sure that prayer did anything. I probably wasted your time," he said.

I creaked my right knee open and shut and winced. It was always stiff after sitting.

"I'm having a bad day." He bit into the apple. "I lost my job three months ago, and my electricity just got turned off. My mother uses a breathing machine at night, but now it won't work."

"I'm sorry. That sounds hard." I thought about Beryl sitting in the lid of her trashcan. I remembered how Axel wheezed with each breath.

"It's not the worst of it, either. I can't buy her heart tablets. She fills up, gets water on the lung when she doesn't take her Lasix, the fluid pill. But I'm out of cash." He threw his apple core into the woods, then pulled a plastic bottle out of his backpack, unscrewed the top and poured water into the lid and set it on the ground for Kippy, who lapped. "I can't keep a job. On account of how I can't finish whatever I start. I can't concentrate when I'm stressed. And work stresses me out."

We sat a while. I thought about everyone's problems and decided I'd keep my sore knees. A hornet spun around our heads, and the man batted it away. Finally, I reached into my purse and took out a twenty. "This won't solve your troubles, but you can get some Lasix for your mom. And call the electric company. It's illegal to turn off power, if she's on oxygen. They must turn it on."

"You think?"

"I know."

He took the twenty. "Okay." Kippy finished the water and nuzzled the man's hands until he scratched her ears. "Good dog." Kippy stretched her neck as he scratched. "Such a good dog."

Bless this tormented child, I thought, watching Kippy lick the man's hands. It was Jesus, after all. Who knew? Who knew he showed up on playgrounds with filthy hands?

"Thanks for your prayer. Thank you for wanting to cure my affliction. I wish I could cure your troubles, too. I wish I could cure lots of people."

"Will you pray for me, too?" The man kept his eyes down on Kippy, who gnawed his wrist.

"I will. You can count on it."

But I was lying again. As sure as I sat on that bench, I was lying. I don't know how to pray.

Carolyn Wolf-Gould, a family doctor in a small town in upstate New York, majored in English at Hamilton College before going to Zaire, Africa, in the Peace Corps to teach rural villagers fish farming. After attending Yale University School of Medicine, where she met her husband, they established a medical practice together.

As medical director of a Gender Wellness Center, Wolf-Gould provides medical care for transgender patients. This part of her practice began in 2007, when a patient asked for assistance managing his hormones. She now cares for hundreds of transitioning men and women from a wide geographic area and appreciates the opportunity to know and care for these patients as they journey toward authentic gender expression.

This essay, adapted from a novel-in-progress, is loosely based on her experiences. Wolf-Gould's professional email is cawolf-gould@aofmh.org; the gender wellness center website is http://www.bassett.org/ao-fox-hospital/services/transgender-health-services/.

Leaving Big Sur

Dennis James

Rattling down the Pacific Coast in the back of a flatbed truck, hitchhiking from San Francisco to the Big Sur, I am sprawled on the deck, my back against the cab. Frank, sprawled next to me, lights a joint in cupped hands, takes a drag and passes it to me. I take a deep drag and pass it back.

The wind has dispersed the morning fog, and the sun beams like a blessing in the azure sky, but visibility is limited as the flatbed exhales a cloud of dust every time the truck hits a pothole. We can't talk; the wind blows away our words. Can't read, because of the jarring ride. The floorboards are unforgiving. One dare not sleep for fear of being flung into eternity on a tight curve. So I hang on to a ringbolt, close my eyes and think back over the last two weeks.

It is November 1967. I am a twenty-nine-year-old bearded lawyer living in Detroit, drifting along in a boring Legal Services program job and volunteering a lot for anti-draft counseling. Plunged in the overwrought politics of the Left, I have given up on the Democratic Party because of its pursuit of the Vietnam War. I have had several relationships since graduating from law school and am now dating a stunning, red-haired, straight-backed, recently-divorced dancer and choreographer named Lena.

I love Lena. But I sense the beginning of that slow, sweet slide into marriage, kids, dogs, cats, mortgages, in-laws—what

Zorba the Greek called "the whole catastrophe." Am I ready for that? Or do I chuck it all, buy a Harley, see the world and like Che Guevara, cast my fate to the winds? Then Nico, my musta-chioed, law school friend and co-employee in the Legal Services program, goes to visit an old rugby teammate, Max, who is living near Golden Gate Park in San Francisco. Two days after Nico arrives, he calls and entreats me to join him, which I regard as an opportunity to explore the question on the table. So, two days later, in the spirit of the times, I fly to San Francisco to examine the option of "dropping out."

Nico is inside the truck cab with his girlfriend of the moment, Pamela, a former divorce client who moved out to the Coast. Frank, bouncing on the flatbed next to me, is an old friend of Max's, one of five or six who live with Max and his compan-ion Gail in a rented flat just off Golden Gate Park. Members of this loose collective take turns working. They pool their pay and unemployment checks for meals, dope and rock concert tickets.

Max, a kind of impresario for his housemates and local fel-low travelers, is a big-shouldered, cheerful man with a booming voice who smiles and laughs a lot. Every morning in the kitchen he presents his ideas and plans for having fun that day, which invariably receive approbation. The plans generally involve some excursion, athletic contest, ethnic restaurant, party, rock concert, or all of the above. Gail says little but keeps an eye on him to head off stunts that might get out of hand. Sort of a one-man Chamber of Commerce for the Golden Gate/Haight-Ashbury experience, Max conducts impromptu tours of the neighborhood, distributes introductory samples of controlled substances and encourages cultural and chemical experimen-tation. Bemused by Eastern visitors' self-conscious reserve, he commends us as we shed our inhibitions.

So for two weeks Nico and I have been on a continuous marijuana high interrupted by occasional inhalations of amyl nitrite. Several times a day, three of us crowd around an amyl nitrite capsule, crack it and inhale. After inhaling amyl, any mildly absurd remark, say like, "rubber baby buggy bumpers," results in our falling on the ground and laughing until our sides hurt. God knows what permanent effects result. We find an alternative to merely falling down is getting into a car around 1:00 a.m., driving to the top of one of the city's insanely steep hills, popping a cap, releasing the brake and rolling down the hill. Once is enough.

These drugs form a kind of mental miasma in which perception is pleasantly distorted. I awake each morning to the unmistakable sweet smell of burning reefer. Proceeding to the kitchen, I find a shot glass on the table bristling with joints like so many toothpicks. A lit one is already making the rounds as residents and guests of Max's flat wander in, get a cup of tea and toke up. They are in various stages of dress or undress, which doesn't seem to matter to anyone.

Stoned, we have played touch football in Golden Gate Park meadows and Stinson Beach, gone to Janis Joplin and Jimi Hendrix concerts, walked the Haight-Ashbury freak show, swum naked in the ocean, viewed old W.C. Fields movies, experiencing most of this in slow motion with exaggerated sensory stimuli. I spend hours staring at art-book reproductions of Magritte paintings. And everyone—everyone in the flat, on the street, in the Park—is toking up, not surreptitiously, but as openly as one drinks a Stroh's long-neck beer on a front porch in my native Detroit. Even the striking young woman with hair down to her ass, in full US Postal Service uniform and cap, takes a friendly toke at every stop, as she hands you your mail.

On Thanksgiving Day, Max's household prepares by opening all the sliding doors separating the rooms of the flat, creating a fifty-foot corridor for an extended dining "table," consisting of a half-dozen folding card tables, several coffee tables and two picnic tables, all of differing heights, covered with a continuous "tablecloth" made of pinned-together bed sheets. Every few feet on the table sits a potted marijuana plant decorated with colored joints. Max and Gale's friends bring casseroles, mostly vegetarian, lots of pasta, mac and cheese, baked veggies, tacos, cakes, pies, cookies, muffins, and a token turkey. Jugs of Napa Valley are passed around like a bucket brigade.

We feast, laugh and smoke all afternoon, then split up into small groups and couples and disperse to various musical venues. Max fixes me up with a woman at the dinner. A nice, very pleasant person, Anita and I go to a club where the Brazilian guitarist Bola Sete is playing. After a couple of sessions, Anita invites me to her apartment, where we listen to soft music, talk, drink wine and make out. Nothing passionate. Just friendly sex. I kiss her good-bye at dawn and make my way back to Max's.

Short on sleep, I crash on the daybed, but there is too much going on. The Doors are on the stereo, people are scrambling around, looking for sleeping bags, tents, camping gear in general. Max has decided Nico and I cannot end our pilgrimage to the Bay without a sortie into the Big Sur, the coastal mountain range that runs from Monterey south to San Luis Obispo. The objective: Lime Kiln Creek, a beautiful cove with a creek running down the mountain to the beach. Frank, who will be our guide, says the creek is privately owned but nobody bothers you. We should have no trouble hitching if we split up and meet at the creek.

In truth, hitching in San Francisco in 1967 is a common form of public transportation. If you have to go somewhere and have no wheels, you walk to the corner, stick out your thumb and get a ride within minutes. There are near-accidents caused by drivers veering to the curb across two lanes to give somebody a lift. A young guy, who says he is a civilian employee at the local Nike Missile base, gives Nico, Pam, Frank and me a lift. There's a club soda bottle in the console between the front seats full of vodka. He says his job is boring, and that's how he gets through the day. Everybody in California wants to talk—about dope, music, scams, beaches, sex, food, tea, karma, yoga, and homeopathic medicine—to name a few common subjects, as well as groove on nature.

By early afternoon, we have thumbed our way to the Cabrillo Highway that hugs the Coast South from San Francisco to Monterey, but the guy's truck only goes as far as Monterey. In the waning sunlight we catch a ride from a New Jersey couple in a new, VW camper van; they've traveled out West to see the hippies. Apparently, the guy has second thoughts about transporting four dirty, smelly, vagabonds, one of whom (Frank) keeps talking about how much he would love to have a camper like this. So in total darkness, New Jersey pulls off the highway and announces he has got to drop us off as he has decided to visit a friend nearby. His wife begins to say something, but he gives her The Look, and she shuts up. Along a wild, unpopulated and very dark section of the Big Sur coastal road, we are left standing on the narrow shoulder, barely able to see each other, watching New Jersey's taillights disappear. We hear nothing but the distant roar and slap of the waves against the cliffs below and countless crickets. No vehicles appear.

As our eyes adjust to the darkness we make out a small highway bridge a few yards away, spanning a stream and discover a trail under the bridge that goes up the stream's left bank. We figure it may lead to shelter or at least an old campsite with enough level ground for our sleeping bags. In single file, we mount the narrow trail bounded by thickly-wooded canyon walls with Frank and his flashlight in the lead until he abruptly stops. Approaching is an apparition that I initially attribute to the THC residue in my cranium. Into our circle of light from the flashlight comes a tall, very thin man with scraggly hair and beard, who looks like one of Donatello's bony, bedraggled saints. Wearing what I always imagined sackcloth to be, as torn and ragged as his hair, he carries an old, Coleman gas lantern. "Hallo," he says. "Who goes there?"

Picking up on the biblical intonation, Frank says, "Four travelers from afar, in need of rest and shelter. We leave on the morrow."

The spectre strokes his beard. "I'm the caretaker of this canyon. Somebody else owns it. You can be my guests for the night. Follow me."

Frank turns to us, smiles and nods. We fall in, trudging up the trail until it branches into a path, and we cross the stream on slippery rocks and head straight up the canyon wall. Eventually, we come to a ledge in the wall, where a shelter has been built of plastic tarp stretched over long branches and anchored by large stones. The entry flap is pulled back revealing piles of carpet, cushions and shelving with jars of beans, rice, grain and canned goods. In front of the shelter is a fire pit with an iron pot suspended above glowing logs. A slight, cameo-faced young woman, no more than twenty, wearing a faded dress and cotton shawl, smiles as she nurses a baby in the firelight. She is a hippie Madonna.

"I offer you the hospitality of my home," says the spectre, whose name is Jeremy. He invites us to sit on a log reserved for guests, hands us wooden bowls and dishes out some pretty good lentil soup. He talks about the mountain's vibrations, how he can feel them, how he communicates with other mountain dwellers by thumping a hollowed out log with his feet, how his many cats all roam free, free, free! He lives on wild herbs, nuts and berries. He goes on and on until the unnamed woman disappears into the shelter. "Time for sleep," he says. "I talk too much. Good night." He follows the woman and closes the flap.

We watch the fire and speak in whispers. Soon we detect grunts and whimpers emanating from the shelter. Discreetly we disperse to various patches of level ground to unroll our bags. I'm on a small ledge just barely enough for a sleeping bag twenty feet down the slope from Jeremy's world headquarters. During the night, a feral cat lands on my bag. I fling him down the slope; he doesn't return.

In the foggy morning we gather for an oatmeal breakfast on the guest log. The young woman and baby remain in the shelter. When we finish eating, Jeremy sticks a pin in what looks like a tiny, clay cube and lights it until it smolders. He offers the hashish to us to inhale the thick smoke and we, of course, accept

"This will put some pep in your step," he says.

Grinning foolishly, we practically cakewalk down the narrow trail to the highway, stand on the shoulder and wait for a sympathetic driver, as in the far distance a low rhythmic booming begins to echo off the canyon walls.

We split up—Nico and Pam moving north about a half-mile around a bend. We figure, as they are a more attractive couple, they'll get picked up first and can persuade the driver to stop for us. This happens. Two young guys bearded and beaded in a VW peace van and dangerously stoned, blasting "Summertime Blues" by Blue Cheer, pull over, nearly driving off the shoulder into the canyon. The side door opens and Pam and her backpack come flying out. "Uh, uh," she mutters, "I'm not riding with these freaks. They'll get us all killed."

Frank cautions patience.

"Peace, brothers," he says to the freaks. "Most kind of you to give us a ride. You going far?"

"Oh, man, yeah," says freak-driver. "From Monterrey to Malibu, straight through, if we don't run out of pills. Gonna hook-up with some producer that Cisco, here, knows. Met him at a party in Carmel where we did some business. Maybe invest in some porn films. Eh, Cisco?"

"Gotta start somewhere," grunts Cisco.

"Awesome. But a good turn deserves another," says Frank. "Why don't you let me drive? You can crash in the back, smoke our stash, eat our cookies, anything you want. Forget the pills. Relax and leave the driving to us. Sound good?"

"Oh. Wow, Man! Take the wheel. Somebody roll me a joint. I got to crash. Cisco?"

Cisco, pissing in the weeds off the shoulder, says, "No brainer. Let 'em drive."

So Frank and I alternate driving and make it to the village of Big Sur, when the van develops a rattle, which means a blown valve. We limp into an auto repair shop. The mechanic makes the official pronouncement of death. Freak driver says, "Put another engine in."

Repairman says, "Cost you twelve hundred dollars cash, no cards.

"No problem" says the freak. "Cisco, get out twelve C's."

Cisco unbelts his jeans, reaches into his Jockey shorts, pulls out a roll of bills and peels off twelve one hundred dollar notes and offers them to the repairman, who puts on his gloves before counting the bills. "Have it by tomorrow," he says.

"Today," says Cisco holding up another one hundred dollar bill.

"Uh, today," says the repairman, "but late."

Nico and Pam get a ride from a kid driving a 1948 Ford woody station wagon, surf board on top, headed for the breakers off Oceanside Beach. Lime Kiln Creek is on the way. Twenty minutes later Gus, a state building inspector driving to San Luis Obispo to inspect a new school, picks us up. "So they build this school with no reinforcement right on top of a major fault line. I'm gonna have to violate them again. That's another nail in my coffin as far as my career goes," Gus says.

Finally, as we go around the hundredth hairpin turn, Frank shouts, "Stop, stop! By that rock!"

The rock, on our right, is a monolith the size of a school bus standing on end. A narrow driveway circles the rock. Beyond, empty space drops down to the Pacific.

"That's it," says Frank. "The big rock on the right just before the bridge. Lime Kiln Creek."

Gus pulls up next to the rock and all three of us get out and look down into the narrow canyon carved by a rivulet glistening in the afternoon sun. The creek, waves and weather have created a tiny inlet. Two black, stalagmite-shaped towers, each at least fifty-feet high, which were once part of the cliffs, stand like sentinels in the sea, breaking the impact of the waves, so that the inlet's sandy beach receives only gentle swells.

We stand and watch waves break against the stone towers, the salt breeze wets our faces and whistles around the rock.

Gus looks down, kicks a stick over the cliff. "Gotta go." he says.

"Stay, man," says Frank. "Take a few hours off. Tell 'em fog closed the road."

"I'd love to. But they're looking to get rid of me. I can't give them a reason. Good luck to you kids."

"Peace, brother," says Frank.

Gus waves and drives off, as we cross the road and climb down to where Nico and Pam are wading in the serpentine creek that cuts through the beach. We decide to climb up the trail and follow the creek upstream. Pam stays behind to watch our stuff. We scramble up the trail, barefoot, until we come to a pool fed by a waterfall, strip and jump bare-assed into the shockingly cold water. When we emerge laughing hysterically, I spy a pretty young woman also in the pool treading water. She smiles hello. I smile back and make a mental note to check her out on the return.

Onward and upward, naked and shouting we follow the creek until dusk. Without glasses, I can't see my footing. I turn back while Nico and Frank disappear whooping into the rocky cascades upstream. The lovely young woman is no longer in the pool; she probably made a mental note, too.

By now the canyon is in shadow. I pull on my clothes and begin climbing up the canyon wall to dry off where the sun lingers, when I slip and fall and something pokes me in the eye. The pain is sharp and lingering. I make my way down in the dark and by the time Nico, Pam, and Frank and I meet up, the eye hurts like hell. I think about the author and humorist James Thurber, whose family failed to take him to a doctor immediately after an eye injury; Thurber's vision was permanently impaired. I am reluctant to mess up the trip, having come all this way. Nevertheless, the others are unanimous: I should go with Frank to the emergency clinic in Monterey.

"How do we get there?" I ask.

"Same way we got here," says Frank.

Thirty minutes later, Frank and I are standing next to the rock on the highway waiting for a ride. Headlights appear, winding around the turns, disappear behind a ridge, then appear again, brighter, until they are upon us, blinding us.

"Hey, man. Need a ride?" The young, bearded guy in jeans, sandals and T-shirt gets out of a worn Chevy Nova and scuffs over to us. We all look at the constellations for long minutes.

"Beautiful," says Frank.

"Yeah. Good karma tonight. Gonna need it. Car steers a little funny. But I drive this stretch all the time. Not to worry. How far you going?"

"Monterey. The emergency clinic. My man here took a stick in the eye."

"Bummer. I'll getcha there. Just relax in the back seat."

His name is Beaufort, but he goes by Bo. He dropped out of college and kind of dropped out of life, sleeps in his car, does odd jobs, sells weed and mostly seeks peace in yoga and meditation. While I stretch out on the back seat, Frank and Bo discuss transcendental esoterica. I close my eyes to avoid seeing us go through the guardrails and sleep fitfully, awakened by the squealing tires and pain stabbing my eye. Hours later we arrive at the clinic, thank Bo for the ride and his karma, and he thanks us for the company.

The ophthalmologist on duty has to be awakened but is in good humor. He, too, is a young guy. Hair in a ponytail, wearing rimless glasses, he is John Lennon in a lab coat and hums as he uses a penlight to gaze into my eyeball. "Nothing serious," he says. "I know it feels like a fence post's in there. But it isn't. Scratched eyeballs are very sensitive. It will heal. Cover it up for a day to rest it, these antibiotic eye drops will lessen the pain and try not to poke the other eye."

By now it is dawn. I tell Frank what the doctor said.

"Hey, great. It's that good karma from the dude last night. We can go back to the creek. Goof on the beach. Smoke and look at the stars again. Zone out."

Suddenly I am tired. I don't want to toke. I don't want to play ball on the beach. I don't want to zone out. I don't want to look at constellations or sunsets or Magritte, DeChirico, the Dadaists, cubists, impressionists, expressionists. I don't want non-stop stimuli, gorging my senses, bypassing reality. It is fun. Just too much fun.

"Frank, thank you so much for coming with me, but I need to go back to the flat and crash. You go to Lime Kiln and tell Nico and Pam. Have a good time. Go nuts. I'll find a bus into town."

"You sure? You'll be all right?"

"Yeah, Frank. My plane is tomorrow night. I want to prepare for re-entry into the real world."

"Man, this is the real world, if you want it. You should stay. But I can dig it. Home is home. I'll see you tomorrow before you leave."

Frank goes back to the highway to hitch to the creek. I find the bus station, pay my fourteen dollars and sleep most of the way to San Francisco. Max, Gail and others of the circle are delighted by my account of the Big Sur adventure. When Nico, Frank and Pam arrive, we all go to Chinatown for my last dinner in the Bay in a place where you go through the kitchen and upstairs to a room serviced by a dumbwaiter. Piles of steaming rice, meat, shrimp, dumplings, noodles, veggies and unidentified things served in dented metal bowls are unceremoniously thumped down on our table.

The next day Max and Frank borrow a car and take me to the airport. Nico decides to stay a few more days. A last toke on some dynamite grass in the car renders me nearly unhinged as I board. I marvel at the Bay and the Sierras below as we wing east to gaunt, rust-belt, Detroit.

On the night of my return, as we lay in bed, Lena says, "I was afraid you weren't coming back."

"So was I," I say.

Within months of my visit, Haight-Ashbury dissolves in a tsunami of hard drugs, which drives the grass purveyors off the street, swamps the free clinics and sends teen-age runaways back home or like Joplin, Hendrix, Morrison, into early graves. This was not what the bell-bottomed, purple-hazed innocents I met envisioned. They assumed free love, hard rock and soft drugs were our generation's immutable legacy.

Maybe for some it was. When last heard from, Max and Gail were happily living in an Airstream trailer in Hawaii, where Max ran a small marijuana business.

Just good karma, I guess.

Dennis James is a retired attorney living and writing in Brooklyn, NY. He previously practiced employment law on behalf of employees in Detroit, Michigan. His short stories have been published in Mobius, The Summerset Review, The Griffin, The MacGuffin, *and* Struggle Magazine. *A collection of ten of his stories and the nonfiction, "Algeria Journal," were published in 2012 in a special supplement of* The Legal Studies Forum, *a quarterly publication of literature by lawyers. His article, "Cuba: State of the Arts," was published in 2013 in the quarterly magazine of the North American Conference on Latin America. Dennis and his wife, Barbara Grossman, travel extensively (but not on a Harley). He is currently working on* Songs of the Baka, *a book based on their travels, to be released by Skyhorse Publishing in 2017. He can be contacted at djames11238@gmail.com*

Isolation

Martha Ellen Hughes

To be or not to be mentally ill is not the question in my family. We are all unbalanced and suffer from depression, neuroses, manic behavior, all the way up to schizophrenia. This dirty little secret is the reason, I now think, that the women, especially the women, in my family worked so hard at indoctrinating the children with the idea we were from an old, exceptionally gifted family: We were blue bloods.

I used to love to sit pressed against my grandmother and stare at the blue veins running through her old hands as proof that it was so. Even later, when I was old enough to know better, I was still buying this carefully-crafted aristocratic family image.

"Your mother thinks you're descended from Charlemagne," my father said one day when I stumbled upon him alone in the living room engrossed in musical laughter. That day Mama and her cousin had received conclusive proof from a South Carolina genealogist that our family sprang through an illegitimate line from the king of the Franks.

"Charlemagne's horse, more like it," Daddy roared.

I had the guile to laugh, too. What does he know, I thought. A Northerner. From a family careless about losing its members. I was sure my mother and her cousin knew what they were talking about. You can't get more blue-blooded than descending from a king.

Many more years had to pass, the older generation had to die, and I had to veer close to madness myself before realizing what all the talk of aristocracy hid. While it is true that my great-grandfather walked home to ruin from the Civil War and built a fortune before his death in 1906, the kind of money most people in the war-ravaged South could not envision even eighty years later, and true that family members founded towns, started the Mississippi Archives, became writers, doctors, lawyers, mathematicians, ministers, and even allowed its women to attend college in the 1890s, what resounds more are the silent souls left out of the chronicle of the family's splendid accomplishments.

For these I have always felt a great affinity, a hungering to know more. There was Aunt Missouri, named according to the fashion of the day for the most recent state to enter the union, who ran away with a Cherokee and disappeared down the Trail of Tears into Oklahoma. Deemed mad by her blue-blooded kin, her name was still whispered almost a century later.

There was Uncle Isaac Newton, who spent his last meals hoisted in the air by a system of pulleys attached to his chair to keep the ants off the food that dribbled down his chin while he ate. (Who, I want to know, was the madder, Uncle Ike or my cousins who cooked up this plan?) There was my great-uncle, who vanished after leaving a movie to smoke a cigarette. Was he murdered? Did he desert from the navy? Or simply walk off pursued by private demons? I do not even know his name.

It is natural to protect children from unpleasant or frightening stories, to not want them to know about family members who have hurt, perplexed or disappointed, but there is a level of desperation apparent in my family's pattern of deleting such relatives from the family's collective memory, from its stories told over and over to the children, while filling the gaps left by these omissions with stories glorifying family members we were allowed to know.

This glorification, I now see, served to justify our family's isolation.

The children in our family knew from an early age that we had no need to mix freely with other people; it was more than sufficient to play with our siblings and cousins. And so we did. Or, more correctly, I did, my brother, the oldest child, always felt blamed for the mischief we got into and thus refused prolonged visits to my mother's family in Mississippi, where my beloved grandmother and aunt were the salient purveyors of the family's glory and attendant isolation.

Isolation is dangerous, I now know. It is the hallmark of troubled people, the breeding ground of addictions and mental illness. It is easier to be perverse when one is hidden. People in trouble know there is something wrong with them—that is why they hide.

When the guardians of small children are troubled, keeping the world at bay is not difficult. Once the children enter school, it becomes more problematic, although still not a daunting task. It is fairly easy to isolate children. Find fault with their friends. Nothing flashy. Point out that their friends' parents don't read much, that their mothers don't supervise them enough. Be less than enthusiastic whenever the names of these friends come up. Wonder why they have continual bad colds, complain that they live too far away. Make fun of a mother's new Sunday hat, a father's tendency to talk with his hands. Anything will do.

I know this is how it's done, not because I was smart enough to pick it up, but because years later, I remembered my mother saying when she was a girl, her mother always found fault with her friends.

Although loneliness and the feeling that I can never quite belong have been hallmarks of my adult life, as a child, I did not feel the isolation much. I was always eager to visit my Mississippi family. I loved playing with my cousins. It seemed then, and does now, a magical time. We were a unit. Four bright, imaginative little children playing together on our own in the days before children got carted everywhere by their mothers; there was little of today's supervised play. No television. No excess of toys. The bamboo clumps growing in the back were teepees or castles, depending on the game. A gold-brown scarf cast off by my aunt provided endless hours of Beautiful Ladies, which my girl cousin and I played by passing the scarf back and forth between us. While one tied and retied the scarf, pulled the golden tresses over her shoulder and preened, the other would say, "My, what beautiful hair!" until it was time for the hair to pass back and the other Beautiful Lady to appear. Often while we were thus engaged my cousin Robin, a year older than I, was in the front yard talking to the mint patch growing under the faucet, although he would grow silent when we approached.

I did not find this odd. It seemed dear and typical of our family sensibility: We were special. We lived on a higher plane.

The only times I felt the isolation were when we came up against children our own age—at vacation Bible school, for example, or the town swimming pool—when occasionally some especially sweet girl who attended my cousins' church would break off from her crowd and paddle over a moment to talk but soon seem alarmed and paddled back. I noticed that boys made a game of jumping into the water on top of Robin, so that he came up coughing and frightened. We said nothing, drew closer together in the water and soon left. Once home, my aunt would rail against the brutes and bullies of the world, of which this Mississippi village of four thousand seemed to have more than its share. We were to watch out for them and come home immediately if threatened. Her fantastical tirade was our only defense.

Most of all, I felt the isolation at the birthday party my aunt gave me every summer. I had always felt my aunt withheld affection from me. That this was done because, in some way, she felt a sort of jealousy on behalf of her own children. I was the oldest granddaughter and, so I thought, the favorite of our grandmother. And yet, in spite of my aunt's withholding, not a summer went by when she did not make a little celebration of and for me. A decorated cake, sometimes even store-bought, in the years when the village had a bakery; flowers on the table; even party decorations and punch. Then she would make out a guest list, suggesting appropriate names of children I knew from frequent visits to my cousins' Sunday school class, and I would be permitted to choose.

There was always something wrong about these parties, something old-fashioned, dated. Always an air of strained finances, in the handmade crepe decorations, the party favors she cooked up. She would take out her good silver and china for these affairs, which contributed to the echoing coldness, the stiffness of the celebration.

Girls went to parties then in their nicest Sunday clothes. You were expected to behave and display nice manners. Not grab food, wait until it was offered. Take a present nicely wrapped with a bow and a name tag. At other birthday parties I had attended, we played Pin the Tail on the Donkey with new cardboard donkeys, whereas at my aunt's, we might play Chinese checkers on a mangy-looking board, its colors rubbed off thirty years before by my mother, aunt, and uncle. Or, I could offer my guests croquet, which in all of Mississippi only my family still played.

My aunt would always limit my guest list to one or two girls, with the result that my aunt, two cousins and I outnumbered the guests. The little girls would arrive in their starched dresses, petticoats and patent leather shoes and, looking very prim and silent, sit in a row on the antique brocade sofa, side by side, hands in laps, eyes cast down, watching us through their lashes. I felt observed, found peculiar, like a wild animal in a zoo.

They were sad little parties. All around the air of great effort to please, the failure hitting me in the face. I wanted so badly for her not to realize this.

And yet, this annual effort my aunt made to celebrate my birth and hers, for she was born at midnight on the same day as I, remains a tender memory of my childhood. My mother did not make much of birthdays or holidays, seemed not to understand the importance of rituals the way my aunt did. Without her, I wonder if I ever would have had a birthday party.

She was a difficult woman. A sometime battle-ax and former schoolteacher, she believed in the eye-for-an-eye kind of justice. She and my female cousin held me down while she instructed Robin to spit on me, as punishment for spitting on him. The primitive impulse still shocks me. But those pitiful birthday parties in some odd way bound me to her, despite her harshness, made me respond to her need years later when the tendency to isolate, which had always been there, became absolute. When Robin was twenty-nine, he was working as a civilian mathematician for the navy. One day, his boss called my aunt and uncle and told them Robin was in the hospital; he had had a breakdown. Eventually, he was diagnosed as schizophrenic, given shock treatments, and, when stable, taken home to live with his parents. This is what many parents do, over the objections of psychiatrists who want the mentally ill to live in group homes, not isolated with their families. My aunt and uncle would not hear of it; it was, they felt, their duty to protect their once-brilliant, now troubled son. Robin never left home again.

For the next thirty years, he lived there with his mother, father, and our grandmother, who was showing every sign of living to a great age, until the early 1980s, when one by one members of the family began to die. First went my aunt's husband, then her brother, and her sister three years later; finally, her mother died in 1986. Robin and his mother were then on their own.

From the moment her mother died, my aunt seemed to stoop and shuffle her feet as an old lady would. The sudden change alarmed me; literally overnight, I saw before me my 102-year-old grandmother. My aunt was mimicking her deceased mother's walk.

The ladies in her Sunday school class must have been alarmed, too. She was only seventy-two, too young to look that way. She had always been tall, erect, and energetic. Now she struggled and gasped for breath to walk from the car to the church door. They began to inquire about her health.

"'What's wrong with you?'" my aunt would say, bitterly mimicking them. "Oh, I don't say a word back to them," she'd say, her eyes flashing defiance.

Not long after that she gave up going to church entirely. Robin continued to go to church and sing in the choir, but she complained about this a lot, nagging him to stop. When I once asked her why, as Robin's singing in the choir was the one social outlet he had, she told me she was scared for him to drive, he had to take so many drugs. Finally, a doctor in the choir made a rude crack about Robin sneezing; he never went back. The walls were closing in.

For a long time after her husband and mother died and she stopped going to church, people my aunt had known all her life would call her on the telephone, sometimes drop by. Robin was always present at these visits. He'd begin by being silent and finish by dominating the conversation in the room. Regardless of what new miracle drug he was on, Robin answered every question exhaustively, speaking so rapidly that all the words ran together, and then he repeated what he'd said again and again. My aunt would grow silent, slump in her chair. The guests would try to be jovial and keep up with his racing, drugged mind, pretending in the Southern way that nothing was amiss. Then everyone in the room would stop trying, and Robin would race on, explaining how income taxes should be done, then explaining it again, then starting anew from the same sentence. Sometimes he giggled wildly at jokes he inserted, which nobody could understand. Or sometimes he would riff on a quotation from the Bible, or something in *Scientific American* that had caught his eye. (He was *ill*, not stupid, we seemed endlessly to have to explain. He had been a mathematician. A National Merit Scholarship finalist!)

When it became clear that my aunt could not be visited alone, that she would always insist her son be present, her lifelong friends stopped coming. One could hardly blame them. To be with a mentally ill person is often frustrating, boring, and ultimately depressing. "What can I do!" she would cry when I urged her not to include him, at the very least to take a drive alone with me in the car. Anything to buy her an hour of silence, relief from Robin's clattering, machine gun mouth. How could she stand being locked up with him day and night, never a moment off? I could barely take him an hour.

On the rare occasions she did go out, she would cut the drive short, insist on getting back. "Robin will worry," she would say. Or, "Poor thing. I hate to leave him alone."

Her "normal" children felt abandoned by my aunt. "She's my mother, too!" my female cousin complained bitterly when we spoke on the phone. "They're so close, they're like an old married couple. I don't think Robin will outlive her." Finally, although they telephoned their mother each week, she and her brother also stopped going to see her.

But I could not stop myself, even though I, too, felt the sense of utter frustration and abandonment my cousin complained about. Twelve years went by in which I traveled from New York to Mississippi three or four times a year, watching her weaken, hearing her angry refusals to walk farther than from her bedroom in the back of the house to the dining room in the front, observing her ever narrowing world closing in. The trips were expensive; they interrupted my work; I had to be strong to deal with my aunt and cousin but paid for this strength with depression upon my return. My therapist said the constant trips south prevented me from developing my own life in New York. It made no difference. I continued to go.

I have always been emotionally attached to the South; nothing ever felt so much like home, despite my having lived in the North since I was twenty-two. I could not leave the South behind. This, of course, can be seen as an emotional problem, this unwillingness to get on with life, to grow up. But I always thought it more complicated than that. I had grown up in this odd family, force-fed since infancy with the notion that it was special, that no one could ever take the place of my family. Now one by one they had died. Of the three strong women in my family—my mother, my grandmother and my aunt—now two were gone; only my aunt remained. My least favorite of the three had become the surrogate for all three women; through her I could maintain touch with them. She was my mother's "baby sister" and needed my help.

It was hard to arrive and never have her to myself. She hadn't my mother's or grandmother's sense of fun, but her voice and accent were the same; being with her, I could call them up at will. Psychologists say the mind sometimes remembers the good longer than the bad. Certainly I remembered the family picnics, the jaunts through the countryside to pick wild blackberries and plums, the fun we used to have, all the women gathered together in the kitchen before our family's holiday meals, when we all traveled great distances to be together. My aunt rejoiced in remembering, too. There was no one else I could share these memories with. My brother, my cousins and I were rarely in touch. Robin's memory had been destroyed by shock treatments. The memories he dredged up were obviously bogus, pitiful remnants he repeated endlessly in a vain attempt to believe his memory was intact despite having had shock therapy.

As the years went by, I realized it was more than my sense of duty that kept me going back to see her, more than a feeling of "paying her back" for those long ago summer birthday parties. As odd as it might seem, I admired her, this stooped-over shell of my aunt, pretending to be her mother. She was intelligent. Either despite or because of her eccentricities, she was more of an independent thinker than most people I knew. Although Southern Baptist to the core, she was appalled at the growing conservative movement in the church and the abandonment of its once-proud belief in the separation of church and state. While the rest of the South was enthralled with Ronald Reagan, she saw the mean-spirited politics behind his congenial mask. The cost to her own sanity was apparent, but I admired her determination to provide as much of a normal life for her son as she could. Despite my growing admiration and love, it was never easy to get in the car and drive 1,600 miles, only to arrive and get a fast hug from her and Robin before they retreated into the television, or behind a book or newspaper. Why on earth did

I come? I would fume to myself the night of my arrival. They hardly notice I'm here! It finally dawned on me that my aunt did not need rescuing. She had secured her own isolation from the world by using her schizophrenic son as a shield.

I wondered if there were something wrong with me for admiring her. Her behavior was at best self-destructive; to keep him out of mental institutions, she was losing her own grip on reality. She became replete with quirky habits. She had always been afraid of "bogeymen" seeing into her house at night, but now she kept the curtains closed throughout the day, held tight with a bobby pin. The windows were always closed and locked, even in the summertime, and the air conditioners off, as Robin was afraid of electricity.

While dust collected on the china and crystal in her china cabinet, she and Robin ate and drank out of plastic food and yogurt containers, which they carefully washed and collected. Whenever I went home, I would open the kitchen cabinets and find hundreds neatly stacked. When I tried to throw them away surreptitiously while washing up after a meal, Robin would sneak into the kitchen and cry out, "Mama! She's throwing away the yogurt cups again!" Ditto everything else I tried to straighten and clean.

Robin's bedroom was filthy. For years he had been dropping his mail and clothes in the middle of the floor, until there was only a narrow path from the door to his bed. When she was stronger, my aunt used to simply close his bedroom door.

"Martha Ellen, I just have to let him do what he wants," was her standard statement to my objections. Despite her growing frailty, her inability to walk or stand for any length of time, my aunt never demanded Robin's help with the house or yard. It was always this lame—*I have to let him do what he wants.* Was she afraid of him? At times, I certainly was. When pressed to do a task he found odious, this ordinarily sweet, childlike man would grow silent, withdrawn, his face a dark mask.

For the last five years of her life, my aunt sat in her recliner by the curtained front window, often with her hands tucked between her legs. She had beautiful hands—the long, tapered fingers of someone who played the piano and the violin. "My hands" she used to cry. "I need to do something with my hands! But I've forgotten how to tat!" There was always a reason she could not do something she wanted to do.

Finally, Robin's mess spilled over into the rest of the house. His mail piled up in the dining room, where they always sat during the day, until it spilled over onto the floor. My aunt began to slip and fall on the numerous magazines he ordered. When I would hear of it and call from New York to express concern, she would say, "These old bones are tough, but, oh, you should see my bruise. It goes from my hip to my knee," then giggle, maddeningly.

Secretive, opinionated, stubborn, she was and always had been a formidable, often irritating woman. But now the fire was gone.

In the spring of 1997, she had a series of strokes. When she was better, her younger son flew down and took her up North to live temporarily in a nursing home near him and his family. She stayed for three months and came back refreshed. The time away from Robin had restored her; she seemed almost the aunt I knew. But before long, the aberrant behaviour began again, or maybe it had never ended. On my next trip home, there were mice droppings on the mail-strewn table where they ate. When I fussed and fumed, my blue-blooded aunt seemed only mildly interested to learn she was eating surrounded by feces.

I went down to visit her in January, in April, and once again in early June. Each time she said as though for the first time, "I keep thinking of how hard we worked to get the few nice things we have, and now, it's come to this. What for? No one wants these big, old antiques. No one has a house or room big enough for them. No one comes to visit anymore. Yes, I've been thinking a lot about that lately."

On that trip in early June, she thanked me for loving her. She wanted to know if I wanted anything. I should have known what that meant. But I am a member of this family, too. I know how to block reality. She died three weeks later.

Robin now lives in an adult assisted-living facility. The house, which my aunt left to him, stands empty; rather, I should say, no one lives there. It is still full of furniture, stacks of mail, the hundreds of little packets of ketchup, duck sauce, soy sauce, sugar and salt they collected over the years from take-out meals, the yogurt cups and plastic containers, the fabulous crystal and china. Robin has put the house on the market, and I am going to buy it.

"What on earth do you want with that house in Mississippi," my friends and therapist say.

I have no answer. I suppose I am still taking care of my aunt and the ghosts of all the people I once loved inside that house.

I do wonder about my own sanity, not solely because of buying the house. In my twenties, I, too, had a rough time, a time when I lay in bed all day pretending to be an inanimate object so the angel of death would not notice me. My therapist and drugs pulled me through. She tells me it is natural for children who grow up with a mentally ill sibling or cousin to question their own sanity. But that's not what I am afraid of; I know I am not schizophrenic. As much as I pitied, admired and finally loved my aunt, I do not want to be like her. Maybe that is the reason I am buying her house. Maybe when I've fixed it up and peopled it with another family, I'll be able to put my family to rest. It is time to stop driving 1,600 miles to find home.

Martha Ellen Hughes founded the nonprofit Peripatetic Writing Workshop, Inc., in 1991. This intensive writing workshop and retreat, lead by herself, Maureen Brady and other writers, meets twice annually, currently in Florida and Italy. She has taught creative writing at New York University for more than twenty-five years and is a freelance editor of novels and nonfiction books. She holds an MFA in creative writing from Bennington College and is a native of Louisiana. For further information, please visit www.peripateticwritingandart.org.

. . . OF LETTING GO

Tools of My Trade

Elena Lelia Radulescu

My love for words began with a peculiar journey one late evening when I didn't want to let myself go into the arms of Morpheus. I was five or six years old and reluctant to fall asleep. Perhaps I was afraid that all the things in the room—the picture books piled on the windowsill, my calico dress hanging on the back of a chair, the clock on the wall, even the house itself—would disappear if I took my eyes off them. But nothing escaped. What did happen was my own running away, the here in body and somewhere in mind, an amphibian life between two worlds which would shape and define my life trajectory.

Hugging a pillow and singing a lullaby to myself, I played one word out loud or to myself, I cannot recall which one, but I do recall the words: apple tree. The moment I said them I realized that there were two apple trees: one in my mind and another one, the real one, outside in the garden. With the same words I could call to mind the image of another apple tree, the crab apple tree, or the Jonathan one and, if I added other words to go along with the initial one, such as "in bloom" or "full of green leaves," the image in my mind changed as a response to the words I used.

The discovery astonished and fascinated me to the point of forgetting the fear of losing my surroundings while asleep. I did not know at that time that my discovery—the specific detail versus the generic one—was the golden nugget, the "show, don't tell" technique employed by a crafty writer in the act of description. What I knew and embraced then was the unlimited power of words to evoke images and my ability to arrange them in a kaleidoscopic pattern.

Shortly after that realization, another event had a snowball effect on my passion for words. Unsatisfied by the common word "beautiful," when telling my severely visually impaired grandfather about the blossoming plum trees on the hills of our village, I compared the trees to a group of bathers covered in soap lather, white foam dangling from the armpits of their branches. The words enabled me to bring the beauty of the landscape closer to my grandfather, helping him see what I had seen, offering an image enriched by analogy. Not knowing it, I was stepping up in the world of words to the level of metaphor. "Nature, after all is only one alphabet in the language of poetry," stated Antonio Machado, the Spanish poet I would read later in my adolescent years. At that time, I didn't know I was learning the first letters of a magic alphabet which would be my gift and my curse for years to come.

"Where the words are coming from?" I asked my father. "Who has made them? And how?"

"Let's find out." My father opened an enormous black book bigger than the Bible my grandmother kept on her night table. "This is a dictionary and contains all the words that there are in our language. We can find their meanings, their past, their own personal history, the family they belong to. The word *casa* comes from Latin, which is the mother of five other languages and aunt to many more. Sometimes words from one language flourish into another. Sometimes they change the sounds, maybe get rid of one syllable but keep the meaning. Some even die or are not in use anymore, like an outdated tool." He pointed to words originating from the German language and chose the word *blitz* as an example of foreign names finding a home in our Romanian language. He turned the pages to the word *yataghan,* a Turkish one which arrived into our language during the Ottoman domination over the Balkans.

My father was not a philologist, but he loved the music of foreign languages, liked to read and had a deep respect for the written word. From him I learned that words have their own stories, and stories stay in your memory longer than a list of facts. Stories, slices of life in motion and movement, are better choices to be stored in mental archives. All the words were there in his big book with hard covers, onion skin pages and a faint smell of gum Arabic rising from its spine each time we opened it. The dictionary. Sitting cross-legged on the rug in my parents' room with the heavy book on my lap, I went on my first linguistic expedition uncovering layer after layer of human history hidden at the core of each word. I fell in love with Father's dictionary, and I desperately wanted one for myself. My wish came true on my eleventh birthday: I received a smaller version of my father's, one with soft covers and light pages. With the gift came another fear: Would I be able to know all the words that were printed there? What if someone would say a word, but I would not know its meaning?

I began to carry a dictionary with me everywhere as if it were my passport to a country whose landscape was made of strict facts and entertaining stories. Over the years I acquired more dictionaries: A French one, a Latin one, Dictionary of Mythological Names, of Synonyms and Antonyms, of Famous Quotations, of Poetic Expressions, of Literary Terminology and even one on trees and shrubs. Growing up I lost some of them or have used them so much that the dog-eared pages became brittle or disappeared.

I don't remember a time when I didn't have a reference book, ready any time to search for a new word or a word whose meaning escaped my memory at the first encounter. A dictionary was my safety blanket and my tool of the trade, since, at the age of sixteen, my first poems appeared in a national literary review, marking my birth as a writer. I held onto words, reaching beyond their meanings, choosing shades of connotations, closer synonyms, driven by a burning desire to unfold the truth about the world inside and around me.

Most of the dictionaries came out in hard cover. By definition they were voluminous and heavy. As a university student, I ended up carrying extra weight, bulging in my backpack like a hump. Many times I found myself thinking of Abdul Kassam Ismael, the Grand Vizir of Persia, who, in the tenth century, travelled everywhere with his whole library: 117,000 volumes loaded on the backs of 400 camels. I felt as if I were one of his camels.

With extra weight on my back I looked like a mountain hiker, an ugly appearance, which mother and her older sister, a former beauty pageant winner before WWII, would not approve of.

"Very unfeminine," my aunt declared at one of our family gatherings, and every woman relative echoed her with a "not lady-like," or "not good for your bone structure" or "it'll damage body posture." I didn't care as much for lady-like behaviors as I cared for the health problems I might develop later in life, so I tried to wean myself from my addictive behavior. I made an effort to let go of the habit of rummaging through the book crates at the antiquary shops in the back of my university building.

For a while I unburdened myself and felt free, light, weightless but somehow exposed to the elements as if I were wandering barefoot in the woods. I kept the habit home. Like faithful pets waiting for their owner to come home from work, my dictionaries waited on my desk, and I would spend most of my evening hours taking their words to the light of my heart, polishing them into a poem or a short story.

Unexpectedly my life changed with the force of a storm over a mental landscape. In my early thirties, I immigrated to the United States. I had to learn a new language, and I had to learn it fast. Carrying an English dictionary in my bag became a vital necessity. I couldn't let it go: I depended on it. The habit was justified by my non-native speaker status and by my eagerness to belong to the new place.

Relying heavily on my knowledge of Latin, I labored over every single word I encountered, trying to make it mine, a piece of my everyday survival kit. I listened to people's talk, learning idioms, understanding meanings. After all, a dictionary is really a record of what people "say." The term *dictionary* comes from the Latin word *dictio* from *dico* "say" or "speak." But I didn't dream to write in a language not given to me at birth. I didn't dare take foreign words to mold them into prose or poetry. They did not belong to me.

"You can write in your own language, find a good translator or translate your own writing. Many writers did that: Nabokov, Norman Manea," advised an old Romanian friend, himself a writer in exile.

For a while I lived between two languages, reading my old poems in my mother's tongue but also tasting the new words, listening to their music, trying desperately to tame them, to make them mine. It was painful, always lagging behind, always measured by the scrutinizing eyes of native English speakers.

I thought of translating my old work into English, so I armed myself with plenty of lexicons, Webster's dictionaries, *The New*

Roget's Thesaurus and began my journey into a linguistic Terra Incognita. My translations seemed light, see-through, something was lost, but I couldn't pinpoint what was missing. The new version of my poems seemed pale shadows of the originals; they were not the poems themselves. I thought of an Irish poet who said that the beauty is in the walking; we are betrayed by our destination. I thought my only beauty was in the learning itself, for I couldn't see the end of my journey.

I stopped writing poems or short stories. For years. In any language. I just lived with a pain inside me as you would live with a chronic illness, a weird arthritis responding to the changes of my heart. I continued to collect dictionaries, this time of the English language.

One day at The Strand, a book store in Manhattan, browsing, touching the backs of books lined up on the shelves, my finger stopped on a sort of a dictionary by Wilfred Funk: *"Word Origins and Their Romantic Stories."* I opened it at random and began to read: "Every word was once a poem. Each began as a picture. Our language is made up by terms that were all figures of speech.... To know the past of an individual helps us to understand him better. To know the life history of a word makes its present meaning clearer and more nearly unforgettable. . . . Words truly are little windows through which we can look into the past. . . ." I was reading Funk's words but in my mind I was hearing my father's voice. Again I was nine years old with a dictionary in my hands, Father explaining patiently how the words could become a habit that would be hard to break; first you would want to know the meanings, then their pronunciation, and after that you would worry about their structure, their origins, and personal lives.

Had my father known the work of this famous lexicographer? Was Wilfred Funk translated into Romanian? I doubted it. These were just common, universal notions about language. Any language. But Funk's words had a powerful effect on me. It was as if an electric jolt of energy set my whole emotional and intellectual being into motion.

James Joyce once said that the first ten years of life are crucial for a writer. Did the author of *Ulysses* have in mind childhood inquiries, perplexities, fears of not knowing the meaning of a word as part of a writer's make-up? That, I do not know. I know that since that day in the bookstore my childhood fears, questions and pure love for words have returned to me. Would I know the meaning of all the English words? Would I be able to invite readers to bask in the light of my images? Old anxieties run deep, like an underground river, only to become an emotional source and writing material.

I began writing. I wrote (and I still do) in a foster language, cautiously testing the words on my tongue, every written line inspected under an invisible magnifying glass, every paragraph weighted on the scale of good grammar and punctuation.

I am still limping in English but walking, nevertheless, with dictionaries as my golden crutches. Luckily, now the reference books are easy to travel with, at the reach of your finger on your iPad or other electronic devices.

I thought I was alone in my journey packed with lexicons and Webster's editions until I read an interview with the novelist Carol Shields. She confessed that the best trick she uses to obtain the mental calmness to create and to get into the flow of writing is to open a dictionary which "puts me in that cool, quiet place of language."

My place of language is not a quiet one but a busy construction site teeming with words, coming and going, crossing imaginary roads, meeting new terms exchanging stories, calling each other—loudly or in a whisper—singing, playing tricks, commanding, shaping, assembling defining, living on pieces of paper. And I at the other side of the page, holding onto words, not letting them go, for if I did, I would lose sight of my own destination.

Elena Lelia Radulescu has a master of philosophy degree from the University of Bucharest, Romania, and a master of education from Columbia University, NY. Her poetry and short stories have been published by Vision International, Square Lake Review, The Spoon River Poetry Review, Chelsea, Karamu, CALYX Journal, Mutabilis Press Anthology of Poetry, Trajectory Journal, Texas Poetry Calendar, Romanian Literary Review, The Cape Rock Review, Magnolia Journal, Twisted Endings *and other literary publications. In 2014, Radulescu was a finalist in The Southern Women Poetry Contest. She lives in Katy, TX, where she is working on a novel-in-verse for middle-grade children.*

Letting Go Isn't Real

Susie Abulhawa

Letting go, as a process initiated by decision or conscious will, is not real. Yet it is something we spend a lot of time talking about, to ourselves, with therapists and each other. The truth is, when there is attachment, there is no such thing as letting go. Attachments happen organically and frequently dissolve on their own, like falling in and out of love. Just as one cannot decide to stop loving another, attachments do not go away simply by one's deliberate will to *let go*.

That's not a bad thing. It means we are biological, spiritual beings who are able to form attachments with our environment and other living creatures in it. But because attachments aren't always healthy, for example think of hurtful relationships or addictions, we are always looking for ways to detach, emotionally. We also struggle to let go of less threatening or dangerous attachments, for example, material objects that give us a sense of security or objects that hold memories of our own lives.

Several years ago, I had a flood in my basement in which old high school yearbooks were damaged. I could have let them dry out and preserved the remains of that chapter in my life. The messages from classmates were still legible and the pages intact. But I was well into my thirties then and felt no attachment to those years. High school was so long ago, and it hadn't been particularly pleasant for me. So I threw them away along with damaged sheetrock and soaked power tools. In my mind, it was a *letting go* decision that put an irrelevant past out by the curb for waste pickup. But years later, when my daughter was in high school, there were several instances when I wanted to share those yearbooks with her, as a way to prove shared experiences, perhaps. More than that, I realized I wanted those yearbooks to safeguard my own memories. The attachment was still there, I just no longer possessed the object to redeem it.

Items of nostalgia, such as photos, mementos, or books are the only material objects I feel tied to in some way. Growing up, I was forced to move around a lot and learned not to form attachments to things or places. Sometimes people, too. So the idea of losing a car, a suitcase full of clothes, or a basement full of mostly replaceable items does not bother me. There are no real attachments to mourn.

Of course, attachment to things, no matter their significance, is not the same as attachment to people. So, what does it mean to let go of relationships or contend with the loss of a loved one? Again, all I have to offer is my own experience. While I do not believe it is within our power to sever emotional and spiritual bonds with others, we can, by conscious decision, walk away from the tangible or identifiable manifestations of attachment.

The most profound instance of this in my life occurred shortly before my fortieth birthday, when I made the decision to sever communication with my mother, deliberately closing a door that had been a source of tremendous hurt. It was not walking away from, letting go, or dissolution of that attachment. It was simply creating a space to contend with what it means to be motherless and perpetually harmed and wounded by one's mother. I cannot let go of this basic fact of me, with all its cruelty, because it is woven into my identity. It is a component of my character from which I have found power. I imagine it to be similar to the experience of an addict. Addiction never goes away, no matter how far the distance from alcohol or drugs. It becomes enmeshed into one's identity, its presence a wounding relief. And in the eventual acceptance and coping comes a personal power.

Trying to *let go* is a futile struggle. Attachments exist of their own volition. They can dissipate or they can stay forever. I find they usually stay. But through deliberate will, I believe one can create a private space where it is possible to contend and reconcile with what we have unconsciously hoarded of pain, objects, loss, addictions, insecurity, demons, and fear. The real process, then, is not of letting go, but of accepting and welcoming them until they are not threatening, hurtful, distracting, or limiting. The process is of coping, which is more of a noun, really. To be in coping, like in mourning, is what is often misunderstood as letting go.

Susan Abulhawa is the author of two bestselling novels, Mornings in Jenin *and* The Blue Between Sky and Water; *a poetry collection,* My Voice Sought the Wind; *and several anthologies. She is a frequent speaker, political essayist, and human rights activist. In 2001, Abulhawa founded a children's NGO, Playgrounds for Palestine, dedicated to upholding the right to play for Palestinian children living under military occupation and in refugee camps elsewhere. She lives in Pennsylvania. Abulhawa is on twitter at @sjabulhawa; her website is susanabulhawa.com.*

Spoiled Fruit
Bears Bad Seeds

Nilo T. Alvarez

Even after almost half a century of American colonization, divorce was never permitted in the Philippines. My country remained a Catholic-dominated society in which only the church could annul marriages. But the process of tearing apart this sacrament of God could take a very long time. Sometimes by the time the holy institution granted separation for the couples, they were already in the kingdom of heaven, facing judgment from God. In my family, when my father could no longer endure my mother's nagging mouth, and vice versa, my parents agreed to end their marriage. But contrary to the common belief that spoiled fruit bears bad seeds, children of a broken family do not necessarily fail in life.

My parents' separation happened when I was a junior in high school. One day when my classmates and I were practicing singing for the choral intramurals, our beloved principal interrupted to ask our instructor if I could be excused. It turned out my father, who was waiting outside, needed me in the municipal office. I had not even taken a seat beside my sisters when the judge, who was also my uncle, asked me to choose between my father and mother. I looked away from the worried eyes of my uncle and stared at a leafless tree outside. Although I loved my mother more, I chose my father.

My father was proud of me. Neither of my parents had finished elementary school. I was the youngest of their twelve children and blessed with intelligence. Unlike my sisters, none of my four brothers made it to college. My father silently hoped I would become a doctor. But after he and my mother separated, like most broken families in my country, misfortune knocked upon our door, and his financial status crumbled like a sandcastle washed away by the sea. My father suffered a heart attack. A few months before his illness, our small plantation of sugarcane had caught fire, and his income evaporated with the smoke. After my father left the hospital, he went completely bankrupt. I can still remember those days when we only ate one meal a day, often soup made from clams I harvested at the seashore, or papaya I plucked from the tree in our yard. Needless to say, my father's dream of sending me for pre-med vanished.

I was embarrassed by what happened to us. We were a respected family looked up to in our town and suddenly our status was reduced to a peasant's. I was devastated that my father could no longer afford to send me to college. I can't remember if I hated my father at that time. All I remember is sometimes we had frustrating arguments, and I turned that hatred toward myself. My life suddenly changed drastically. I became a loner. I rarely went out with my friends. I learned to gamble and did stupid tricks in the street. I would have smoked marijuana if my father had not caught me and skinned my butt with a bamboo stick. When college was about to begin, I didn't bother to ask my father if we had money for my schooling. I knew the answer. I always saw him sitting on a bench in our front yard under the Bitter tree, as if waiting for a hopelessly late ship.

Fortunately, before I graduated from high school, a new technical school was built in our town. I took its entrance examination just to boost my ego and prove to my classmates I was still the best. I wasn't really interested in this school, because it only offered an associate degree; I wanted a bachelor's. Nevertheless, when I scored high, my friends came to my house and convinced me to go to this school because I had only to pay one hundred pesos, or two dollars at that time, for the registration. Since my father's bank vault was as clean as our empty house, I took their advice.

During my studies in this school, I met a lot of friends—poorer friends but with minds like mine. Through them I realized that being poor wasn't the end of the world. Through my teachers I learned that knowledge was the best financial weapon. Later, our school offered me a loan, which I accepted and sent part of the money to my sister, who was working at that time in rural services for the poor living in barrios, so that she would be able to complete her nursing career. The other part of the loan, I used to feed our family—my unmarried sister, niece and my father. When I graduated, the school found me a job. Once I started to work, through self-determination, I kept studying until I finished a chemical engineering course.

While I was still studying, my father suffered another heart attack; this time it was serious. Ever since the plantation had caught fire, he'd never recovered financially. The bank seized half of his land to pay his debts, and the remaining half was never planted, because nobody would provide him with another loan. Since that time his mind had remained barren like his land.

On his dying day in the hospital, my father summoned me to his room. His breathing was laboured, and there were many tubes attached to him, yet he greeted me with the weary smile I had seen many times as he sat and waited under the Bitter tree for a ship that never came. But this day, he was different.

"Never give up on yourself," he said, eyes teary yet full of hope. "Your destiny lies in your hands."

Nilo Alvarez was born on Negroes, one of many Pacific Ocean islands discovered in 1521 by the Portuguese explorer, Ferdinand Magellan. Named the Philippines for Spain's King Philip II, eleven of the archipelago's original 7,113 islands are under water, the victim of global warming. In his fiction, Alvarez often uses his small, friendly town of Talisa, where from the top of the water tower during his childhood all one could see were waving green sugarcane fields, planted during American colonization. Few people lived on Negroes; his aunt, a midwife, delivered all the babies. His mother often took him to movies and told him stories about her life. What he most enjoyed were her stories about World War II. Her colourful stories plus the movies inspired him to become a writer. His email address is niloalv56@gmail.com.

On Not Letting Go of Grief

Marion Cuba

People meant well. They were nearly as stricken as I was to learn that my son had died. Long-time friends, those who knew him best, were positively devastated. I felt almost guilty for being the bearer of such horrific news.

They all struggled for words. "This is unbelievable." "So sorry for your loss; I can't imagine . . ." "You are so strong; how did you ever live through this?"

I felt their pain and sincerity. I could also feel their desperation for some comfort. *From me.*

What was I to say? "Oh, that's all right?"

I simply said to them what I say to myself: "There are no words."

After the initial news, many people called to invite me for lunch or dinner. Again: they meant well, thinking to soothe and distract me. Some tried to nudge me along in my grief. I sensed that a few wanted me back to being the old me. For my sake, they said. But for theirs, too, I realized.

What they didn't—and couldn't—know was that when my son died, the old me died with him. I would never be that person again. That person had enjoyed restaurants, museums, intense conversations with friends, going to theatre, sleeping late, writing, and—my favorite—listening to music. No more.

My son couldn't eat normal food. Instead, he was nourished

by intravenous nutrients through a tube. If he couldn't eat, then I couldn't eat.

He had restless, pain-filled, sleepless nights as the I-V pumped the solution into his body for twelve hours. So how could *I* sleep? I could not, often lying awake till two and three in the morning.

Many days when I visited, he didn't wish or was too debilitated to talk at all. Unable to speak with him, I found I couldn't bear to talk with my own friends either. Unusual for me, I often didn't pick up the phone or listen to my messages, or read or answer e-mails.

My son was a gifted writer, earning his master's degree at the American Film Institute and working for a time at Disney in Hollywood. I had published my first book, realizing a years-long dream. And I was nine chapters into my second novel—with reams of historical research, interviews, and testimony from people all over the world via the Internet. Finishing and publishing this book was the cynosure of my existence.

Until my son's illness. With him unable to write, I could not write. I could not even walk across the room to my computer or set foot in the subscription library where I'd always worked on it. Part of the reason was I did not have the heart. The other part, I realized, was that when writing in the privacy of my library, I entered another zone, an island of peace, where I could escape the grueling truths of what was happening outside.

But I did not want to escape. I did not even want to check out a book. I couldn't really read, which could have been another possible escape. But that seemed to me a betrayal of him. My sole drive was to be with my son in his pain, and, in some mystical way, help carry it for him. And to agonize over him when I wasn't with him, hoping—irrational as it was—that my worry could help cure him. To be ready on a moment's notice to dash to his apartment or the hospital for an emergency.

And what about my love of music? My son played the guitar, wrote songs, and sang; now he could not. So I could not bear to listen to my treasured collection of tapes and CDs, or switch on the radio, or go to a concert. Hearing the rhapsodic beauty, rather than soothing me, would unleash ravaging tears and sorrow. Inflicting almost physical pain.

So these are the things I did—and did not do—for the three-and-a-half years my son fought cancer.

And after he died? I hibernated in my apartment for more than four months. Living in New York, I could have almost anything delivered: food, drugstore needs, liquor. If I wanted a book, which I rarely did, I could order it on the Internet. My building employees sent up my mail and packages. Any boxes needing to be mailed could be picked up by UPS or FedEx. The *New York Times*, filled with nothing but bad news, it seemed, often lay at my door until evening. Nor did I accept invitations, however heartfelt.

I did not need to leave my house for anything. I could be alone with my grief to mourn and weep for my son

Some people had a problem with that. When was I going to get on with my life? They wanted to know. Traditionally, the unveiling of the gravestone takes place eleven months after the death—signaling the time to throw off mourning and no longer dwell in sadness. To return to "normal" life.

A once-notable theory of Elisabeth Kübler-Ross supported this view. In her 1969 book, *On Death and Dying,* she defined five stages of grief one should go through in order to be "successful": denial, anger, bargaining, depression, and acceptance.

Denial. How could I deny my son's death? I'd been standing at the foot of his bed in the hospital, when a young doctor looked up from the computer we were all watching—a YouTube video of my son playing the guitar and singing a song he'd written. "He's gone," she said. She walked over to check his monitor. "He's gone," she repeated. There was no denying it. And, later, no denying the pounding on his casket as I shoveled dirt into his grave.

Anger. I'm not sure I ever felt that. Devastated. Shocked. Numb, yes. But whom would I be angry with? Yes, I had previously prayed to God to intervene, to spare my son. But after reading several modern books by Jewish scholars, explaining that God did not have power over everything, how could I be angry at Him? Besides, anger took vehemence and energy. Neither of which I had.

Bargaining. Again, with whom would I bargain? I was newly educated: God created the world, but did not affect human events.

Depression. There is a big difference between depression and grief. I have suffered depression. It is a weighty mass that grinds in your stomach and metastasizes to your entire body, mind and soul, leaving you immobilized and imprisoned. But in most cases, it is manageable. Even curable. Grief, on the other hand, is an ineffable sadness engulfing you, but it is also intertwined with love and yearning. It is a cosmic spiritual entity all its own that provides a sheltered place when there is nowhere else to go. There is no cure for it.

Acceptance? Never. That would be like saying I accept the Holocaust, the horror of 9/11, or all the other cruelties and obscenities visited upon our world.

I am not alone in rejecting Kübler-Ross and other theorists who define grief in predictable stages that lead to "recovery." In recent bereavement studies, there has been a shift away from the idea that successful grieving requires "letting go" of the death. And, furthermore, that continuing the bond with a loved one can play a potentially healthy role for the griever.

Another theory describes grief as the process of oscillation. In a loose way, this theory describes my own mourning path. I do oscillate: between intense visceral sadness, where I am bereft as if for the first time—and the matter-of-fact calm of paying my bills or going to the hardware store.

I now accept more invitations with friends—or even offer some: enjoying a dinner out, getting lost in a movie or play or lecture. Enjoying the snow. And I have returned to my abandoned writing, which propels me into a rarefied zone.

Little by little, I've also begun listening to music. And for some minutes I may be glorying in its beauty, believing the world is whole—only to break down in tears, thrust back into my sealed world of grief. *My son is gone and cannot experience this exquisite joy.*

When enjoying the good moments, I feel much different from before, when my joy and appreciation enhanced my certitude about life. Now these experiences exist in an isolated bubble, and when they are over, it is as if they had never happened.

No matter which way I oscillate—toward grief or joy—I am hugely diminished. My "new life" is narrowed, and I am proceeding like someone who is naked. As I walk down the street, my step is no longer sure, my balance no longer steady. I lose keys, break glasses. Spill red wine on pristine tablecloths, sob at old family pictures.

So this is a map of my schizoid grief. When I am out, I exist in a small, mindless zone. When I come back, my grief meets me at the door. I rush into its arms. Gladly.

Many people simply cannot understand this: *Why would I want to dwell in this pain?*

Shakespeare understood.

In 1596, while writing *King John,* one of his history plays, Shakespeare lost his own eleven-year-old son. In Act III he reflects his grief, depicting Constance, the widowed sister-in-law of the king, openly and deeply mourning the death of her son, Arthur.

Cardinal Pandulph reproaches her: "You hold too heinous a respect for grief."

To which Constance replies: "He talks to me that never had a son."

And she goes on further, intoning Shakespeare's words:

> Grief fills the room up of my absent child,
> Lies in his bed, walks up and down with me,
> Puts on his pretty looks, repeats, his words,
> Remembers me of all his gracious parts,
> Stuffs out his vacant garments with his form;
> Then, have I reason to be fond of grief?
> Fare you well: had you such a loss as I,
> I could give better comfort than you do.
> I will not keep this form upon my head,
> When there is such disorder in my wit.
> O Lord! My boy, my Arthur, my fair son!
> My life, my joy, my food, my all the world!
> My widow-comfort, and my sorrow's cure.

O my boy, my Jonathan, my fair son! I hold, I cherish my grief for you.

I will never let it go.

Marion Cuba *comes from a family that loves to write and debate ideas, especially those concerning how we behave in life. Writing has always been her best means of expression—in her novels, fundraising for non-profit causes, poetry and twenty years of journaling. The ideal of doing good in the world is a theme that impels her work. In her previous historical novel,* Shanghai Legacy *and in the book she's currently writing, she focuses on little-known chapters of the Holocaust when humane groups and ordinary individuals of all religions rose up to save countless lives. She lives in New York City.*

Acknowledgments

I am deeply indebted to my own teachers of writing—David McHam, formerly of Baylor University and recently retired from the University of Houston; Nicholas Delbanco, recently retired from the University of Michigan, who developed the first master of fine arts program at Bennington College in Vermont; and his colleague in the MFA program, the late novelist and poet, Richard Elman.

I am also beholden to four writers in this collection—Sue Parman, Mina Samuels, Norma Nixon Schofield and Joe Levine—for their patience and exceptional good manners in never bringing up to me the long wait to see their essays in print. I wish to thank Michele Orwin, the founder of Bacon Press Books, for her friendship over the years and the much-appreciated guidance in producing this work, and to Maureen Ellen Brady, for her love, support and encouragement now and in all things.

For further information, see www.peripateticwritingandart.org.

About the Editor

M.E. Hughes has guided and edited a small army of writers since receiving her MFA in creative writing from Bennington College in 1986. The joy of experiencing the thriving artistic community that existed at Bennington at that time, under the leadership of Nicolas Delbanco and the late Richard Elman, led her to start her own summer writing program, the nonprofit Peripatetic Writing Workshop, Inc. (www.peripateticwritingandart.org) in 1991. The Peripatetic meets each winter and summer and lives up to its name by meeting in the United States and abroad, to date in Sicily and Italy, Guatemala and Ireland. She has taught creative writing at New York University for many years and is also a freelance book doctor/editor. She has published two nonfiction books and the novel, *Precious In His Sight* (Viking Penguin).

A native of New Orleans, Hughes grew up in New Iberia, Louisiana, in the heart of cajun country.

Made in the USA
Charleston, SC
21 June 2016